LEAVING CERTIF

CW00496910

LESS STRESS MORE SUCCESS

Maths Revision
Higher Level
Paper 2

Brendan Guildea, Louise Boylan & George Humphrey

g **GILL** EDUCATION

Gill Education

Hume Avenue

Park West

Dublin 12

www.gilleducation.ie

Gill Education is an imprint of M.H. Gill & Co.

ISBN 978 07171 8625 9

Design by Liz White Designs Artwork and print origination by MPS Limited

At the time of going to press, all web addresses were active and contained information relevant to the topics in this book. Gill Education does not, however, accept responsibility for the content or views contained on these websites. Content, views and addresses may change beyond the publisher or authors' control. Students should always be supervised when reviewing websites.

For permission to reproduce photographs, the authors and publisher gratefully acknowledge the following:

© Alamy: 101, 240, 241.

The authors and publisher have made every effort to trace all copyright holders, but if any have been inadvertently overlooked we would be pleased to make the necessary arrangement at the first opportunity.

Acknowledgements

The authors would like to thank Colm Kelleher, Elaine Guildea, Joe Heron and Colman Humphrey who helped with the proofreading, checked the answers and made valuable suggestions that are included in the final text.

CONTENTS

Please note:

- The philosophy of your mathematics course is that topics can overlap, so you may encounter Paper 1 material on Paper 2 and vice versa.
- The exam questions marked by the symbol in this book are selected from the following:

    1. SEC exam papers (relevant year indicated)

    2. Sample exam papers

    3. Original and sourced exam-type questions

Introduction

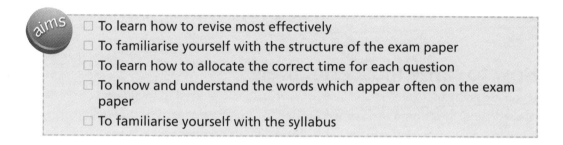

aims
- ☐ To learn how to revise most effectively
- ☐ To familiarise yourself with the structure of the exam paper
- ☐ To learn how to allocate the correct time for each question
- ☐ To know and understand the words which appear often on the exam paper
- ☐ To familiarise yourself with the syllabus

The aim of this revision book is to help you enhance your grade in your Leaving Certificate. The book is designed to be exam focused. To do this, the book is based not just on the syllabus, but also on the examination paper. Because of this, this revision book can be used in conjunction with **any** textbook.

Throughout this book, **examples and exam-type questions are graded by level of difficulty**.

This level of difficulty is indicated by calculator symbols, as follows:

The number of calculators shown beside a question helps you know how difficult the question is. One calculator indicates a question which is relatively basic. As the questions get harder, there will be more calculators. Three calculators indicates an average-level question, whereas five calculators indicates that it is a very challenging question. These questions may be beyond some students, but give them a go! **Students hoping to achieve a high grade should aim to complete all of the five calculator questions. The calculator symbol given for each question relates to the most difficult part of that question. Don't be discouraged by a challenging question.** As in the Leaving Certificate exam, difficult questions can sometimes begin with one or two simple parts. You should attempt as much as you can.

It is very important to realise that **you are your own best teacher**. Revision is when you begin to teach yourself. Thus, it is very important for you to start your revision as soon as possible. Make notes while you are revising. If you are having difficulty with a particular question, seek help from your teacher, a friend or a member of your family. As with all subjects, the best examination preparation is to work through past examination or sample papers so that you are familiar with the layout and the style of questions.

Let's start at the beginning. If you want to do well in your Leaving Certificate, then two things are essential:

- Revise effectively.
- Be familiar with the exam paper and so be prepared on the day of the exam.

These may seem obvious, but it's worth taking a moment to think about what these tips mean.

How to revise most effectively

If you are going to do well in the Leaving Certificate, you need to spend quite a bit of time revising. Spending a little time learning how to revise effectively will help you get more from your time and will help you absorb and understand more of the material on the course. Here are some tips to help you revise for maths.

- Find a quiet place where you can work. This place should be dedicated to study and free of potential distractions. Turn off music, the TV, computer and mobile phone.
- Write a study plan. Don't be afraid to ask your parents/teachers/guidance counsellor for help at this stage.
- Do the more challenging revision first, when you are fresh. Trying to focus on difficult problems when you are tired can be counter-productive.
- Maths is based on understanding, so while you can 'learn' some elements of the course, it is important that you develop an understanding of the material.

Study in small chunks of time lasting 25 to 35 minutes. Your memory and concentration will work better if you study in short, frequent bursts.

- Drill and practice are essential ingredients for success in maths.
- Try to link any new material to things you know already. This is learning through association and helps long-term retention.

Don't get hung up on more difficult material. Concentrate on understanding the fundamental concepts and being able to answer all straightforward questions. Then, with time, you can build up to the more challenging problems.

Leaving Certificate examination

Exam focus is critical to exam success. It is important to prepare yourself for the challenges you will face. By learning about the structure of the exam, you will learn how to maximise your points, allocate your time effectively and manage the paper in a calm manner.

The examination paper will be presented in two sections.

Section A – 150 marks
Concepts and Skills

Read the exam paper right through at the start in order to determine which question is the easiest one to start with. Your mind may also be subconsciously processing some of the other problems.

Section B – 150 marks
Contexts and Applications

Start with your best question, then your next best and so on. This way, if you are short of time, at least your best questions will be done.

Time yourself as follows

- Read the paper at the start: 5 minutes
- Section A: 70 minutes
- Section B: 70 minutes
- Review your answers at the end: 5 minutes
- Try to stick closely to these times. If you run out of time on a question, leave it and come back at the end.
- Keep moving through the questions and follow the procedures you have learned.

Attempt marks are valuable, so it is vital that you attempt all questions. Leave **NO** blanks.

Further exam tips

- There is no such thing as rough work in Maths – all work is relevant. If the examiner doesn't know how you reached an answer, even a correct answer, then full marks may not be awarded. Thus, **show all your work**.
- Attempt marks will be awarded for any step in the right direction. Therefore, **make an attempt at each part of the question**. Even if you do not get the correct answer, you can still pick up most of the marks on offer if you show how you worked it out. Also, **draw a diagram where possible** because this can help you see the solution.
- If you cannot finish part of a question, leave a space and come back to it later. **Never scribble out any work or use Tipp-Ex**. Put a single line through it so that the examiner can still read it. In many cases, work that had a line through it received more marks. **Avoid using pencil** because the writing can be very faint and difficult to read.

- It is a good idea to show each stage of a calculation when using a calculator (in case you press a wrong key). Familiarise yourself with your calculator. Know your *booklet of formulae and tables* well and write down any formula that you use.

> Your calculator and *booklet of formulae and tables* are two extremely valuable resources to have in the exam. Make sure that you are very familiar with how your calculator works and that you know how to perform all functions on it. Also familiarise yourself with the *booklet of formulae and tables* so that you don't waste any time in the exam trying to find formulae.

Glossary of words used on the examination paper

Write down, state
You can write down your answer without showing any work. However, if you want you can show some workings.

Calculate, find, show that, determine, prove
Obtain your answers by showing all relevant work. Marks are available for showing the steps leading to your final answer or conclusion.

Solve
Find the solution, or root, of an equation. The solution is the value of the variable that makes the left-hand side balance with the right-hand side.

Evaluate
Work out, or find, a numerical value by putting in numbers for letters.

Comment on
After studying the given information or answers, give your opinion on their significance.

Plot
Indicate the position of points on a graph, usually on the *x*- and *y*-planes.

Construct
Draw an accurate diagram, usually labelled, using a pencil, ruler, set square, compass and protractor. Leave all constructions on your diagram.

Sketch
Make a rough diagram or graph, labelled if needed.

Hence
You **must** use the answer, or result, from the previous part of the question.

Hence or otherwise
It is recommended that you use the answer, or result, from the previous part of the question, and it is usually best to do this, but other methods are acceptable.

Syllabus checklist for Leaving Certificate Higher Level Maths Paper 2 exam

The philosophy of your mathematics course is that topics can overlap, so you may encounter Paper 1 material on Paper 2 and vice versa.

The syllabus stresses that in all aspects of the Leaving Certificate Maths course, students should be able to:

- ☐ Explore patterns and formulate conjectures
- ☐ Explain findings
- ☐ Justify conclusions
- ☑ Communicate mathematics verbally and in written form
- ☐ Apply their knowledge and skills to solve problems in familiar and unfamiliar contexts
- ☐ Analyse information presented verbally and translate it into mathematical form
- ☐ Devise, select and use appropriate mathematical models, formulae or techniques to process information and to draw relevant conclusions

Coordinate geometry of the line

- ☐ Use slopes to show that two lines are:
  - ○ parallel
  - ○ perpendicular.
- ☐ Recognise the fact that the relationship $ax + by + c = 0$ is linear.
- ☐ Solve problems involving slopes of lines.
- ☐ Calculate the area of a triangle.
- ☐ Solve problems involving:
  - ○ the perpendicular distance from a point to a line
  - ○ the angle between two lines.
- ☐ Divide a line segment internally in a given ratio $m : n$.

Coordinate geometry of the circle

- ☐ Recognise that $(x - h)^2 + (y - k)^2 = r^2$ represents the relationship between the x and y coordinates of points on a circle with centre (h, k) and radius r.
- ☐ Recognise that $x^2 + y^2 + 2gx + 2fy + c = 0$ represents the relationship between the x and y coordinates of points on a circle with centre $(-g, -f)$ and radius r where $r = \sqrt{g^2 + f^2 - c}$.
- ☐ Solve problems involving a line and a circle.

Trigonometry

- ☐ Use the theorem of Pythagoras to solve problems.
- ☐ Define $\sin \theta$, $\cos \theta$ and $\tan \theta$ for all values of θ.
- ☐ Work with trigonometric ratios in surd form.
- ☐ Use trigonometry to calculate the area of a triangle.
- ☐ Solve problems using the sine and cosine rules.
- ☐ Solve problems involving the area of a sector of a circle and the length of an arc.
- ☐ Use trigonometry to solve problems in 3D.
- ☐ Graph the trigonometric functions sine, cosine, tangent.
- ☐ Graph trigonometric functions of type $f(\theta) = a + b\sin c\theta$ and $g(\theta) = a + b\cos c\theta$ for $a, b, c \in \mathbb{R}$.
- ☐ Solve trigonometric equations such as $\sin n\theta = 0$ and $\cos n\theta = \dfrac{1}{2}$, giving all solutions.
- ☐ Use the radian measure of angles.
- ☐ Derive the trigonometric formulae 1, 2, 3, 4, 5, 6, 7, 9.
- ☐ Apply the trigonometric formulae 1–24.

Geometry

Synthetic geometry

- ☐ Perform constructions 1–22.
- ☐ Construct $\sqrt{2}$ and $\sqrt{3}$ geometrically.
- ☐ Use the following terms related to logic and deductive reasoning:

  theorem, proof, axiom, corollary, converse, implies, is equivalent to, if and only if, proof by contradiction

- ☐ Investigate theorems 7, 8, 11, 12, 13, 16, 17, 18, 20, 21 and corollary 6 and use them to solve problems.
- ☐ Prove theorems 11, 12, 13.

Transformation geometry, enlargements

- ☐ Investigate enlargements, paying attention to:
  - ○ centre of enlargement
  - ○ scale factor k, where $0 < k < 1$, $k \in \mathbb{Q}$
  - ○ scale factor k, $k > 1$, $k \in \mathbb{Q}$
  - ○ area.
- ☐ Solve problems involving enlargements.

Length, area and volume

- [ ] Select and use suitable strategies to find:
  - o the length of the perimeter and the area of the following plane figures: parallelogram, trapezium and figures made from combinations of these
  - o surface area and volume of the following solid figures: cylinder, right cone, right prism and sphere.
- [ ] Use the trapezoidal rule to approximate area.
- [ ] Investigate the nets of prisms (polygonal bases), cylinders and cones.
- [ ] Solve problems involving the length of the perimeter and the area of the following plane figures: disc, triangle, rectangle, square, parallelogram, trapezium, sectors of discs and figures made from combinations of these.
- [ ] Solve problems involving surface area and volume of the following solid figures: rectangular block, cylinder, right cone, triangular-based prism (right angle, isosceles and equilateral), sphere, hemisphere and solids made from combinations of these.

Probability

Counting

- [ ] List outcomes of an experiment.
- [ ] Apply the fundamental principles of counting.
- [ ] Count the arrangements of n distinct objects ($n!$).
- [ ] Count the number of ways of arranging r objects from n distinct objects (nPr).
- [ ] Count the number of ways of selecting r objects from n distinct objects (nCr).

Concepts of probability

- [ ] Decide whether an everyday event is likely or unlikely to occur.
- [ ] Recognise that probability is a measure on a scale of 0–1 of how likely an event is to occur.
- [ ] Use set theory; discuss experiments, outcomes, sample spaces.
- [ ] Use the language of probability to discuss events, including those with equally likely outcomes.
- [ ] Estimate probabilities from experimental data.
- [ ] Recognise that if an experiment is repeated, there will be different outcomes and that increasing the number of times an experiment is repeated generally leads to better estimates of probability.
- [ ] Associate the probability of an event with its long-run relative frequency.
- [ ] Discuss basic rules of probability (and/or, mutually exclusive) through the use of Venn diagrams.

- [ ] Calculate expected value and understand that this does not need to be one of the outcomes.
- [ ] Recognise the role of expected value in decision-making and explore the issue of fair games.
- [ ] Extend your understanding of the basic rules of probability (and/or, mutually exclusive) through the use of formulae:
  - ○ addition rule: $P(A \cup B) = P(A) + P(B) - P(A \cap B)$
  - ○ multiplication rule (independent events): $P(A \cap B) = P(A) \times P(B)$
  - ○ multiplication rule (general case): $P(A \cap B) = P(A) \times P(B \mid A)$
- [ ] Solve problems involving conditional probability in a systematic way.
- [ ] Appreciate that in general, $P(A \mid B) \neq P(B \mid A)$.
- [ ] Examine the implications of $P(A \mid B) \neq P(B \mid A)$ in context.

Outcomes of random processes

- [ ] Construct sample spaces for two independent events.
- [ ] Apply the principle that in the case of equally likely outcomes, the probability is given by the number of outcomes of interest divided by the total number of outcomes (examples using coins, dice, spinners, urns with coloured objects, playing cards, etc.).
- [ ] Find the probability that two independent events both occur.
- [ ] Apply an understanding of Bernoulli trials.
- [ ] Solve problems involving up to three Bernoulli trials.
- [ ] Calculate the probability that the first success occurs on the nth Bernoulli trial where n is specified.
- [ ] Solve problems involving calculating the probability of k successes in n repeated Bernoulli trials (normal approximation not required).
- [ ] Calculate the probability that the kth success occurs on the nth Bernoulli trial.
- [ ] Use simulations to explore the variability of sample statistics from a known population, to construct sampling distributions and to draw conclusions about the sampling distribution of the mean.
- [ ] Solve problems involving reading probabilities from the normal distribution tables.

Statistics
Statistical reasoning with an aim of becoming a statistically aware consumer

- [ ] Engage in discussions about the purpose of statistics and recognise misconceptions and misuses of statistics.
- [ ] Discuss populations and samples.

☐ Decide to what extent conclusions can be generalised.

☐ Work with different types of data – categorical, nominal or ordinal numerical, discrete or continuous – in order to clarify the problem at hand.

☐ Work with different types of bivariate data.

Finding, collecting and organising data

☐ Clarify the problem at hand.

☐ Formulate one (or more) questions that can be answered with data.

☐ Explore different ways of collecting data.

☐ Generate data or source data from other sources, including the internet.

☐ Select a sample (simple random sample).

☐ Recognise the importance of representativeness so as to avoid biased samples.

☐ Discuss different types of studies: sample surveys, observational studies and designed experiments.

☐ Recognise the importance of randomisation and the role of the control group in studies.

☐ Recognise biases, limitations and ethical issues of each type of study.

☐ Select a random sample (know the definitions of stratified, cluster, quota).

☐ Design a plan and collect data on the basis of the above knowledge.

Representing data graphically and numerically

Graphical:

☐ Describe the sample (both univariate and bivariate data) by selecting appropriate graphical or numerical methods.

☐ Evaluate the effectiveness of different displays in representing the findings of a statistical investigation conducted by others.

☐ Use stem and leaf plots and histograms (equal intervals) to display data.

☐ Explore the distribution of data, including concepts of symmetry and skewness.

☐ Compare data sets using appropriate displays, including back-to-back stem and leaf plots.

☐ Determine the relationship between variables using scatterplots.

☐ Recognise that correlation is a value from -1 to $+1$ and that it measures the extent of the linear relationship between two variables.

☐ Match correlation coefficient values to appropriate scatterplots.

☐ Understand that correlation does not imply causality.

☐ Analyse plots of the data to explain differences in measures of centre and spread.

☐ Draw the line of best fit by eye.

☐ Make predictions based on the line of best fit.

☐ Calculate the correlation coefficient by calculator.

Numerical:

☐ Use a variety of summary statistics to describe the data:

    ○ central tendency: mean, median, mode

    ○ variability: range.

☐ Recognise standard deviation and interquartile range as measures of variability.

☐ Use a calculator to calculate standard deviation.

☐ Find quartiles and the interquartile range.

☐ Use the interquartile range appropriately when analysing data.

☐ Recognise the existence and the effect of outliers.

☐ Use percentiles to assign relative standing.

Analysing, interpreting and drawing inferences from data

☐ Recognise how sampling variability influences the use of sample information to make statements about the population.

☐ Use appropriate tools to describe variability, drawing inferences about the population from the sample.

☐ Interpret the analysis.

☐ Relate the interpretation to the original question.

☐ Interpret a histogram in terms of the distribution of data.

☐ Make decisions based on the empirical rule.

☐ Recognise the concept of a hypothesis test.

☐ Calculate the margin of error for a population proportion.

☐ Conduct a hypothesis test on a population proportion using the margin of error.

1 Coordinate Geometry of the Line

☐ To know where to find the coordinate geometry formulae in the *booklet of formulae and tables*

☐ To learn how to apply these formulae to procedural and in-context examination questions

☐ To gain the ability, with practice, to recall relevant techniques and tactics for the exam

Coordinate geometry formulae

Nine formulae for coordinate geometry are on pages 18 and 19 of the *booklet of formulae and tables*. Here they are:

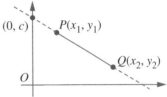
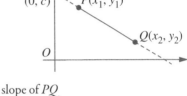

$$m = \frac{y_2 - y_1}{x_2 - x_1}$$ slope of PQ

$$|PQ| = \sqrt{(x_2 - x_1)^2 + (y_2 - y_1)^2}$$ length of $[PQ]$

$$\left(\frac{x_1 + x_2}{2}, \frac{y_1 + y_2}{2} \right)$$ midpoint of $[PQ]$

$$y - y_1 = m(x - x_1)$$
$$y = mx + c$$ equation of PQ

$$\frac{1}{2}|x_1y_2 - x_2y_1|$$ area of triangle OPQ

$$\left(\frac{bx_1 + ax_2}{b + a}, \frac{by_1 + ay_2}{a + b} \right)$$ point dividing $[PQ]$ in the ratio $a : b$

$$\frac{|ax_1 + by_1 + c|}{\sqrt{a^2 + b^2}}$$ distance from (x_1, y_1) to the line $ax + by + c = 0$

$$\tan \theta = \pm \frac{m_1 - m_2}{1 + m_1m_2}$$ angles between two lines of slopes m_1 and m_2

In addition, we must also know the following rules:

(i) Parallel lines have equal slopes.

If $l \| k \Leftrightarrow m_l = m_k$

(ii) If two lines are perpendicular then the product of their slopes equals -1.

If $l \perp k \Leftrightarrow (m_l)(m_k) = -1$

(iii) $y = 0$ is the equation of the x-axis.

$x = 0$ is the equation of the y-axis.

key point

m_l is the slope of l and m_k is the slope of k.

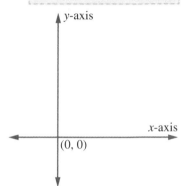

exam focus

Rules (i), (ii) and (iii) are not in the *booklet of formulae and tables.* You have to know them!

To verify that a point belongs to a line

Substitute the coordinates of the point into the equation of the line. If the coordinates satisfy the equation, then the point is on the line, otherwise, the point is not on the line.

Example

Is the point $(4, -7)$ on the line $2x - 3y = 27$? Justify your answer.

Solution

If $(4, -7) \in 2x - 3y = 27$

then $2(4) - 3(-7) = 27$

$\qquad 8 + 21 \neq 27$

Hence $(4, -7)$ is not on the line $2x - 3y = 27$.

Example

The point $P(k^2, k)$ is on the line $x - 2y = 8$.

Find the coordinates of P where $k \in \mathbb{R}$.

Solution

$(k^2, k) \in x - 2y = 8$

$(k^2) - 2(k) = 8$

$k^2 - 2k - 8 = 0$

Factorising: $(k + 2)(k - 4) = 0$

$k = -2$ or $k = 4$

$P = (k^2, k)$

$k = -2$ then $P = (4, -2)$

$k = 4$ then $P = (16, 4)$

key point

Both points are on the line $x - 2y = 8$

Equation of a line, and finding the point of intersection of two lines

In this section, we revise some straightforward coordinate geometry by tackling an exam question.

(2018 Q.5 (a) and (b))

The line m: $2x + 3y + 1 = 0$ is parallel to the line n: $2x + 3y - 51 = 0$.

(a) Verify that $A(-2, 1)$ is on m.

(b) Find the coordinates of B, the point on the line n closest to A as shown

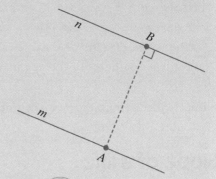

Solution

(a) Is $A(-2,1) \in 2x + 3y + 1 = 0$

$$2(-2) + 3(1) + 1 = 0?$$
$$-4 + 3 + 1 = 0$$

This is true. Therefore the point $A(-2, 1)$ is on the line.

Part (a) was awarded 10 marks.
Part (b) was awarded 10 marks.

(b) Slope of line m: $2x + 3y + 1 = 0$

$$3y = -2x - 1 \text{ has slope } = \frac{-2}{3}$$

Slope of $AB = +\frac{3}{2}$ because AB is perpendicular to line m.

Equation of AB given by $y - y_1 = m(x - x_1)$ $m = \frac{3}{2}$ $(x_1, y_1) = (-2, 1)$

$$y - 1 = \frac{3}{2}(x - (-2))$$
$$2y - 2 = 3x + 6$$
$$-3x + 2y = 8$$

Now find B, the point of intersection of AB and the line n.

$2x + 3y = 51$ multiply by 3	Now sub $y = 13$ into (say) $-3x + 2y = 8$
$-3x + 2y = 8$ multiply by 2	$-3x + 2(13) = 8$
$6x + 9y = 153$	$-3x = 8 - 26$
$-6x + 4y = 16$	$-3x = -18$
$13y = 169$	$x = 6$
$y = 13$	

Answer: $B = (6, 13)$

Transformations of the plane

(a) Translation: A translation moves a point in a straight line.

(b) Central symmetry: Central symmetry is a reflection in a point.

(c) Axial symmetry: Axial symmetry is a reflection in a line.

(d) Axial symmetry in the axes or central symmetry in the origin.

The following three patterns emerge and it is worth memorising them:

1. Axial symmetry in the x-axis → change the sign of y
2. Axial symmetry in the y-axis → change the sign of x
3. Central symmetry in the origin, $(0, 0)$ → change the sign of both x and y

Note: Under a translation or a central symmetry, a line is mapped onto a parallel line.

Slope of a line

Slope of a line, m, given two points.
$$m = \frac{y_2 - y_1}{x_2 - x_1}$$

Slope is $\dfrac{\text{rise}}{\text{run}} = \tan \theta$, where θ is the angle the line makes with the positive sense of the x-axis.

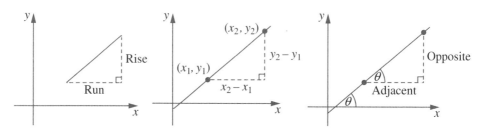

We say θ, the angle of inclination, is the angle formed between a line and the positive side of the x-axis.

The angle of inclination is always between 0° and 180°.

- It is always measured anticlockwise from the positive side of the x-axis.
- The slope m of any line is equal to the tangent of its angle of inclination: then $m = \tan\theta$ (where θ = angle of inclination).

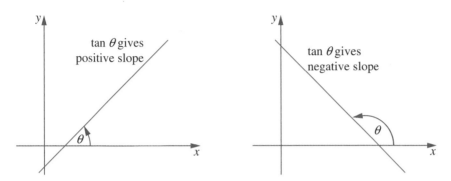

The slope of a line when given its equation

To find the slope of a line when given its equation, do the following.

Method 1:

> Get y on its own, and the number in front of x is the slope.

Note: The number in front of x is called the **coefficient** of x.

The number on its own is called the y-**intercept**.

In short: write the line in the form

$y = mx + c$.

$$y = \quad mx \quad + \qquad\qquad\qquad c \quad \text{(see } booklet\ of\ formulae\ and\ tables, \text{page 18)}$$

$$\qquad\quad \downarrow \qquad\qquad\qquad\qquad\qquad \downarrow$$

$y = (\text{slope})x + (\text{where the line cuts the } y\text{-axis})$

Method 2:

> If the line is in the form $ax + by + c = 0$, then $-\dfrac{a}{b}$ is the slope.

In other words: Slope $= -\dfrac{\text{Number in front of } x}{\text{Number in front of } y}$

key point

When using this method, make sure every term is on the left-hand side in the given equation of the line.

Lines parallel to the axes

$y = 1$ is a line parallel to the x-axis through the point $(0, 1)$.

$x = 2$ is a line parallel to the y-axis through the point $(2, 0)$.

key point

$y = 0$ is the equation of the x-axis.

$x = 0$ is the equation of the y-axis.

All horizontal lines have an angle of inclination of 0°.

Their slopes are zero.

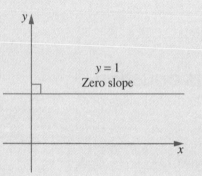

All vertical lines have an angle of inclination of 90°.

Their slopes are infinitely steep.

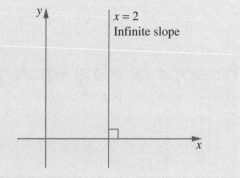

exam Q

(2013 Q.3 (a))

The equations of six lines are given:

Line	Equation
h	$x = 3 - y$
i	$2x - 4y = 3$
k	$y = -\frac{1}{4}(2x - 7)$
l	$4x - 2y - 5 = 0$
m	$x + \sqrt{3}y - 10 = 0$
n	$\sqrt{3}x + y - 10 = 0$

Complete the table below by matching each description given to one or more of the lines.

Description	Line(s)
A line with a slope of 2.	
A line which intersects the y-axis at $(0, -2\frac{1}{2})$	
A line which makes equal intercepts on the axes	
A line which makes an angle of 150° with the positive sense of the x-axis	
Two lines which are perpendicular to each other.	

Solution

Use $y = mx + c$ six times

h: $x = 3 - y$
$\quad\quad y = 3 - x$

h has slope $= -1$

i: $2x - 4y = 3$
$\quad\quad 2x - 3 = 4y$
$\quad\quad \frac{1}{2}x - \frac{3}{4} = y$

i has a slope $= \frac{1}{2}$

Very few candidates answered all five correctly. The marking scheme reflected this.

3 marks for any one correct.

7 marks for any two correct.

9 marks for any four correct.

10 marks for all five correct.

k: $y = -\frac{1}{4}(2x - 7)$
$\quad\quad y = -\frac{1}{2}x + \frac{7}{4}$

k has a slope $= -\frac{1}{2}$

l: $4x - 2y - 5 = 0$
$\quad\quad 4x - 5 = 2y$
$\quad\quad 2x - \frac{5}{2} = y$

l has a slope $= 2$

m: $x + \sqrt{3}y - 10 = 0$
$\quad\quad \sqrt{3}y = 10 - x$
$\quad\quad y = \frac{10}{\sqrt{3}} - \frac{1}{\sqrt{3}}x$

n: $\sqrt{3}x + y - 10 = 0$
$\quad\quad y = 10 - \sqrt{3}x$
$\quad\quad m$ has slope $= -\sqrt{3}$

m has slope $= -\frac{1}{\sqrt{3}}$

The six slopes above tell us:

- l has slope 2

- $k \perp l$ because $\left(-\frac{1}{2}\right)(2) = -1$

- $\tan 150° = $ slope $= -\frac{1}{\sqrt{3}}$ slope m

- Equal intercepts $\rightarrow$ slope $= \tan 135° = -1$
  Then h has slope $= -1$.

- Finally $\left(0, -2\frac{1}{2}\right) \in l$

$\quad\quad \left(0, -2\frac{1}{2}\right) \in 4x - 2y - 5 = 0$

$\quad\quad 0 + 5 - 5 = 0$

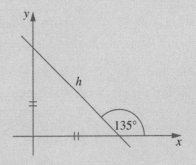

Answer:

Description	Line(s)
A line with a slope of 2.	l
A line which intersects the y-axis at $(0, -2\frac{1}{2})$	l
A line which makes equal intercepts on the axes	h
A line which makes an angle of 150° with the positive sense of the x-axis	m
Two lines which are perpendicular to each other.	l, k

Example

Investigate whether $A(-4, 3)$, $B(-1, 6)$ and $C(7, 10)$ are collinear.

key point

Collinear: If three or more points lie on the same line, then the points are said to be collinear.

Note: Two points always lie on a line.

Solution

Method 1

The three points either form a straight line or they do not.
To decide which, we will find the slopes of AB and BC.

$$m_{AB} = \frac{y_2 - y_1}{x_2 - x_1}$$

$$= \frac{6 - 3}{-1 - (-4)} = \frac{3}{3} = 1$$

$$m_{BC} = \frac{y_2 - y_1}{x_2 - x_1}$$

$$= \frac{10 - 6}{7 - (-1)} = \frac{4}{8} = \frac{1}{2}$$

As $m_{AB} \neq m_{BC}$, the points A, B and C are not collinear.

Note: We could have found the slope of m_{AC} as one of the two slopes.

Method 2

To find the area of $\triangle ABC$, use translation $(-4, 3) \rightarrow (0, 0)$ to get:

$$A = (-4, 3) \rightarrow (0, 0) \qquad \text{(Add 4 to } x \text{, subtract 3 from } y)$$

$$B = (-1, 6) \rightarrow (3, 3) = (x_1, y_1)$$

$$C = (7, 10) \rightarrow (11, 7) = (x_2, y_2)$$

$\therefore$ Area $\triangle ABC = \frac{1}{2}|x_1y_2 - x_2y_1|$ (see *booklet of formulae and tables*, page 18)

$$= \frac{1}{2}|(3)(7) - (11)(3)|$$

$$= \frac{1}{2}|21 - 33| = \frac{1}{2}|-12| = 6$$

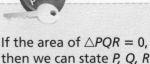

Since the area of $\triangle ABC \neq 0$, the three points A, B and C do not form a straight line $\Rightarrow A$, B and C are not collinear.

If the area of $\triangle PQR = 0$, then we can state P, Q, R are collinear.

Division of a line segment in a given ratio

The coordinates of the point $C(x, y)$ which divides the line segment $P(x_1, y_1)$ and $Q(x_2, y_2)$ internally in the ratio $a : b$ is given by:

Internal divisor

(see *booklet of formulae and tables*, page 18)

$$C(x, y) = \left(\frac{bx_1 + ax_2}{b + a}, \frac{by_1 + ay_2}{b + a}\right)$$

Example

(i) $P(7, -11)$ and $Q(-5, 5)$ are two points. C is a point on $[PQ]$ such that $|PC| : |CQ| = 5 : 3$. Find the coordinates of C.

(ii) The point $R\left(-\frac{1}{2}, -1\right)$ divides the line segment $|VW|$ such that $|VR| : |RW| = 1 : 4$. If the coordinates of V are $(3, -3)$, find the coordinates of W.

Solution

(i) $C = \left(\frac{(5)(-5) + (3)(7)}{5 + 3}, \frac{(5)(5) + (3)(-11)}{5 + 3}\right)$

$C = \left(\frac{-25 + 21}{8}, \frac{25 - 33}{8}\right) = \left(-\frac{1}{2}, -1\right)$

(ii) Using a translation

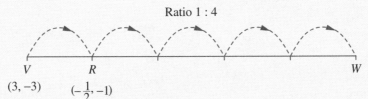

Notice translation $V \rightarrow R$ means $(3, -3) \rightarrow \left(-\frac{1}{2}, -1\right)$

x-component $-3\frac{1}{2}$

y-component $+2$

V　　R　　　　　　　　　　　　　　W

$\left(-\frac{1}{2}, -1\right)$

x-component $-\frac{1}{2} - 3\frac{1}{2} - 3\frac{1}{2} - 3\frac{1}{2} - 3\frac{1}{2} = -14\frac{1}{2}$

y-component $-1 + 2 + 2 + 2 + 2 = 7$

$$W = \left(-14\frac{1}{2}, 7\right)$$

exam
Q

(i) The line $4x - 5y + k = 0$ cuts the x-axis at P and the y-axis at Q. Write down the coordinates of P and Q in terms of k.

(ii) The area of the triangle OPQ is 10 square units, where O is the origin. Find two possible values of k.

Solution

(i) P is on the x-axis $\Rightarrow y = 0$ 　　　　　　Q is on the y-axis $\Rightarrow x = 0$

　$4x - 5y + k = 0$ 　　　　　　　　　　　$4x - 5y + k = 0$

　$4x - 5(0) + k = 0$ 　　　　　　　　　$4(0) - 5y + k = 0$

　　　　$x = -\frac{k}{4}$ 　　　　　　　　　　　　$y = \frac{k}{5}$

Thus, P has coordinates $\left(-\frac{k}{4}, 0\right)$. 　　Thus, Q has coordinates $\left(0, \frac{k}{5}\right)$.

(ii) Points: $(0, 0)$, $\left(-\frac{k}{4}, 0\right)$, $\left(0, \frac{k}{5}\right)$ 　　Given: area of $\triangle OPQ = 10$

$$\text{Area of } \triangle = \frac{1}{2}|x_1y_2 - x_2y_1| = 10$$

$$\frac{1}{2}\left|\left(-\frac{k}{4}\right)\left(\frac{k}{5}\right) - (0)(0)\right| = 10 \quad \text{(multiply by 2)}$$

$$\left|-\frac{k^2}{20}\right| = 20$$

$$-\frac{k^2}{20} = 20 \text{ or } -\frac{k^2}{20} = -20$$

$$k^2 = -400 \text{ or } k^2 = 400$$

Reject $k = \pm 20$

key point

k^2 is always positive where $k \in \mathbb{R}$, hence we reject $k^2 = -400$.

exam Q

(i) Show that the point (1, 5) is on the line $2x - 5y + 23 = 0$.

(ii) If $2x - 5y + 23 = 0$, express y in terms of x.

(iii) A triangle ABC lies entirely in the first quadrant and has an area of $4\frac{1}{2}$ square units. The equation of one side of the triangle is $2x - 5y + 23 = 0$ and the vertices of A and B are (1, 5) and (3, 4), respectively. Find the coordinates of C.

Solution

(i) $2x - 5y + 23 = 2(1) - 5(5) + 23 = 2 - 25 + 23 = 0$
∴ (1, 5) is on the line $2x - 5y + 23 = 0$.

(ii) Rearrange the equation of the line:

$$2x - 5y + 23 = 0$$

$$-5y = -2x - 23$$

$$y = \frac{2}{5}x + \frac{23}{5} \text{ or } \frac{2x + 23}{5}$$

(iii) As $B(3, 4)$ is not on $2x - 5y + 23 = 0$ (because $2(3) - 5(4) + 23 \neq 0$), we can deduce that C must be on it. From **(ii)**, we can describe C as $\left(x, \frac{2}{5}x + \frac{23}{5}\right)$. We need to move (translate) the points so that one of them is at the origin (0, 0).

$$A(1, 5) \quad B(3, 4) \quad\quad C\left(x, \frac{2}{5}x + \frac{23}{5}\right)$$
$$\downarrow \quad\quad\quad \downarrow \quad\quad\quad\quad\quad \downarrow$$
$$(0, 0) \quad (2, -1) \quad\quad \left(x - 1, \frac{2}{5}x + \frac{23}{5} - 5\right)$$
$$= \left(x - 1, \frac{2}{5}x - \frac{2}{5}\right)$$

Area of triangle: $\dfrac{1}{2}\left|x_1 y_2 - x_2 y_1\right| = 4\dfrac{1}{2}$

$$\frac{1}{2}\left|(2)\left(\frac{2}{5}x - \frac{2}{5}\right) - (x - 1)(-1)\right| = \frac{9}{2}$$

$$\left|(2)\left(\frac{2}{5}x - \frac{2}{5}\right) - (x - 1)(-1)\right| = 9 \quad \text{(multiply both sides by 2)}$$

$$\left| \frac{4}{5}x - \frac{4}{5} + x - 1 \right| = 9$$

$$\left| \frac{9}{5}x - \frac{9}{5} \right| = 9$$

$$|9x - 9| = 45 \quad \text{(multiply both sides by 5)}$$

$$|x - 1| = 5 \quad \text{(divide both sides by 9)}$$

$$x - 1 = 5 \qquad \text{or} \qquad x - 1 = -5$$
$$x = 6 \qquad\qquad\qquad x = -4$$

$$y = \frac{2x + 23}{5}$$

Reject $x = -4$, as C must lie inside the first quadrant.

$$= \frac{2(6) + 23}{5}$$

$$= \frac{35}{5}$$

$$= 7$$

∴ C is (6, 7).

Concurrencies of a triangle

1. Centroid *G*

A **median** of a triangle is a line segment from a vertex to the midpoint of the opposite side. The three medians of a triangle meet at a point called the centroid, *G*. *G* divides each median in the ratio 2 : 1.

The following three geometry constructions using concurrencies may be easily incorporated into a coordinate geometry exam question. They are worth remembering.

$$\text{Coordinates of } G = \left(\frac{x_1 + x_2 + x_3}{3}, \frac{y_1 + y_2 + y_3}{3} \right).$$

(see *booklet of formulae and tables*, page 52)

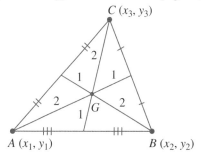

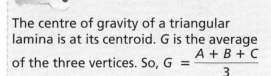

The centre of gravity of a triangular lamina is at its centroid. *G* is the average of the three vertices. So, $G = \dfrac{A + B + C}{3}$

2. Circumcentre O

The circumcentre of a triangle is the point of intersection of the perpendicular bisectors of the sides.

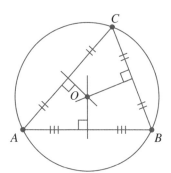

3. Orthocentre H

An altitude of a triangle is a perpendicular line from a vertex to its opposite side. The orthocentre is the point of intersection of the altitudes.

Note: The centroid, circumcentre and orthocentre in a triangle all lie on a straight line called **Euler's line.**

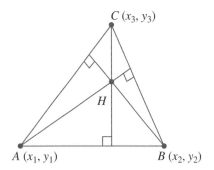

exam
Q

(2017 Q.3)

ABC is a triangle where the co-ordinates of A and C are $(0, 6)$ and $(4, 2)$ respectively. $G(\frac{2}{3}, \frac{4}{3})$ is the centroid of the triangle ABC. AG intersects BC at the point P.

$$|AG| : |GP| = 2:1$$

(a) Find the co-ordinates of P.

(b) Find the co-ordinates of B.

(c) Prove that C is the orthocentre of the triangle ABC.

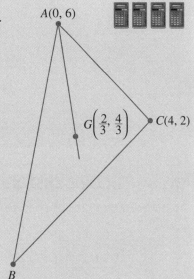

Solution

(a) and (b) Rule for centroid

$$G = \frac{A + B + C}{3}$$

$$\left(\frac{2}{3}, \frac{4}{3}\right) = \frac{(0, 6) + B + (4, 2)}{3}$$

$$(2, 4) = (0, 6) + B + (4, 2)$$

$$(2, 4) = (4, 8) + B$$

$$(2, 4) - (4, 8) = B$$

$$(-2, -4) = B$$

P is mid-point of BC

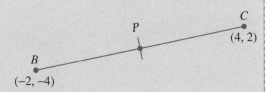

$$P = \left(\frac{-2+4}{2}, \frac{-4+2}{2}\right) = (1, -1)$$

(c)

key point

A note on the location of orthocentre: The orthocentre of a triangle is
  (i) <u>inside</u> the triangle if all three angles are less than 90°.
  (ii) <u>outside</u> the triangle if one angle is greater than 90°.
  (iii) <u>at</u> the perpendicular vertex in a right-angled triangle.

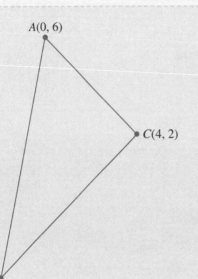

Slope $AC = \dfrac{6-2}{0-4} = \dfrac{4}{-4} = -1$

Slope $BC = \dfrac{-4-2}{-2-4} = \dfrac{-6}{-6} = 1$

Since $(-1)(1) = -1$ Therefore, $AC \perp BC$

$\triangle ABC$ is right-angled at C and so, the orthocentre is at the point C.

Perpendicular distance from a point to a line

The perpendicular distance, d, from the point (x_1, y_1) to the line $ax + by + c = 0$ is given by:

$$d = \frac{|ax_1 + by_1 + c|}{\sqrt{a^2 + b^2}}$$

(see *booklet of formulae and tables*, page 19)

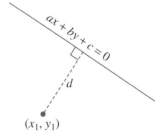

Example

Find the perpendicular distance of the point $(7, -2)$ from the line
$5y - 12x + 3 = 0$

Solution

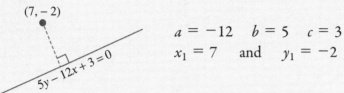

$a = -12$ $b = 5$ $c = 3$

$x_1 = 7$ and $y_1 = -2$

$$\text{The perpendicular distance} = \frac{|ax_1 + by_1 + c|}{\sqrt{a^2 + b^2}}$$

$$= \frac{|(-12)(7) + (5)(-2) + 3|}{\sqrt{144 + 25}}$$

$$= \frac{|-84 - 10 + 3|}{13}$$

$$= 7$$

Example

l is the line $x - 2y + 1 = 0$. The point $(3, k)$ is a distance $2\sqrt{5}$ from the line l. Find two possible values of k.

Solution

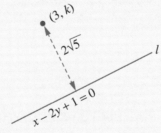

We have been given an equation in disguise, so using the formula:

$$\frac{|ax_1 + by_1 + c|}{\sqrt{a^2 + b^2}} = d$$

$$\frac{|1(3) - 2(k) + 1|}{\sqrt{1^2 + (-2)^2}} = 2\sqrt{5}$$

$$\frac{|4 - 2k|}{\sqrt{5}} = 2\sqrt{5}$$

$$|4 - 2k| = 2(5) = 10$$

$4 - 2k = 10$ or $4 - 2k = -10$

     $-2k = 6$ $-2k = -14$

       $k = -3$ $k = 7$

Thus, $k = -3$ or   7.

key point

Recall how to solve a modulus equation from Algebra.

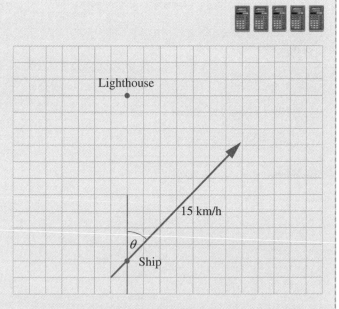

A ship is 10 km due south of a lighthouse at noon.

The ship is travelling at 15 km/h on a bearing of θ, as shown below,

where $\theta = \tan^{-1}\dfrac{4}{3}$.

(i) On the given diagram, draw a set of coordinate axes that takes the lighthouse as the origin, the line east–west through the lighthouse as the x-axis and kilometres as units.

(ii) Find the equation of the line along which the ship is moving.

(iii) Find the shortest distance between the ship and the lighthouse during the journey.

(iv) At what time is the ship closest to the lighthouse?

This question contains all the basic ingredients examiners like to use:

(a) Apply a simple diagram.

(b) Requires a standard formula but with a twist. In this case, $m \neq \tan\theta$, since θ is not the angle in the positive direction.

(c) Apply a more advanced formula.

(d) To make the candidate think and use some techniques from other topics. In this instance, speed and time and Pythagoras's theorem.

Solution

(i)

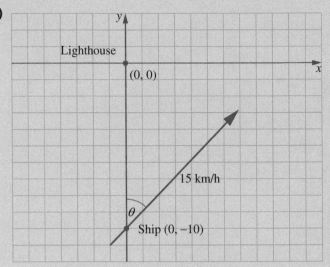

(ii)

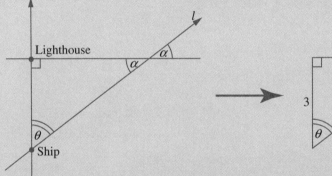

Given $\theta = \tan^{-1}\left(\dfrac{4}{3}\right)$

Then $\tan\theta = \dfrac{4}{3}$

Hence $\tan\alpha = \dfrac{\text{opp}}{\text{adj}} = \dfrac{3}{4}$, from the diagram above.

Alternatively, $\dfrac{\text{rise}}{\text{run}} = \dfrac{3}{4}$.

The slope of line l is given by $m = \tan\alpha = \dfrac{3}{4}$

$$(x_1, y_1) = (0, -10)$$

The equation of l is given by $y - y_1 = m(x - x_1)$

$$y - (-10) = \frac{3}{4}(x - 0)$$

$$4y + 40 = 3x$$

$$-3x + 4y + 40 = 0$$

(iii) The shortest distance is given by the perpendicular distance.

Perpendicular distance $= \left| \dfrac{ax_1 + by_1 + c}{\sqrt{a^2 + b^2}} \right|$

$(x_1, y_1) = (0, 0)$

$a = -3$

$b = 4$

$c = 40$

Shortest distance $= \dfrac{|(-3)(0) + (4)(0) + 40|}{\sqrt{(-3)^2 + (4)^2}}$

$\qquad\qquad = \dfrac{0 + 0 + 40}{\sqrt{9 + 16}} = 8$ km

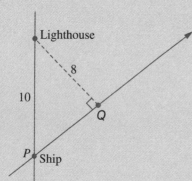

• $(0, 0)$

$-3x + 4y + 40 = 0$

l

(iv)

Lighthouse

8

10

Q

P

Ship

To find $|PQ|$, use the theorem of Pythagoras:

$$(10)^2 = (8)^2 + |PQ|^2$$

$$100 = 64 + |PQ|^2$$

$$36 = |PQ|^2$$

$$6 \text{ km} = |PQ|$$

Time required by the ship to travel 6 km given by:

Time $= \dfrac{\text{Distance}}{\text{Speed}} = \dfrac{6}{15} = 0{\cdot}4$ hours

$\therefore$ Time in minutes $= 0{\cdot}4 \times 60 = 24$ minutes

Hence, the ship is closest to the lighthouse at noon + 24 minutes = 12:24

Angle between two lines

If two lines, l_1 and l_2, have slopes m_1 and m_2 respectively, and θ is the angle between them, then:

$$\tan \theta = \pm \frac{m_1 - m_2}{1 + m_1 m_2}$$

(see *booklet of formulae and tables*, page 19)

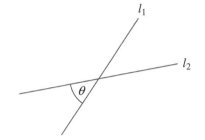

key point

If $\tan \theta$ is positive $\Rightarrow$ smaller angle = acute angle

If $\tan \theta$ is negative $\Rightarrow$ larger angle = obtuse angle

Example

Find the larger angle between the lines $2x + y + 5 = 0$ and $3x - 4y + 1 = 0$, in degrees correct to one decimal place.

Solution

$$2x + y + 5 = 0 \implies y = -2x - 5 \implies m_1 = -2$$

$$3x - 4y + 1 = 0 \implies y = \tfrac{3}{4}x + \tfrac{1}{4} \implies m_2 = \tfrac{3}{4}$$

Use $\tan \theta = \pm \dfrac{m_1 - m_2}{1 + m_1 m_2}$

$$\tan \theta = \left| \frac{m_1 - m_2}{1 + m_1 m_2} \right| = \left| \frac{-2 - \tfrac{3}{4}}{1 + (-2)\left(\tfrac{3}{4}\right)} \right|$$

$$= \left| \frac{-\tfrac{11}{4}}{1 - \tfrac{3}{2}} \right| = \frac{11}{2}$$

$$\theta = \tan^{-1} \frac{11}{2} = 79 \cdot 7°$$

The larger angle $= 180° - 79 \cdot 7° = 100 \cdot 3°$

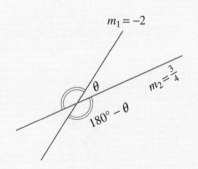

Find the slopes and the equations of the two lines that pass through the point (6, 1) and make an angle of $\theta = \tan^{-1}(1)$ with the line $x + 2y = 0$.

Solution

We will use the angle between two lines to find the slope(s) of the unknown line(s). Of the three values in this formula (m_1, m_2 and θ), we know the last two.

$$\tan \theta = \tan (\tan^{-1}(1)) = 1$$

Let the slope of the unknown line(s) be m. We expect to get two values for this. The slope of the given line must be found by rearranging its equation.

$x + 2y = 0$

$2y = -x$

$y = -\dfrac{1}{2}x$

$\therefore \quad m_2 = -\dfrac{1}{2}$

$\tan \theta = \pm \dfrac{m_1 - m_2}{1 + m_1 m_2}$

$1 = \pm \dfrac{m - \left(-\frac{1}{2}\right)}{1 + m\left(-\frac{1}{2}\right)}$ (multiply each term on the RHS by 2)

$1 = \pm \dfrac{2m + 1}{2 - m}$

$1 = \dfrac{2m + 1}{2 - m}$

$2 - m = 2m + 1$

$-3m = -1$

$m = \dfrac{1}{3}$

$1 = -\dfrac{2m + 1}{2 - m}$

$2 - m = -2m - 1$

$m = -3$

The equations of the lines:

$y - y_1 = m(x - x_1)$

$y - 1 = \dfrac{1}{3}(x - 6)$

$3y - 3 = x - 6$

$x - 3y - 3 = 0$

$y - y_1 = m(x - x_1)$

$y - 1 = -3(x - 6)$

$y - 1 = -3x + 18$

$3x + y - 19 = 0$

2 Coordinate Geometry of the Circle

- ☐ To know where to find the given coordinate geometry formulae in the *booklet of formulae and tables*
- ☐ To learn how to apply these formulae to procedural and in-context examination questions
- ☐ To know and apply the necessary formulae that are not in the booklet of formulae and tables
- ☐ To gain the ability, with practice, to recall relevant techniques and tactics necessary to succeed in the exam

Coordinate geometry formulae

The formulae for coordinate geometry of a circle are on page 19 of the *booklet of formulae and tables*. Here they are:

given centre (h, k) and radius r

$(x - h)^2 + (y - k)^2 = r^2$ equation

$(x - h)(x_1 - h) + (y - k)(y_1 - k) = r^2$ tangent at (x_1, y_1)

given equation $x^2 + y^2 + 2gx + 2fy + c = 0$

$(-g, -f)$ centre

$\sqrt{g^2 + f^2 - c}$ radius

$xx_1 + yy_1 + g(x + x_1) + f(y + y_1) + c = 0$ tangent at (x_1, y_1)

Definitions

A circle is a set of points (a locus), each of which is equidistant from a fixed point called the **centre**.

The distance from the centre to any point on the circle is called the **radius**.

The centre, C, of a wind turbine and the tip of a blade, P, are indicated on the diagram.

The path (locus) traced out in one revolution of P is a circle, centre C, with radius $|CP|$.

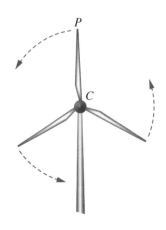

The equation of a circle

Circle with centre (0, 0)

Two quantities are needed to find the equation of a circle.

> **1.** Centre **2.** Radius
>
> If the centre is (0, 0), the equation of the circle will be of the form $x^2 + y^2 = r^2$.

Circle with centre (h, k)

Two quantities are needed to find the equation of a circle.

> **1.** Centre, (h, k) **2.** Radius, r (see *booklet of formulae and tables*, page 19)
>
> Then use the formula $(x - h)^2 + (y - k)^2 = r^2$.

The general equation of a circle is written as:

> $$x^2 + y^2 + 2gx + 2fy + c = 0$$ (see *booklet of formulae and tables*, page 19)

When the equation of a circle is given in this form, we use the following method to find its centre and radius.

> 1. Make sure every term is on the left-hand side and the coefficients of x^2 and y^2 are equal to 1.
> 2. Centre $= (-g, -f) = (-\frac{1}{2}$ coefficient of x, $-\frac{1}{2}$ coefficient of $y)$
> 3. Radius $= \sqrt{g^2 + f^2 - c}$ (provided $g^2 + f^2 - c > 0$)

key point

> When we talk about the 'equation of a circle' we should really say 'the equation of the circumference of the circle'.

Example

Find the centre and radius of the following circles.

(i) $x^2 + y^2 = 9$ (ii) $(x - 2)^2 + (x + 3)^2 = 20$

(iii) $(x + 7)(x + 3) + (y - 2)(y + 2) = 0$

Solution

(i) $x^2 + y^2 = 9$ (ii) $(x - 2)^2 + (y + 3)^2 = 20$

     Centre $= (0, 0)$ and radius $= 3$ Centre $= (2, -3)$ and radius $= \sqrt{20}$

(iii) $(x + 7)(x + 3) + (y - 2)(y + 2) = 0$

     First write the equation in the form $x^2 + y^2 + 2gx + 2fy + c = 0$.

$$(x + 7)(x + 3) + (y - 2)(y + 2) = 0$$
$$x^2 + 10x + 21 + y^2 - 4 = 0$$
$$x^2 + y^2 + 10x + 0y + 17 = 0$$

     Centre $= (-g, -f) = (-5, 0)$

     Radius $= \sqrt{g^2 + f^2 - c} = \sqrt{(-5)^2 + (0)^2 - 17} = \sqrt{8}$

Example

A circle with centre $(-3, 7)$ passes through the point $(5, -8)$. Find the equation of the circle.

Solution

We have the centre and require the radius.

Radius $r = $ distance between the points $(-3, 7)$ and $(5, -8)$.

$r = \sqrt{(5 + 3)^2 + (-8 - 7)^2}$

$= \sqrt{8^2 + (-15)^2} = \sqrt{64 + 225} = \sqrt{289} = 17$

Equation of the circle: $(x - h)^2 + (y - k)^2 = r^2$
$$(x + 3)^2 + (y - 7)^2 = 17^2$$
$$x^2 + 6x + 9 + y^2 - 14y + 49 = 289$$
$$x^2 + y^2 + 6x - 14y - 231 = 0$$

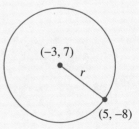

The starting point for the majority of exam questions on the circle will involve either one of the previous two examples. You must be totally familiar with both exam techniques.

Finding the equation of a circle

In many questions it is difficult to find the centre and radius. In these questions we have to use an algebraic approach, or rely on our knowledge of the geometry of a circle to find the centre and radius.

The points $A(-2, 4)$, $B(0, -10)$ and $C(6, -2)$ are the coordinates of the vertices of triangle ABC.

(i) Verify that the triangle is right-angled at C.

(ii) Hence or otherwise, find the equation of the circumcircle of triangle ABC.

Solution

(i) Draw a diagram.

Slope of $AC = m_1 = \dfrac{-2 - 4}{6 + 2} = \dfrac{-6}{8} = -\dfrac{3}{4}$

Slope of $BC = m_2 = \dfrac{-2 + 10}{6 - 0} = \dfrac{8}{6} = \dfrac{4}{3}$

$m_1 \times m_2 = -\dfrac{3}{4} \times \dfrac{4}{3} = -1$

$\therefore$ $AC \perp BC$

$\therefore$ Triangle is right-angled at C.

(ii) $[AB]$ is the diameter of the circumcircle, as triangle ABC is right-angled at C. The midpoint, P, of $[AB]$ is the centre of the circumcircle.

The coordinates of the centre $P = \left(\dfrac{-2 - 0}{2}, \dfrac{4 - 10}{2} \right) = \left(\dfrac{-2}{2}, \dfrac{-6}{2} \right) = (-1, -3)$

Radius $= |PA|$ or $|PB|$ or $|PC|$.

Radius $= |PA| = \sqrt{(-1 + 2)^2 + (-3 - 4)^2} = \sqrt{(1)^2 + (-7)^2}$

$\qquad = \sqrt{1 + 49} = \sqrt{50}$

Diagram labels: $A\,(-2, 4)$; $C\,(6, -2)$; $B\,(0, -10)$

We have the centre $= (-1, -3) = (h, k)$ and the radius $= \sqrt{50} = r$.

$(x - h)^2 + (y - k)^2 = r^2$

$(x + 1)^2 + (y + 3)^2 = (\sqrt{50})^2$

$(x + 1)^2 + (y + 3)^2 = 50$

     or

$x^2 + y^2 + 2x + 6y - 40 = 0$

From a theorem in geometry, you should know that the angle in a semicircle is right-angled. Hence $[AB]$ is a diameter of the required circle. This is yet another case of course content overlap: coordinate geometry with Euclidean geometry.

Touching circles

Two circles are said to be **touching** if they have only one point of intersection. To investigate whether two circles touch, we compare the distance between their centres with the sum or difference of their radii.

Consider two circles of radius r_1 and r_2 (where $r_1 > r_2$) and let d be the distance between their centres.

1. Circles touch externally	2. Circles touch internally
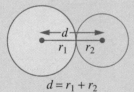	
$d = r_1 + r_2$	$d = r_1 - r_2$
Distance between their centres = sum of their radii	Distance between their centres = difference of their radii

Common chord or common tangent

If $s_1 = 0$ and $s_2 = 0$ are the equations of two circles in standard form, then $s_1 - s_2 = 0$ is the equation of the common chord or common tangent of the two circles.

Common chord	Common tangent
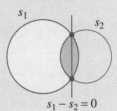	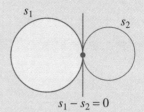
Two points of intersection	One point of intersection

To find the equation of the common chord, or common tangent, of two circles, $s_1 = 0$ and $s_2 = 0$, the coefficients of x^2 and y^2 must be the same for both circles.

(2013 Q.4)

The circles c_1 and c_2 touch externally as shown.

(a) Complete the following table

Circle	Centre	Radius	Equation
c_1	$(-3,-2)$	2	
c_2			$x^2 + y^2 - 2x - 2y - 7 = 0$

(b) (i) Find the coordinates of the point of contact of c_1 and c_2.

   (ii) Hence, or otherwise, find the equation of the tangent, t, common to c_1 and c_2.

Solution

(a) $x^2 + y^2 - 2x - 2y - 7 = 0$

$g = -1, f = -1, c = -7$

Centre $= (-g, -f) = (1, 1)$

Radius $= \sqrt{g^2 + f^2 - c} = \sqrt{1 + 1 + 7} = \sqrt{9} = 3$

Circle	Centre	Radius	Equation
C_1	$(-3, -2)$	2	$(x + 3)^2 + (y + 2)^2 = 4$
C_2	$(1, 1)$	3	$x^2 + y^2 - 2x - 2y - 7 = 0$

(b) (i)

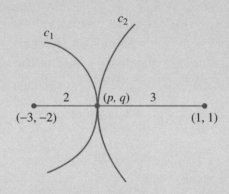

key point

Ratio of radii of $C_1 : C_2 = 2 : 3$

Let (p, q) be the coordinates of the point of contact

$(p, q) = \left(\dfrac{bx_1 + ax_2}{b + a}, \dfrac{by_1 + ay_2}{b + a} \right)$ where $a = 2$ and $b = 3$

$(x_1, y_1) = (-3, -2)$ and $(x_2, y_2) = (1, 1)$

Then $(p, q) = \left(\dfrac{(3)(-3) + (2)(1)}{3 + 2}, \dfrac{(3)(-2) + (2)(1)}{3 + 2} \right) = \left(\dfrac{-7}{5}, \dfrac{-4}{5} \right)$

(b) (ii) $t = C_1 - C_2 = 0$

$t = (x + 3)^2 + (y + 2)^2 - 4 - (x^2 + y^2 - 2x - 2y - 7) = 0$

$t = x^2 + 6x + 9 + y^2 + 4y + 4 - 4 - x^2 - y^2 + 2x + 2y + 7 = 0$

$t = 8x + 6y + 16 = 0$

$4x + 3y + 8 = 0$

Position of points in relation to a circle

The equation of a circle can be of the form:

$$x^2 + y^2 = r^2$$
$$(x - h)^2 + (y - k)^2 = r^2$$
$$x^2 + y^2 + 2gx + 2fy + c = 0$$

If the coordinates of a point satisfy the equation of a circle, then the point is **on** the circle. Otherwise, the point is either **inside** or **outside** the circle. By substituting the coordinates into the equation of the circle, one of the following situations can arise:

1. LHS < RHS: the point is **inside** the circle.
2. LHS = RHS: the point is **on** the circle.
3. LHS > RHS: the point is **outside** the circle.

Example

$x^2 + y^2 - 6x + 4y - 12 = 0$ is the equation of a circle, c.
Determine whether each of the points $(7, -3), (-1, -5)$ and $(9, 2)$ is inside, on or outside c.

Solution

$$x^2 + y^2 - 6x + 4y - 12$$

$(7, -3)$: $\quad 7^2 + (-3)^2 - 6(7) + 4(-3) - 12$
$$= -8 < 0$$
$$\therefore (7, -3) \text{ is inside } c.$$

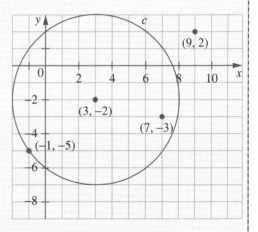

$(-1, -5)$: $(-1)^2 + (-5)^2 - 6(-1)$
$$+ 4(-5) - 12$$
$$= 0$$
$$\therefore (-1, -5) \text{ is on } c.$$

$(9, 2)$: $\quad (9)^2 + (2)^2 - 6(9) + 4(2) - 12$
$$= 27 > 0$$
$$\therefore (9, 2) \text{ is outside } c.$$

(2017 Q.4 (a))

$A(0, 0)$, $B(6{\cdot}5, 0)$ and $C(10, 7)$ are three points on a circle.

Find the equation of the circle.

Solution

Equation of circle	$x^2 + y^2 + 2gx + 2fy + c = 0$
Substitute $(0, 0)$:	$0 + 0 + 0 + 0 + c = 0$
	$c = 0$
Substitute $(6{\cdot}5, 0)$:	$42{\cdot}25 + 0 + 13g + 0 + 0 = 0$
	$13g = -42{\cdot}25$
	$g = -3{\cdot}25$

Substitute $(10, 7)$: $100 + 49 + (2)(-3{\cdot}25)(10) + 2f(7) + 0 = 0$

$$149 - 65 + 14f = 0$$
$$4f = -84$$
$$f = -6$$

Answer: $x^2 + y^2 - 6{\cdot}5x - 12y = 0$

Circles intersecting the axes

To find where a circle intersects the axes, we use the following.

> The circle intersects the x-axis at $y = 0$.
> The circle intersects the y-axis at $x = 0$.

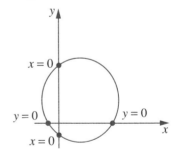

Example

$A\,(3, 5)$ and $B\,(-1, -1)$ are the end points of a diameter of a circle, s.

(i) Find the centre and radius length of s.

(ii) Find the equation of s.

(iii) s intersects the x-axis at P and Q, $P < Q$. Find the coordinates of P and Q.

Solution

(i) Centre is the midpoint of $[AB]$.

$A\,(3, 5) = (x_1, y_1)$ $\qquad$ $B\,(-1, -1) = (x_2, y_2)$

The midpoint of $[AB] = \left(\dfrac{3-1}{2}, \dfrac{5-1}{2}\right) = (1, 2)$.

The radius is the distance from $(1, 2)$ to $(3, 5)$ or $(-1, -1)$.

Thus, the radius $= \sqrt{(3-1)^2 + (5-2)^2} = \sqrt{2^2 + 3^2} = \sqrt{13}$.

Centre $= (1, 2)$ and radius $= \sqrt{13}$

exam focus

In many circle questions it will be very worthwhile to draw a sketch of the situation. The sketch can help you focus on what is given and what is required.

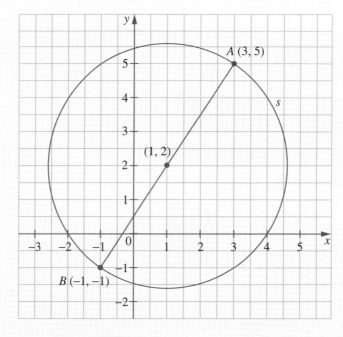

(ii) Centre $(1, 2)$ and radius $\sqrt{13}$

$$(x - h)^2 + (y - k)^2 = r^2$$
$$(x - 1)^2 + (y - 2)^2 = (\sqrt{13})^2$$
$$x^2 - 2x + 1 + y^2 - 4y + 4 = 13$$
$$x^2 + y^2 - 2x - 4y - 8 = 0$$

(iii) On the x-axis, $y = 0$.

$$x^2 + y^2 - 2x - 4y - 8 = 0$$
$$x^2 + 0^2 - 2x - 4(0) - 8 = 0$$
$$x^2 - 2x - 8 = 0$$
$$(x + 2)(x - 4) = 0$$
$$x = -2 \text{ or } x = 4$$

Thus, s intersects the x-axis at $P(-2, 0)$ and $Q(4, 0)$.

Applying the perpendicular distance formula to the circle

key point

The perpendicular distance from the centre of a circle to the tangent is always equal to the radius.

Find the values of $k \in \mathbb{R}$ for which the line $x - y + k = 0$ is a tangent to the circle $(x - 3)^2 + (y + 4)^2 = 50$.

Solution

$(x - 3)^2 + (y + 4)^2 = 50$

Centre $= (3, -4)$ and radius $= \sqrt{50}$

$x - y + k = 0$ is a tangent to the circle.

$\therefore$ The distance from the centre $(3, -4)$ to the line $x - y + k = 0$ must equal the radius.

$$\frac{|ax_1 + by_1 + c|}{\sqrt{a^2 + b^2}} = d$$

$$\frac{|1(3) - 1(-4) + k|}{\sqrt{1^2 + (-1)^2}} = \sqrt{50}$$

$$\frac{|k + 7|}{\sqrt{2}} = 5\sqrt{2} \qquad \text{(multiply both sides by } \sqrt{2}\text{)}$$

$$|k + 7| = 10$$

$$k + 7 = 10 \quad \text{or} \quad k + 7 = -10$$
$$k = 3 \quad \text{or} \quad k = -17$$

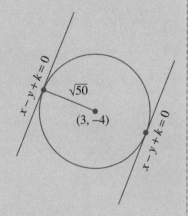

LESS STRESS MORE SUCCESS

(2016 Q.2)

A point X has co-ordinates $(-1, 6)$ and the slope of the line XC is $\dfrac{1}{7}$.

(a) Find the equation of XC. Give your answer in the form $ax + by + c = 0$ where $a, b, c \in \mathbb{Z}$.

(b) C is the centre of a circle s, of radius 5 cm. The line l: $3x + 4y - 21 = 0$ is a tangent to s and passes through X, as shown. Find the equation of one such circle S.

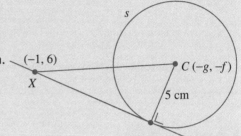

Solution

(a) Use $y - y_1 = m(x - x_1)$

$$m = \frac{1}{7} \qquad (x, y_1) = (-1, 6)$$

$$y - 6 = \frac{1}{7}(x - (-1))$$

$$7y - 42 = x + 1$$

$$-x + 7y - 43 = 0$$

$$x - 7y + 43 = 0$$

(b) Use perpendicular distance $= \dfrac{|ax_1 + by_1 + c|}{\sqrt{a^2 + b^2}}$

$$5 = \frac{|3(-g) + 4(-f) - 21|}{\sqrt{3^2 + 4^2}}$$

$$5 = \frac{|-3g - 4f - 21|}{5}$$

$$25 = |-3g - 4f - 21|$$

$+25 = -3g - 4f - 21$ [or] $-25 = -3g - 4f - 21$

$3g + 4f = -46 \dots (P)$ [or] $3g + 4f = 4 \dots (Q)$

In addition $(-g, -f) \in x - 7y + 43 = 0$ from part (a)

$$-g + 7f + 43 = 0$$

$$-g + 7f = -43$$

Now solve either $3g + 4f = -46 \dots (P)$ or solve $3g + 4f = 4 \dots (Q)$

$$-g + 7f = -43 \qquad\qquad\qquad -g - 7f = -43$$

$$\downarrow$$

Not using this pair of equations

$$3g + 4f = -46$$

$$-3g + 21f = -129$$

$$25f = -175$$

$$f = -7$$

Then $-g + 7f = -43$ becomes $-g - 49 = -43$

$$-g = 6$$

$$g = -6$$

Now circle centre (6, 7) and radius 5 has equation

$$(x - 6)^2 + (y - 7)^2 = 25$$

exam focus

A tough question. We only require either Equation (*P*) or equation (*Q*) for success. This left many good candidates floundering.

Intersection of a line and a circle

To find the points where a line and a circle meet, the **method of substitution** between their equations is used.

The method involves the following three steps:

1. Get *x* or *y* on its own from the equation of the line.
   (Look carefully and select the variable which will make the work easier.)
2. Substitute for this same variable into the equation of the circle and solve the resultant quadratic equation.
3. Substitute **separately** the value(s) obtained in step 2 into the linear equation in step 1 to find the corresponding value(s) of the other variable.

key point

If there is only **one point of intersection** between a line and a circle, then the line is a **tangent** to the circle.

 exam focus

To develop the exam question on page 31, it could ask, for example, to describe the relationship between the given circle $(x - 3)^2 + (y + 4)^2 = 50$ and the system of lines $x - y + k = 0$ when $-17 < k < 3$, $x \in \mathbb{R}$.

Answer using the previous solution:

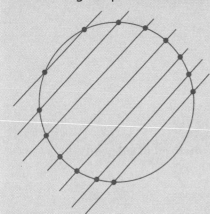

The lines are all parallel to each other and each line intersects the circle twice.

This type of 'what if' testing will be a common feature at the end of procedural exam questions. It will be useful for candidates to know this and develop strategies to cope with such features.

Example

The point $A(5, 2)$ is on the circle $c: x^2 + y^2 + px - 2y + 5 = 0$.

(i) Find the value of p.

(ii) The line $l: x - y - 1 = 0$ intersects the circle c. Find the coordinates of the points of intersection.

Solution

(i) $A(5, 2)$ is on the circle $x^2 + y^2 + px - 2y + 5 = 0$.

$$\therefore \quad (5)^2 + (2)^2 + p(5) - 2(2) + 5 = 0$$
$$25 + 4 + 5p - 4 + 5 = 0$$
$$5p + 30 = 0$$
$$5p = -30$$
$$p = -6$$

(ii) Intersection of the line $l: x - y - 1 = 0$ and the circle c:
$$x^2 + y^2 - 6x - 2y + 5 = 0$$

$$x - y - 1 = 0$$
$$x = y + 1 \qquad (x \text{ on its own})$$
$$x^2 + y^2 - 6x - 2y + 5 = 0$$
$$(y + 1)^2 + y^2 - 6(y + 1) - 2y + 5 = 0 \qquad (\text{put in } (y + 1) \text{ for } x)$$
$$y^2 + 2y + 1 + y^2 - 6y - 6 - 2y + 5 = 0$$
$$2y^2 - 6y = 0$$
$$y^2 - 3y = 0$$
$$y(y - 3) = 0$$
$$y = 0 \text{ or } y = 3$$

$x = y + 1$	
$y = 0$	$y = 3$
$x = 0 + 1$	$x = 3 + 1$
$x = 1$	$x = 4$
$(1, 0)$	$(4, 3)$

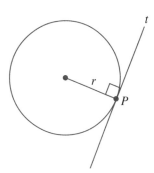

$(4, 3)$

$(1, 0)$ $(3, 1)$

$x - y - 1 = 0$

Tangents and chords

Equation of a tangent to a circle at a given point

A tangent is perpendicular to the radius that joins the centre of a circle to the point of tangency.

This fact is used to find the slope of the tangent.

In the diagram on the right, the radius, r, is perpendicular to the tangent, t, at the point of tangency, P.

The equation of a tangent to a circle at a given point is found with the following steps.

1. Find the slope of the radius to the point of tangency.
2. Turn this slope upside down and change its sign. This gives the slope of the tangent.
3. Use the coordinates of the point of contact and the slope of the tangent at this point in the formula:

$$(y - y_1) = m(x - x_1)$$

This gives the equation of the tangent.

key point

A diagram is often very useful.

Example

Find the equation of the tangent to the circle $x^2 + y^2 - 4x - 8y - 5 = 0$ at the point $(6, 7)$ on the circle.

Solution

Method 1

Centre of the circle $= (-g, -f) = (2, 4)$

Slope of the radius, r, from $(2, 4)$ to the point $(6, 7)$

$$= m = \frac{y_2 - y_1}{x_2 - x_1} = \frac{7 - 4}{6 - 2} = \frac{3}{4}$$

$\therefore$ The slope of the tangent at $(6, 7)$ is $-\dfrac{4}{3}$.

Equation of the tangent, t:

$$(y - y_1) = m(x - x_1)$$

$$(y - 7) = -\frac{4}{3}(x - 6)$$

$$3y - 21 = -4x + 24$$

$$4x + 3y - 45 = 0$$

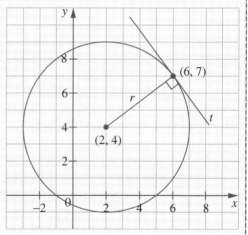

Method 2

Equation of tangent given by $xx_1 + yy_1 + g(x + x_1) + f(y + y_1) + c = 0$
(see *booklet of formulae and tables, page 19*)

$$\left.\begin{array}{l} x_1 = 6 \\ y_1 = 7 \\ g = -2 \\ f = -4 \\ c = -5 \end{array}\right\}$$

$$6x + 7y - 2(x + 6) - 4(y + 7) - 5 = 0$$
$$6x + 7y - 2x - 12 - 4y - 28 - 5 = 0$$
$$4x + 3y - 45 = 0$$

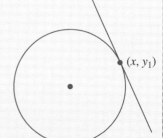

Radius perpendicular to a chord

A radius (or part of a radius) that is perpendicular to a chord bisects that chord. This also enables us to use Pythagoras' theorem:

$$d^2 + x^2 = r^2$$

Thus, knowing two of d, x and r, we can find the third.

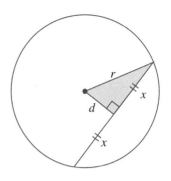

Example

The point $(4, 1)$ is the midpoint of a chord of the circle $x^2 + y^2 - 6x + 2y - 15 = 0$.
Find the length of this chord.

Solution

The centre of the circle is $(3, -1)$.

Its radius length is $\sqrt{g^2 + f^2 - c} = \sqrt{(-3)^2 + 1^2 - (-15)} = 5$.

Draw a sketch.

$d = \sqrt{(x_2 - x_1)^2 + (y_2 - y_1)^2}$

$\quad = \sqrt{(4 - 3)^2 + (1 - (-1))^2} = \sqrt{5}$

Applying Pythagoras's theorem:

$$d^2 + x^2 = 5^2$$
$$(\sqrt{5})^2 + x^2 = 25$$
$$5 + x^2 = 25$$
$$x = \sqrt{20} = 2\sqrt{5}$$

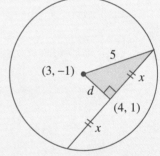

Thus, the length of the chord $= 2x = 2(2\sqrt{5}) = 4\sqrt{5}$ units.

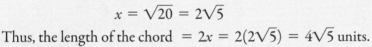

Many circle problems where chords are mentioned are easily solved by drawing a sketch and reviewing the information given. In particular, you should remember that a chord is bisected by a diameter, or radius, perpendicular to the chord.

Length of a tangent to a circle from a point outside the circle

The **length of a tangent** from a point outside a circle is the distance, **d**, from the point outside the circle to the point of tangency.

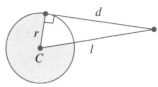

1. Find the centre, C, and radius length, r, of the circle.
2. Find the distance, l, between the centre and the point outside the circle.
3. Use Pythagoras's theorem to find d, i.e. $l^2 = r^2 + d^2$.

exam Q

An earring is to be made from silver wire.

The design is two touching circles with two tangents to the larger circle, as shown in diagram 1.

Diagram 2 is a drawing of this earring imposed on the coordinated axes.

The equation of the inner circle is $x^2 + y^2 + 3y = 0$.

The outer circle intersects the y-axis at (0, −4).

The tangents meet the y-axis at (0, −6).

Find the total length of silver wire required to make this earring. Give your answer correct to the nearest integer.

Diagram 1

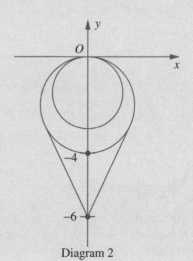

Diagram 2

Solution

We need to find the lengths of the circumferences of the inner and outer circles and the lengths of the two tangents.

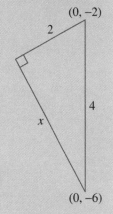

Inner circle	Outer circle
$x^2 + y^2 + 3y = 0$	Centre = midpoint of (0, 0) and (0, −4)
Centre $= (-g, -f) = \left(0, -\frac{3}{2}\right)$	$= (0, -2)$
$\therefore$ Radius $= \dfrac{3}{2}$	$\therefore$ Radius $= 2$
Circumference $= 2\pi r = 2\pi\left(\frac{3}{2}\right) = 3\pi$	Circumference $= 2\pi r = 2\pi(2) = 4\pi$

Lengths of the two tangents

Using Pythagoras's theorem:

$$x^2 + 2^2 = 4^2$$
$$x^2 + 4 = 16$$
$$x^2 = 12$$
$$x = \sqrt{12}$$

$\therefore$ Length of the two tangents $= 2x = 2\sqrt{12}$.

Total length of silver wire required to make the earring

$$= 3\pi + 4\pi + 2\sqrt{12} = 29 \quad \text{(correct to the nearest integer)}$$

Circles with the axes as tangents

If a circle touches an axis (the x- or y-axis is a tangent to the circle), then one of the coordinates of the centre of the circle is equal to the radius.

1. Circle touching the x-axis

$$\text{Radius} = |-f|$$
$$\sqrt{g^2 + f^2 - c} = |-f|$$
$$g^2 + f^2 - c = f^2$$
$$g^2 - c = 0$$
$$g^2 = c$$

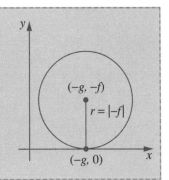

2. Circle touching the y-axis

$$\text{Radius} = |-g|$$
$$\sqrt{g^2 + f^2 - c} = |-g|$$
$$g^2 + f^2 - c = g^2$$
$$f^2 - c = 0$$
$$f^2 = c$$

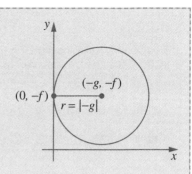

key point

- If the circle touches both the x- and y-axes, then $g^2 = f^2 = c$.
- If the centre is in the 1st or 3rd quadrant, its centre will lie on the line $y = x$.
- If the centre is in the 2nd or 4th quadrant, its centre will lie on the line $y = -x$.

exam Q

(i) The y-axis is a tangent to the circle
$x^2 + y^2 + 2gx + 2fy + c = 0$. Prove that $f^2 = c$.

(ii) Find the equations of the circles that pass through the points $(-3, 6)$ and $(-6, 3)$ and have the y-axis as a tangent.

Solution

(i) Already done in the introduction to this section.

(ii) Let the circle be $x^2 + y^2 + 2gx + 2fy + c = 0$.

Touches the y-axis, $\therefore f^2 = c$. ①

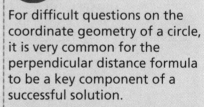

For difficult questions on the coordinate geometry of a circle, it is very common for the perpendicular distance formula to be a key component of a successful solution.

This equation contains f^2 so we should use this equation last and substitute into it.
The points $(-3, 6)$ and $(-6, 3)$ are on the circle.

Substitute each point into the equation for a circle: $x^2 + y^2 + 2gx + 2fy + c = 0$

$\therefore (-3)^2 + (6)^2 + 2g(-3)$
$+ 2f(6) + c = 0$
$9 + 36 - 6g + 12f + c = 0$
$-6g + 12f + c = -45$
$6g - 12f - c = 45$ ②

$(-6)^2 + (3)^2 + 2g(-6)$
$+ 2f(3) + c = 0$
$36 + 9 - 12g + 6f + c = 0$
$-12g + 6f + c = -45$
$12g - 6f - c = 45$ ③

There is no g in the equation $f^2 = c$. ①

Thus, we eliminate g using equations ② and ③.

$$12g - 24f - 2c = 90 \qquad ② \times 2$$
$$\underline{-12g + 6f + c = -45 \qquad ③ \times -1}$$
$$-18f - c = 45$$
$$-c = 18f + 45$$
$$c = -18f - 45$$

(put this into equation ①)

$$f^2 = c \qquad ①$$
$$f^2 = -18f - 45$$
$$f^2 + 18f + 45 = 0$$
$$(f + 3)(f + 15) = 0$$
$$f = -3 \quad \text{or} \quad f = -15$$

Case 1	Case 2
$f = -3$	$f = -15$
$c = f^2 = (-3)^2 = 9$	$c = f^2 = (-15)^2 = 225$
$6g - 12f - c = 45$ ②	$6g - 12f - c = 45$ ②
$6g - 12(-3) - 9 = 45$	$6g - 12(-15) - 225 = 45$
$6g + 36 - 9 = 45$	$6g + 180 - 225 = 45$
$6g = 18$	$6g = 90$
$g = 3$	$g = 15$
$x^2 + y^2 + 2(3)x + 2(-3)y + 9 = 0$	$x^2 + y^2 + 2(15)x + 2(-15)y + 225 = 0$
$x^2 + y^2 + 6x - 6y + 9 = 0$	$x^2 + y^2 + 30x - 30y + 225 = 0$

Equations of tangents from a point outside a circle

From a point outside a circle, two tangents can
be drawn to touch the circle.

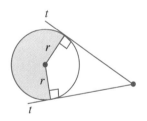

Method for finding the two equations of tangents from a point (x_1, y_1) outside a circle:

1. Find the centre and radius length of the circle (a rough diagram can help).
2. Let the equation be $y - y_1 = m(x - x_1)$ and write the equation in the form $ax + by + c = 0$.
3. Let the perpendicular distance from the centre of the circle to the tangent equal the radius.
4. Solve this equation to find two values of m.
5. Using these two values of m and the point (x_1, y_1), write down the equations of the two tangents.

Example

Find the equations of the two tangents from the point $(6, -4)$ to the circle $x^2 + y^2 - 6x + 10y + 26 = 0$.

Solution

$x^2 + y^2 - 6x + 10y + 26 = 0$

Centre $= (-g, -f) = (3, -5)$

Radius $= \sqrt{g^2 + f^2 - c} = \sqrt{(3)^2 + (-5)^2 - 26} = \sqrt{8}$

We have a point $(6, -4)$ on both tangents.

We need the slopes of the two tangents.

Equation of the tangents (in terms of m):

$$(y + 4) = m(x - 6)$$
$$y + 4 = mx - 6m$$
$$mx - y + (-6m - 4) = 0$$

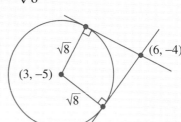

The distance from the centre of the circle, $(3, -5)$, to the line $mx - y + (-6m - 4) = 0$ is equal to the radius, $\sqrt{8}$.

$$\therefore \frac{|m(3) + (-1)(-5) + (-6m - 4)|}{\sqrt{m^2 + (-1)^2}} = \sqrt{8} \quad \text{(perpendicular distance formula)}$$

$$\frac{|3m + 5 - 6m - 4|}{\sqrt{m^2 + 1}} = \sqrt{8}$$

$$\frac{|-3m + 1|}{\sqrt{m^2 + 1}} = \sqrt{8}$$

key point

> When a question requires the equation of two circles that satisfy the same conditions, try to form a quadratic equation in g or f. For example, $g^2 - 2g - 8 = 0$, $f^2 - f - 6 = 0$.

$$\frac{9m^2 - 6m + 1}{m^2 + 1} = 8 \quad \text{(square both sides)}$$

$$9m^2 - 6m + 1 = 8m^2 + 8 \quad \text{(multiply both sides by } (m^2 + 1))$$

$$m^2 - 6m - 7 = 0$$

$$(m + 1)(m - 7) = 0$$

$$m = -1 \quad \text{or} \quad m = 7$$

Equations of the two tangents

Slope $= -1$, point $= (6, -4)$

$$(y + 4) = -1(x - 6)$$
$$y + 4 = -x + 6$$
$$x + y - 2 = 0$$

Slope $= 7$, point $= (6, -4)$

$$(y + 4) = 7(x - 6)$$
$$y + 4 = 7x - 42$$
$$7x - y - 46 = 0$$

3 > Geometry Theorems

aims

- ☐ To know the definitions of the geometry terms listed in the glossary
- ☐ To know all theorems, corollaries and axioms
- ☐ To be able to reproduce the proofs for theorems 11, 12 and 13
- ☐ To be able to solve problems by applying the theorems, corollaries and axioms

Glossary of examinable terms

Axiom:	A statement which is assumed to be true. It can be accepted without a proof and used as a basis for an argument.
Converse:	The converse of a theorem is formed by taking the conclusion as the starting point and having the starting point as the conclusion.
Corollary:	A corollary follows after a theorem and is a statement which must be true because of that theorem.
If and only if:	Often shortened to 'iff'. One statement is true if and only if the second statement is true, so both statements must be true or both statements must be false.
Implies:	Implies indicates a logical relationship between two statements, such that if the first is true then the second must be true.
Is congruent to:	Two things are said to be congruent if they are identical in size and shape.
Is equivalent to:	Two things are said to be equivalent if they have the same value but different forms.
Proof:	A sequence of statements (made up of axioms, assumptions and arguments) that follow logically from the preceding one, starting at an axiom or previously proven theorem and ending with the statement of the theorem to be proven.
Proof by contradiction:	A proof which establishes the truth of a statement by proving that the statement being false leads to a contradiction. Proving its falsity to be impossible proves that the statement must be true.
Theorem:	A statement which has been proven to be true, deduced from axioms by logical argument.

exam focus

You must understand these terms and be able to explain them, if required in the exam.

You are required to know the following axioms, theorems and corollaries and you must be able to apply them in answering geometric questions.

Axioms

Axiom 1: There is exactly one line through any two given points.

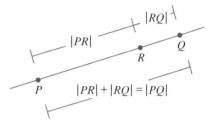

Axiom 2: **Ruler axiom**
The distance between points P and Q has the following properties:

1. The distance $|PQ|$ is never negative.
2. The distance between two points is the same whether we measure from P to Q or from Q to P.
3. If there exists some point R between P and Q, then the distance from P to Q is equal to the sum of the distances from P to R and R to Q.

$$|PR| + |RQ| = |PQ|$$

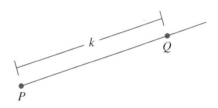

$$|PR| + |RQ| = |PQ|$$

4. Marking off a distance:
   Given any ray from P, and given any real number $k \geq 0$, there is a unique point Q on the ray whose distance from P is k.

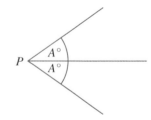

Axiom 3: **Protractor axiom**
The number of degrees in an angle (also known as its degree-measure) is always a number between 0° and 360°.
It has these properties:

1. A straight angle has 180°.
2. If we know the angle $A°$, opened up at a point P, then there are two possible rays from P that form that angle.

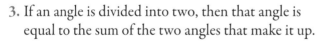

3. If an angle is divided into two, then that angle is equal to the sum of the two angles that make it up.

$$|\angle QPR| = |\angle QPS| + |\angle SPR|$$
$$|\angle QPR| = A° + B°$$

Axiom 4: **Congruent triangles**
We can say that two triangles are congruent if:

1. SAS: Two sides and the angle in between are the same in both.

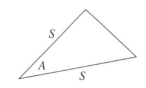

2. **ASA:** Two angles and a side are the same in both.

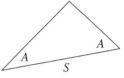

3. **SSS:** All three sides are the same in both.

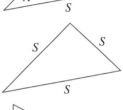

4. **RHS:** Right angle, hypotenuse and another side.

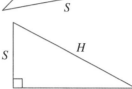

Axiom 5: Given any line *l* and a point *P*, there is exactly one line through *P* that is parallel to *l*.

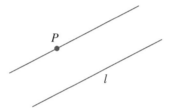

Theorems

- The application of all theorems can be examined.
- Only proofs for theorems 11, 12 and 13 are examinable (marked with *).
- You will be presented with a worded statement of a theorem, without reference to the theorem number.
- Proofs are expected to begin with a diagram, followed by the following headings: 'Given', 'To prove', 'Construction' and 'Proof'.
- You must explain all construction steps fully.
- You may be asked for an example of a proof by contradiction.

Theorem 1: **Vertically opposite angles**
Vertically opposite angles are equal in measure.

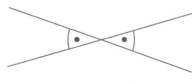

Theorem 2: **Isosceles triangles**
1. In an isosceles triangle, the angles opposite the equal sides are equal.
2. Conversely, if two angles are equal, then the triangle is isosceles.

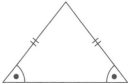

Theorem 3: **Alternate angles**
If a transversal makes equal alternate angles on two lines, then the lines are parallel (and converse).

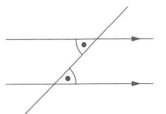

Theorem 4: **Angles in a triangle**
The angles in any triangle add up to 180°.
$$A° + B° + C° = 180°$$

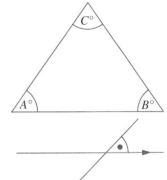

Theorem 5: **Corresponding angles**
Two lines are parallel if, and only if, for any transversal, the corresponding angles are equal.

Theorem 6: **Exterior angle**
Each exterior angle of a triangle is equal to the sum of the interior opposite angles.
$$E° = A° + B°$$

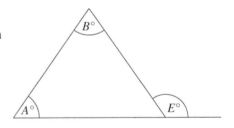

Theorem 7: **Angle–side relationship**
1. In a triangle, the angle opposite the greater of two sides is greater than the angle opposite the lesser side.
2. Conversely, the side opposite the greater of two angles is greater than the side opposite the lesser angle.

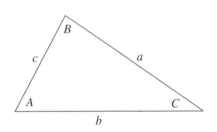

Theorem 8: **Triangle inequality**
Any two sides of a triangle are together greater than the third.
$$a + b > c$$
$$b + c > a$$
$$a + c > b$$

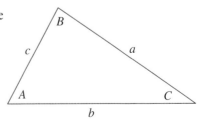

Theorem 9: **Parallelograms**

In a parallelogram, opposite sides are equal and opposite angles are equal. Two converses of this theorem are true:

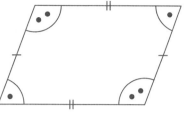

1. If the opposite angles of a quadrilateral are equal, then it is a parallelogram.
2. If the opposite sides of a quadrilateral are equal, then it is a parallelogram.

Corollary: A diagonal divides a parallelogram into two congruent triangles.

Theorem 10: **Diagonals of a parallelogram**

The diagonals of a parallelogram bisect each other.

Converse:

If the diagonals of a quadrilateral bisect one another, then it is a parallelogram.

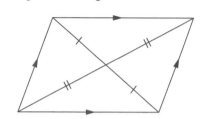

*Theorem 11: **Transversals**

If three parallel lines cut off equal segments on some transversal line, then they will cut off equal segments on any other transversal.

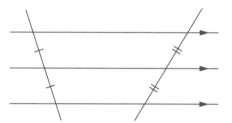

*Theorem 12: **Proportional sides**

Let ABC be a triangle. If a line XY is parallel to BC and cuts $[AB]$ in the ratio $s : t$, then it also cuts $[AC]$ in the same ratio.

Converse:

If a line XY cuts the sides AB and AC in the same ratio, then it is parallel to BC.

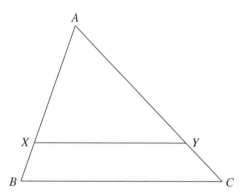

*Theorem 13: **Similar triangles**

If two triangles are similar, then their sides are proportional, in order.

$$\frac{|PQ|}{|AB|} = \frac{|PR|}{|AC|} = \frac{|QR|}{|BC|}$$

Converse:

If the corresponding sides of two triangles are proportional, then they are similar.

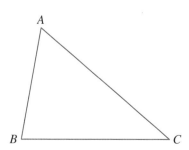

Theorem 14: **Theorem of Pythagoras**

In a right-angled triangle, the square of the hypotenuse is the sum of the squares of the other two sides.

$$|AC|^2 = |AB|^2 + |BC|^2$$

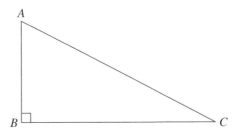

Theorem 15: **Converse to Pythagoras**

If the square of one side is the sum of the squares of the other two, then the angle opposite the first side is a right angle.

Theorem 16: **Area**

For a triangle, base × height does not depend on the choice of base.

Definition:

The area of a triangle is half the base by the height, regardless of which side you choose as the base.

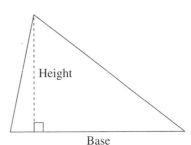

Theorem 17: **Parallelogram bisector**

A diagonal of a parallelogram bisects the area.

$$\text{Area} \triangle ABD = \text{Area} \triangle CDB$$

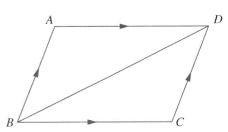

Theorem 18: **Area of a parallelogram**

The area of a parallelogram is the base × height.

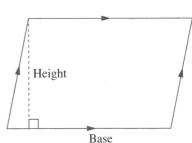

Theorem 19: **Circle theorem**

The angle at the centre of a circle standing on a given arc is twice the angle at any point of the circle standing on the same arc.

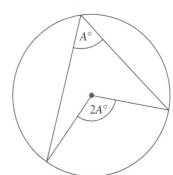

Corollary 1: All angles at points of a circle standing on the same arc are equal.

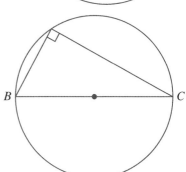

Corollary 2: Each angle in a semicircle is a right angle.

Corollary 3: If the angle standing on a chord $[BC]$ at some point on the circle is a right angle, then $[BC]$ is a diameter.

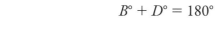

Corollary 4: If $ABCD$ is a cyclic quadrilateral, then opposite angles sum to 180°.

$$A° + C° = 180°$$
$$B° + D° = 180°$$

Converse:
If the opposite angles of a quadrilateral sum to 180°, the quadrilateral is cyclic.

Theorem 20: **Tangents**
1. Each tangent is perpendicular to the radius that goes to the point of contact.
2. If P lies on the circle s, and a line l is perpendicular to the radius at P, then l is a tangent to s.

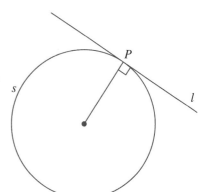

Corollary 5: If two circles intersect at one point only, then the two centres and the point of contact are collinear.

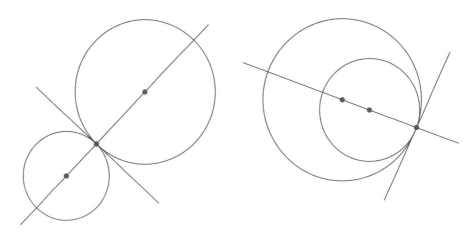

Theorem 21: **Perpendicular bisector of a chord**

1. The perpendicular from the centre of a circle to a chord bisects the chord.
2. The perpendicular bisector of a chord passes through the centre of the circle.

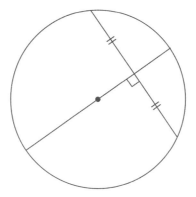

When solving questions which involve diagrams, it is often helpful to do rough copies, in pencil, of the diagram on a separate piece of paper. This allows you to mark things on the diagram and try different approaches, **without drawing on the original image**. This can be useful if you take the wrong approach the first time. You still have a clean diagram to work from.

Proof of theorems

Theorem 11: If three parallel lines cut off equal segments on some transversal line, then they will cut off equal segments on any other transversal.

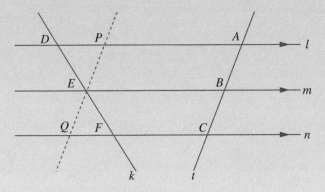

Given: Three parallel lines, l, m and n, intersecting the transversal, t, at the points A, B and C such that $|AB| = |BC|$. Another transversal, k, intersects the lines at D, E and F.

To prove: $|DE| = |EF|$

Construction: Through E, construct a line parallel to t and intersecting l at the point P and n at the point Q.

Proof: $PEBA$ and $EQCB$ are parallelograms.

Then $|PE| = |AB|$ and $|EQ| = |BC|$ (opposite sides)

But $|AB| = |BC|$

So $|PE| = |EQ|$

In $\triangle DEP$ and $\triangle FEQ$

$|PE| = |EQ|$

$|\angle PED| = |\angle FEQ|$ (vertically opposite angles)

$|\angle DPE| = |\angle FQE|$ (alternate angles)

$\therefore \triangle DEP$ and $\triangle FEQ$ are congruent (ASA rule)

$\therefore |DE| = |EF|$

Theorem 12: Let *ABC* be a triangle. If a line *XY* is parallel to *BC* and cuts [*AB*] in the ratio *s* : *t*, then it also cuts [*AC*] in the same ratio.

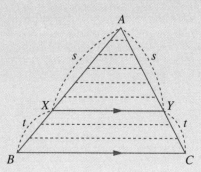

Given: The triangle *ABC* with *XY* parallel to *BC*.

To prove: $\dfrac{|AX|}{|XB|} = \dfrac{|AY|}{|YC|}$

Construction: Divide [*AX*] into *s* equal parts and [*XB*] into *t* equal parts.

Draw a line parallel to *BC* through each point of the division.

Proof: The parallel lines make intercepts of equal length along the line [*AC*]. (converse of transerval theorem)

∴ [*AY*] is divided into *s* equal intercepts and [*YC*] is divided into *t* equal intercepts.

∴ $\dfrac{|AY|}{|YC|} = \dfrac{s}{t}$

But $\dfrac{|AX|}{|XB|} = \dfrac{s}{t}$

∴ $\dfrac{|AX|}{|XB|} = \dfrac{|AY|}{|YC|}$

Theorem 13:   If two triangles, *ABC* and *DEF,* are similar, then their sides are proportional in order:

$$\frac{|AB|}{|DE|} = \frac{|BC|}{|EF|} = \frac{|AC|}{|DF|}$$

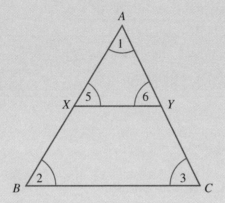
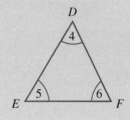

Given: The triangles *ABC* and *DEF* in which $|\angle 1| = |\angle 4|$, $|\angle 2| = |\angle 5|$ and $|\angle 3| = |\angle 6|$.

To prove: $\dfrac{|AB|}{|DE|} = \dfrac{|BC|}{|EF|} = \dfrac{|AC|}{|DF|}$

Construction: Mark the point *X* on [*AB*] such that $|AX| = |DE|$.

Mark the point *Y* on [*AC*] such that $|AY| = |DF|$.

Join *XY*.

Proof: The triangles *AXY* and *DEF* are congruent.   (SAS)

$\therefore |\angle AXY| = |\angle DEF| = |\angle 5|$ (corresponding angles)

$\therefore |\angle AXY| = |\angle ABC|$

$\therefore XY \parallel BC$ (corresponding angles)

$\therefore \dfrac{|AB|}{|AX|} = \dfrac{|AC|}{|AY|}$ (a line parallel to one side divides the other side in the same ratio)

$\therefore \dfrac{|AB|}{|DE|} = \dfrac{|AC|}{|DF|}$

Similarly, it can be proven that $\therefore \dfrac{|AB|}{|DE|} = \dfrac{|BC|}{|EF|}$

$\therefore \dfrac{|AB|}{|DE|} = \dfrac{|BC|}{|EF|} = \dfrac{|AC|}{|DF|}$

exam focus

You must learn, and be able to reproduce, the proofs for theorems 11, 12 and 13.

Proof by contradiction

This method of proof takes a proposition of the form

If certain conditions, **then** a result will follow.

And examines the consequences of assuming that

If certain conditions, **then** the *opposite* result will follow.

To prove:	A triangle has at most one obtuse angle.
Proof:	Consider a triangle with angles A, B and C.

Assume that the opposite of the 'to prove' statement is true, i.e. the triangle has **more** than one obtuse angle.

Suppose A and B are both obtuse.

$\therefore A$ is more than 90° and B is more than 90°.

$\therefore A + B$ is more than 90° + 90°, which is more than 180°.

But this is impossible, as the *three* angles must add up to 180°.

Therefore, it is not possible for the triangle to have two obtuse angles.

Therefore, a triangle has at most one obtuse angle.

The method of 'proof by contradiction' is a vital skill that can be easily transferred to other aspects of this course. It does not relate purely to the topic of geometry.

Application and use of theorems

You must know all of the theorems very well and be able to apply them when solving geometric problems.

- Be aware that there may be more than one method of proof for answering questions by the application of theorems.
- Many geometry problems will involve aspects of trigonometry.

Example

O is a point inside an acute-angled triangle ABC. The feet of the perpendiculars from O to BC, CA and AB respectively are P, Q and R. Prove that:

$$|PB|^2 - |PC|^2 = |OB|^2 - |OC|^2$$

Solution

Start by drawing a diagram of the triangle.

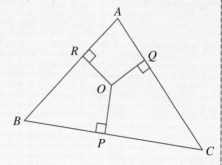

Construction

Join O to B.
Join O to C.
Join O to A.

Proof

In $\triangle BOP$, $|PB|^2 = |OB|^2 - |OP|^2$
    (Pythagoras' theorem).

In $\triangle POC$, $|PC|^2 = |OC|^2 - |OP|^2$
    (Pythagoras' theorem).

Subtracting $|PC|^2$ from $|PB|^2$ gives:

$$|PB|^2 - |PC|^2 = [|OB|^2 - |OP|^2] - [|OC|^2 - |OP|^2]$$
$$|PB|^2 - |PC|^2 = |OB|^2 - |OP|^2 - |OC|^2 + |OP|^2$$
$$\therefore \ |PB|^2 - |PC|^2 = |OB|^2 - |OC|^2$$

It is important to give reasons and explanations for statements made during a proof. This shows that you understand the steps you are taking and thus will help ensure that you get maximum marks in a question.

Example

The diagram shows a circle of centre O, with two tangents CA and CB.

Prove that $\triangle CAO$ and $\triangle CBO$ are congruent.

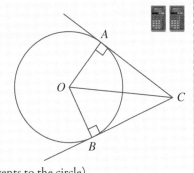

Solution

$|AO| = |BO|$ (both radii of the circle)

$|CO| = |CO|$ (common side)

$|\angle CAO| = |\angle CBO| = 90°$ (CA and CB are both tangents to the circle)

$\therefore \triangle CAO \equiv \triangle CBO$ (right angle, hypotenuse, side RHS)

In the diagram, l_1, l_2, l_3 and l_4 are parallel lines that make intercepts of equal length on the transversal, k.

FG is parallel to k and HG is parallel to ED.

Prove that the triangles $\triangle CDE$ and $\triangle FGH$ are congruent.

 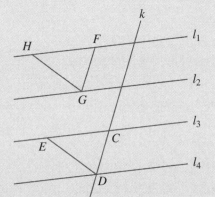

Solution

Construction:

Label the points A and B on the diagram.

    $|AB| = |CD|$ (given)

    $|AB| = |FG|$ (opposite sides of a parallelogram)

$\therefore \ |CD| = |FG|$ (marked with double dashes)

    $HG \| ED$ (given)

    $CD \| AB \| FG$ (given)

$\therefore \ |\angle EDC| = |\angle HGF|$

    (corresponding angles)

    (marked with a •)

Similarly,

    $HF \| EC$ (given)

    $CD \| FG$ (given)

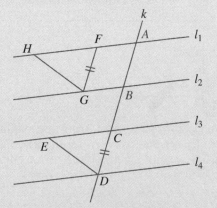

∴ $|\angle ECD| = |\angle HFG|$
(corresponding angles)
(marked with an *)

∴ $\triangle CDE \equiv \triangle FGH$ (ASA)

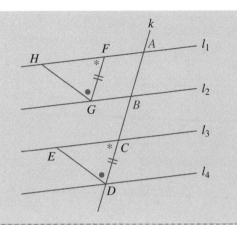

In the triangle ABC, $|AB| = q$ and $|CB| = p$.

Find the shortest distance from the vertex, B, to the side $[AC]$, in terms of p and q.

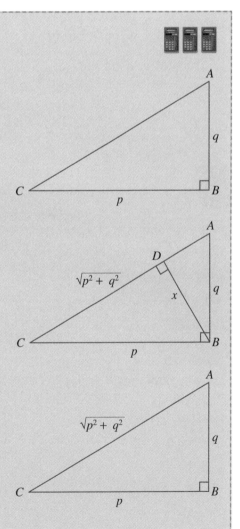

Solution

Draw a perpendicular line from B to $[AC]$. Label this new point D.

Mark this new length x.

This is the required shortest distance.

Using Pythagoras' theorem on $\triangle ABC$, we find:

$$|AC| = \sqrt{p^2 + q^2}$$

Consider $\triangle ABC$ and $\triangle ADB$:

$|\angle CAB| = |\angle BAD|$ (common angle)

$|\angle CBA| = |\angle BDA|$ (both 90°)

∴ $\triangle ABC$ and $\triangle ADB$ are similar.

∴ Their sides are in proportion.

$$\frac{|BD|}{|CB|} = \frac{|AB|}{|AC|}$$

$$\frac{x}{p} = \frac{q}{\sqrt{p^2 + q^2}}$$

$$x = \frac{pq}{\sqrt{p^2 + q^2}}$$

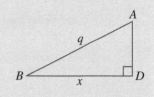

Alternative method:

Area of $\triangle ABC = \dfrac{1}{2}$ (base) ($\perp$ height)

Area of $\triangle ABC = \dfrac{1}{2}\left(\sqrt{p^2 + q^2}\right)(x)$

Area of $\triangle ABC = \dfrac{1}{2}(p)(q)$

$\therefore \quad \dfrac{1}{2}\left(\sqrt{p^2 + q^2}\right)(x) = \dfrac{1}{2}(p)(q)$

$\left(\sqrt{p^2 + q^2}\right)(x) = (p)(q)$

$$x = \frac{pq}{\sqrt{p^2 + q^2}}$$

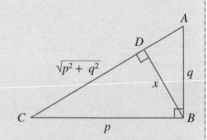

exam Q

(2018 Q.6 (b))

In the triangle *ABC* shown:

$|\angle CAB| = 90°, |AX| = 4$ cm,

$|AY| = 3$ cm, $XY \parallel BC$,

$XZ \parallel AC$, and $|AX|:|XB| = 1:2$.

Find $|BZ|$

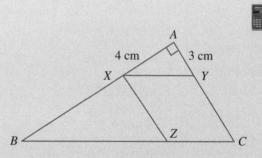

Solution

Start by finding $|XY|$, using Pythagoras's theorem:

$|XY|^2 = 3^2 + 4^2$

$|XY|^2 = 9 + 16$

$|XY|^2 = 25$

$\quad |XY| = 5$ cm

Since, $XY \parallel BC$ and $XZ \parallel AC$, triangles AXY and XBZ are similar.

Given that $|AX|:|XB| = 1:2$

Then $|XY|:|BZ| = 1:2$

Therefore, $|BZ| = 2|XY|$

$\quad |BZ| = 2(5)$

$\quad |BZ| = 10$ cm

(2017 Q.5)

ABCD is a rectangle.

$F \in [AB]$, $G \in [BC]$, $[FD] \cap [AG] = \{E\}$, and $FD \perp AG$.

$|AE| = 12$ cm, $|EG| = 27$ cm, and $|FE| = 5$ cm

(a) Prove that $\triangle AFE$ and $\triangle DAE$ are similar.
(equiangular)

(b) Find $|AD|$.

(c) $\triangle AFE$ and $\triangle AGB$ are similar. Show that $|AB| = 36$ cm.

(d) Find the area of the quadrilateral GCDE.

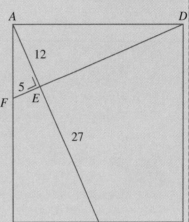

Solution

(a) $|\angle AEF| = |\angle AED|$ (right angles)

$|\angle FAE| + |\angle EAD| = 90°$ (corner of a rectangle)

$|\angle EAD| + |\angle ADE| = 90°$ (remaining angles in $\triangle AED$)

$\therefore |\angle FAE| = |\angle ADE|$

$\therefore \triangle AFE$ and $\triangle DAE$ are equiangular

(b) Find $|AF|$, using Pythagoras's theorem:

$|AF|^2 = 12^2 + 5^2$

$|AF|^2 = 144 + 25$

$|AF|^2 = 169$

$|AF| = 13$ cm

Since $\triangle AFE$ and $\triangle DAE$ are similar:

$$\frac{|AD|}{|AF|} = \frac{|AE|}{|FE|}$$

$$\frac{|AD|}{13} = \frac{12}{5}$$

$$|AD| = 13\left(\frac{12}{5}\right)$$

$$|AD| = 31 \cdot 2 \text{cm}$$

(c) Since $\triangle AFE$ and $\triangle AGB$ are similar:

$$\frac{|AG|}{|AF|} = \frac{|AB|}{|AE|}$$

$$\frac{39}{13} = \frac{|AB|}{12}$$

$$12\left(\frac{39}{13}\right) = |AB|$$

$$36 \text{ cm} = |AB|$$

(d) Since $\triangle AFE$ and $\triangle AGB$ are similar:

$$\frac{|BG|}{|EF|} = \frac{|AB|}{|AE|}$$

$$\frac{|BG|}{5} = \frac{36}{12}$$

$$|BG| = 5\left(\frac{36}{12}\right)$$

$$|BG| = 15 \text{ cm}$$

Area $GCDE$ = Area $ABCD$ − Area $\triangle AFD$ − Area $\triangle ABG$ + Area $\triangle AFE$

Area $GCDE = (31 \cdot 2)(36) - \frac{1}{2}(31 \cdot 2)(13) - \frac{1}{2}(36)(15) + \frac{1}{2}(5)(12)$

Area $GCDE = 1123 \cdot 2 - 202 \cdot 8 - 270 + 30$

Area $GCDE = 680 \cdot 4 \text{ cm}^2$

This question was worth 25 marks. Part (a) was worth 10 marks and all other parts were worth 5 marks each. For part (d), 2 of the 5 marks were awarded for having the correct formula for finding the area.

(2014 Q.6 (b))

[AB] and [CD] are chords of a circle that intersect externally at E, as shown.

(a) Name two similar triangles in the diagram and give reasons for your answer.

(b) Prove that $|EA| \cdot |EB| = |EC| \cdot |ED|$

(c) Given that $|EB| = 6 \cdot 25$, $|ED| = 5 \cdot 94$ and $|CB| = 10$, find $|AD|$

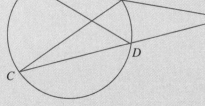

Solution

(a) $|\angle EAD| = |\angle ECB|$ (both on arc BD)

$|\angle DEA| = |\angle BEC|$ (same angle)

Therefore, $\triangle ADE$ and $\triangle CBE$ are similar

Let $AD \cap BC = \{X\}$

$|\angle DAB| = |\angle BCD|$ (both on arc BD)

$|\angle AXB| = |\angle CXD|$ (vertically opposite)

Therefore, $\triangle AXB$ and $\triangle CXD$ are similar

(b) Since, $\triangle ADE$ and $\triangle CBE$ are similar

$$\frac{|EA|}{|EC|} = \frac{|ED|}{|EB|}$$

So, $|EA| \cdot |EB| = |EC| \cdot |ED|$

(c) Since, $\triangle ADE$ and $\triangle CBE$ are similar

$$\frac{|AD|}{|CB|} = \frac{|ED|}{|EB|}$$

$$\frac{|AD|}{10} = \frac{5 \cdot 94}{6 \cdot 25}$$

$$|AD| = 10\left(\frac{5 \cdot 94}{6 \cdot 25}\right)$$

$$|AD| = 9 \cdot 504$$

In the diagram, [PQ] is a bisector of |∠TPR|.

Prove that |QP| = |QR|.

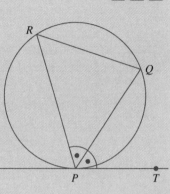

Solution

You need to prove that △PQR is isosceles.

Construct the line [PS] perpendicular to the tangent.

Since this line is perpendicular to the tangent, it must be a diameter of the circle.

∴ |∠PQS| = 90°   (angle in a semicircle is 90°)

Label angles 1, 2, 3, 4, 5 as in the diagram.

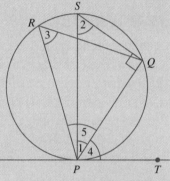

|∠1| + |∠2| = 90°   (remaining angles in a right-angled triangle)

|∠1| + |∠4| = 90°   (since PT is a tangent)

∴ |∠2| = |∠4|

   |∠2| = |∠3| (both standing on arc PQ)

∴ |∠3| = |∠4|

   |∠4| = |∠5| (given)

∴ |∠3| = |∠5|

∴ △PQR is isosceles.

∴ |QP| = |QR|

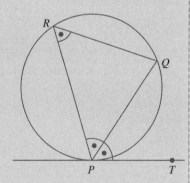

Labelling the angles with numbers often makes the solution simpler.

4 Enlargements and Constructions

aims
- ☐ To know how to find the centre of enlargement
- ☐ To know how to find the scale factor of enlargement
- ☐ To be able to solve problems involving missing sides and the area of enlarged shapes
- ☐ To be able to complete all 22 constructions
- ☐ To be able to use your knowledge of constructions to solve practical problems

Enlargements

An **enlargement** changes the size of a shape to give a similar image. To enlarge a shape, we need a centre of enlargement and a scale factor.

When a shape is enlarged, all lengths are multiplied by the scale factor and all angles remain unchanged. A slide projector makes an enlargement of a shape. In this case, the light bulb is the **centre of enlargement**.

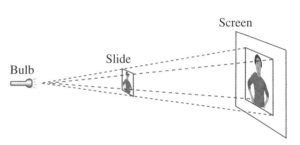

Ray method

In the diagram below, the triangle ABC is the **object** (the starting shape) and the triangle $A'B'C'$ is the **image** under an enlargement, centre O and a scale factor of $\frac{1}{2}$.

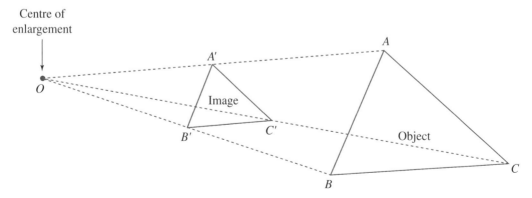

The rays have been drawn from the centre of enlargement, O, to each vertex and beyond. The distance from the centre of enlargement, O, to each vertex on triangle ABC was measured and multiplied by $\frac{1}{2}$. Thus, $|OA'| = \frac{1}{2}|OA|, |OB'| = \frac{1}{2}|OB|$ and $|OC'| = \frac{1}{2}|OC|$.

Also, $|A'B'| = \frac{1}{2}|AB|, |A'C'| = \frac{1}{2}|AC|$ and $|B'C'| = \frac{1}{2}|BC|$.

Note: All measurements are made from the centre of enlargement, O.

Properties of enlargements:

1. The shape of the image is the same as the shape of the object (only the size has changed).
2. The amount by which a figure is enlarged is called the **scale factor** and is denoted by k.
3. Image length = k(object length)   or $k = \dfrac{\text{Image length}}{\text{Object length}}$
4. Area of image = k^2(area of object)   or $k^2 = \dfrac{\text{Area of image}}{\text{Area of object}}$

key point

1. The scale factor can be less than 1 (i.e. $0 < k < 1$). In these cases, the image will be smaller than the object. Though smaller, the image is still called an enlargement.
2. The centre of enlargement can be a vertex on the object figure, inside it or outside.

To find the centre of enlargement, do the following:

1. Choose two points on the image and their corresponding points on the original figure.
2. From each of these points on the larger figure, draw a line to the corresponding point on the smaller figure.
3. Produce these lines until they intersect at a point. This point is the centre of enlargement.

Example

Triangle OAB is the image of triangle OXY under the enlargement, centre O, with $|XY| = 8, |OX| = 10$ and $|AB| = 18$.

(i) Find the scale factor of the enlargement.
(ii) Find $|XA|$.
(iii) The area of triangle OAB is 101·25 square units. Find the area of triangle OXY.

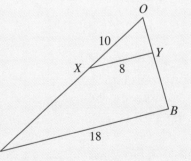

Solution

(i) Since we are told that the triangle OAB is the image of the triangle OXY:

$$\text{Scale factor} = k = \frac{\text{Image length}}{\text{Object length}} = \frac{|AB|}{|XY|} = \frac{18}{8} = \frac{9}{4}$$

(ii) $\text{Scale factor} = k = \dfrac{\text{Image length}}{\text{Object length}}$

$$k = \frac{9}{4} = \frac{\text{Image length}}{\text{Object length}} = \frac{|OA|}{|OX|}$$

$$\frac{9}{4} = \frac{|OA|}{10}$$

$$9(10) = 4|OA|$$

$$22{\cdot}5 = |OA|$$

$$|OA| = |XA| + |OX|$$

$$22{\cdot}5 = |XA| + 10$$

$$\therefore \ 12{\cdot}5 = |XA|$$

(iii)

$$k^2 = \frac{\text{Area of image}}{\text{Area of object}}$$

$$\left(\frac{9}{4}\right)^2 = \frac{\text{Area of } \triangle OAB}{\text{Area of } \triangle OXY}$$

$$\frac{81}{16} = \frac{101{\cdot}25}{\text{Area of } \triangle OXY}$$

$$81(\text{area of } \triangle OXY) = 16(101{\cdot}25)$$

$$\text{Area of } \triangle OXY = \frac{1{,}620}{81}$$

$$\text{Area of } \triangle OXY = 20 \text{ sq. units}$$

exam Q

(2011 Q.4)

Two triangles are drawn on a square grid, as shown. The points P, Q, R, X and Z are on vertices of the triangles, and the point Y lies on $[PR]$. The triangle PQR is an enlargement of the triangle XYZ.

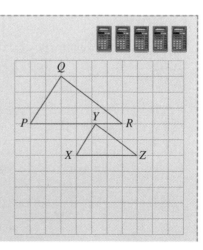

(i) Calculate the scale factor of the enlargement, showing your work.

(ii) By construction or otherwise, locate the centre of enlargement on the diagram.

(iii) Calculate $|YR|$ in grid units.

Solution

(i) Since we are told that the triangle *PQR* is an enlargement of the triangle *XYZ*, we take triangle *XYZ* as the object and triangle *PQR* as the image.

$$\text{Scale factor} = k = \frac{\text{Image length}}{\text{Object length}} = \frac{|PR|}{|XZ|} = \frac{6}{4} = \frac{3}{2}$$

(ii) To find the centre of enlargement:

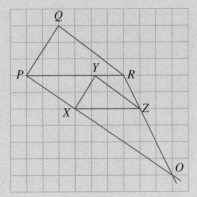

1. Choose two points on the image and their corresponding points on the original image.

2. From each of these points on the larger figure, draw a line to the corresponding point on the smaller figure.

3. Produce these lines until they intersect at the point *O*, which is the centre of enlargement.

(iii) Drop a vertical down from *Q* and *Y* and mark the new points *A* and *B*, respectively.

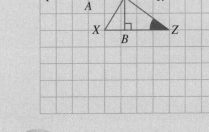

Since triangle *PQR* is an enlargement of triangle *XYZ*, we know that the triangles are similar and so $\angle PRQ = \angle XZY$.

∴ $\triangle QAR$ and $\triangle YBZ$ are similar.

∴ $\dfrac{|QA|}{|YB|} = \dfrac{|AR|}{|BZ|}$ (by theorem)

$$\frac{3}{2} = \frac{4}{|BZ|}$$

$$3|BZ| = 4(2)$$

$$|BZ| = \frac{8}{3}$$

$|BZ|$ is one unit longer than $|YR|$.

∴ $|YR| = |BZ| - 1$

∴ $|YR| = \frac{8}{3} - 1$

∴ $|YR| = \frac{5}{3}$

An alternative method would be to use trigonometry.

Most students were not successful in answering part **(iii)**. Consequently it was awarded only 5 marks, while part **(i)** was awarded 15 marks.

Constructions

There are 22 constructions that you must be able to perform on the Leaving Certificate Higher Level course.

1. Bisector of an angle, using only a compass and straight edge
2. Perpendicular bisector of a segment, using only a compass and straight edge
3. Line perpendicular to a given line l, passing through a given point not on l
4. Line perpendicular to a given line l, passing through a given point on l
5. Line parallel to a given line, through a given point
6. Division of a line segment into two or three equal segments without measuring it
7. Division of a line segment into any number of equal segments without measuring it
8. Line segment of a given length on a given ray
9. Angle of a given number of degrees with a given ray as one arm
10. Triangle, given length of three sides (SSS)
11. Triangle, given two sides and the included angle (SAS)
12. Triangle, given two angles and the common side (ASA)
13. Right-angled triangle, given length of hypotenuse and one other side (RHS)
14. Right-angled triangle, given one side and one of the acute angles
15. Rectangle, given side lengths
16. Circumcentre and circumcircle of a given triangle, using only a straight edge and compass
17. Incentre and incircle of a given triangle, using only a straight edge and compass
18. Angle of 60° without using a protractor or set square
19. Tangent to a given circle at a given point on it
20. Parallelogram, given the length of the sides and the measure of the angles
21. Centroid of a triangle
22. Orthocentre of a triangle

- The steps required for completing each of these constructions are detailed in your textbook.
- Computer simulations of these constructions can be found at www.mathopenref.com.
- Any work involving accurate constructions requires a good pencil, eraser, a compass, a ruler, a set square and a protractor.

Example

Construct √3.

Solution

Consider a right-angled triangle, one side of which is 1 unit in length and with a hypotenuse of 2 units.

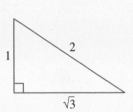

By applying Pythagoras's theorem, we find the third side equals √3.

Draw a rough sketch of this triangle.

Now construct this triangle accurately.

Start by drawing a vertical line 1 unit in length and draw a horizontal line out from its base.

Draw an arc 2 units in length from the top of the vertical line to the horizontal line.

This is the hypotenuse.

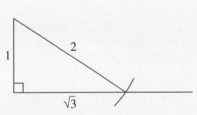

The length marked off the bottom equals √3.

You may be asked to construct √3 in the exam. **You must also be able to construct √2 accurately.** In this case, construct a right-angled isosceles triangle with perpendicular sides 1 unit in length. The hypotenuse of this triangle equals √2.

(2013 Q.6A)

(a) Complete each of the following statements.

(i) The circumcentre of a triangle is the point of intersection of

_____

(ii) The incentre of a triangle is the point of intersection of

_____

(iii) The centroid of a triangle is the point of intersection of

_____

(b) In an equilateral triangle, the circumcentre, the incentre and the centroid are all in the same place. Explain why this is the case.

(c) Construct the orthocentre of the triangle *ABC*. Show all construction lines clearly.

Solution

(a) **(i)** The circumcentre of a triangle is the point of intersection of *the perpendicular bisectors of the sides of the triangle.*

(ii) The incentre of a triangle is the point of intersection of *the bisectors of the angles of the triangle.*

(iii) The centroid of a triangle is the point of intersection of *the medians of the triangle.*

(b) In an equilateral triangle the medians are perpendicular to the opposite sides and bisect the angles. Therefore, the perpendicular bisectors of the sides, the bisectors of the angles and the median are the same line and intersect at one point.

(c) Draw a line from vertex *C*, perpendicularly through the line *AB* produced. This line is called an altitude.

Draw a line from vertex *B*, perpendicularly through the line *AC* produced. This line is also called an altitude.

The point where these altitudes intersect is the orthocentre of the triangle *ABC*.

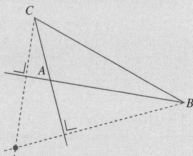

Parts (a) was worth 10 marks, (b) was worth 5 marks and part (c) was worth 10 marks.

(2015 Q.6 (a))

Construct the centroid of the triangle *ABC* given.

Show all construction lines.

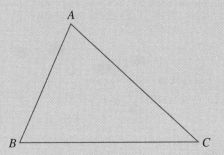

Solution

1. Construct the perpendicular bisector of [*AC*]. Label the midpoint of [*AC*] as *X*.

2. Join the point *X* to the vertex *B*, constructing a median.

3. Construct the perpendicular bisector of [*BC*]. Label the midpoint of [*BC*] as *Y*.

4 Join the point *Y* to the vertex *A*, constructing a median.

5. The point where these two medians intersect is the centroid.

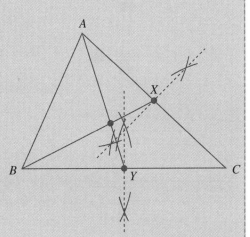

Cavan, Monaghan and Dundalk are three large towns in Ireland. These towns are indicated on the map. Each town has a local hospital for minor needs and emergencies. The Department of Health wants to build an advanced, modern medical facility, which can be shared by the three towns and their surrounding communities.

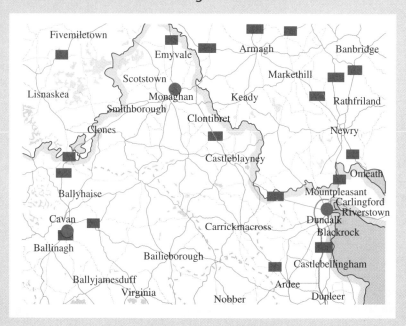

You have been asked to determine the best location for this facility.

(i) What do you think is the most important issue when deciding the location of the new medical facility?

(ii) Accurately construct the most appropriate position of the new medical facility.

(iii) By studying the map, do you think this location is the best place for the new medical facility? Give a reason for your answer.

Solution

(i) The medical facility should be equidistant (the same distance) from each of the three towns.

(ii) The point which is equidistant from each of the towns is known as the circumcentre.

To construct the circumcentre:

1. Join the towns to form a triangle.

2. Label the points C, M and D.

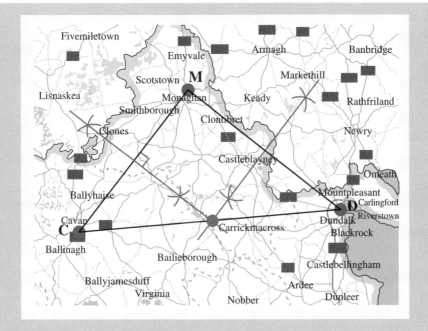

3. Construct the perpendicular bisectors of [CM] and [MD].

4. The point where these bisectors intersect is the circumcentre of the triangle.

The new medical facility should be placed at the circumcentre, which is indicated by a large blue dot on the map.

(iii) No, I do not think the location of the circumcentre is the best place for the new medical centre, as it is away from the main roads. It may be better to place the medical facility slightly closer to some main roads. Even though it will be physically further away from one town than the others, it may make it quicker to access. Also, one town may have a much bigger population and so it may be wiser to place the medical centre closer to that town.

OR

Yes, I think the location of the circumcentre is the best place for the new medical centre, as it is an equal distance from each of the towns, so it is the fairest place to put it.

exam focus

In the exam, when you are asked for your opinion you must be aware that more than one answer can be valid. Whatever opinion you give, it is important that you give reasons to back it up.

Fintan has a triangular garden, as shown. He intends to build a circular pond within the garden.

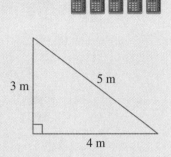

(i) Describe how Fintan would determine where the largest pond can be placed.

(ii) Find the radius of the largest pond that could fit.

(iii) Why might Fintan choose not to build the largest pond possible? Suggest a practical change he should make.

Solution

(i) To create the largest circular pool, Fintan would need to create a circle that touches all sides of the plot of land.

Therefore, Fintan needs to construct the incircle of the triangle.

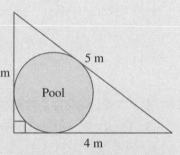

(ii) Label the vertices *A*, *B* and *C*.

Draw a radius perpendicularly to each side. Join each vertex to the centre of the circle, *O*, to divide the big triangle into three smaller triangles.

Area of △*ABC* = Area of △*AOB* + Area of △*BOC* + Area of △*AOC*

$$\frac{1}{2}(4)(3) = \frac{1}{2}(3)(r) + \frac{1}{2}(4)(r) + \frac{1}{2}(5)(r) \quad (\times)$$

$$12 = 3r + 4r + 5r$$

$$12 = 12r$$

$$1 = r$$

Therefore, the radius length is 1 m.

(iii) If Fintan chooses to build the circular pond, as in the diagram, he would have no space to walk around the pond. He should reduce the radius of the pond to allow space for a path around the pond.

Other suggestions would be acceptable answers as long as they are practical, functional and realistic for this situation.

(2016 Q.4)

(a) The diagram shows a semi-circle standing on a diameter $[AC]$, and $[BD] \perp [AC]$.

   (i) Prove that the triangles ABD and DBC are similar.

   (ii) If $|AB| = x$, $|BC| = 1$, and $|BD| = y$, write y in terms of x.

(b) Use your result from part **(a)(ii)** to construct a line segment equal in length (in centimetres) to the square root of the length of the line segment $[TU]$ which is drawn below.

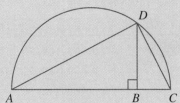

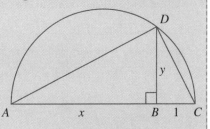

Solution

(a) **(i)** $|\angle ABD| = |\angle CBD| = 90°$ (given)

       $|\angle BDC| + |\angle BCD| = 90°$ (remaining angles in a triangle)

       $|\angle BDC| + |\angle ADB| = 90°$ (angle in a semicircle)

       $\therefore |\angle BDC| + |\angle BCD| = |\angle BDC| + |\angle ADB|$

          $\therefore |\angle BCD| = |\angle ADB|$

    Two pairs of equal angles, therefore the triangles ABD and DBC are similar

   (ii) Since the triangles are similar, the corresponding sides are in proportion:

$$\frac{|BD|}{|BC|} = \frac{|AB|}{|BD|}$$

$$\frac{y}{1} = \frac{x}{y}$$

$$y^2 = x \implies y = \sqrt{x}$$

(b) **1.** Add a length of 1 cm onto the end of $[TU]$ and label the far point as S.

   2. Construct the perpendicular bisector of $[TS]$

   3. Construct the circle with diameter $[TS]$.

   4. Draw a line perpendicularly upright from the point U.

   5. This upright line has a length of $\sqrt{|TU|}$.

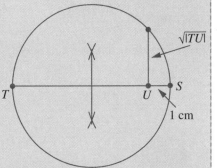

This question was badly answered. Subsequently part **(a) (i)** was worth 15 marks and parts **(a) (ii)** and **(b)** were worth 5 marks each.

☐ To learn how to solve triangles to find missing sides or angles
☐ To learn how to find the area of a triangle
☐ To learn how to find the area and perimeter of a sector of a circle
☐ To learn how to solve trigonometric equations

Formulae for solving triangles

Formulae for right-angled triangles only

(see *booklet of formulae and tables*, page 16)

Pythagoras's theorem:

$$a^2 = b^2 + c^2$$

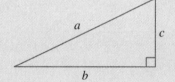

The three trigonometric ratios for a right-angled triangle, $0° < \theta < 90°$, are:

(similar diagram in *booklet of formulae and tables*, page 16)

$$\sin \theta = \frac{O}{H}$$

$$\cos \theta = \frac{A}{H}$$

$$\tan \theta = \frac{O}{A}$$

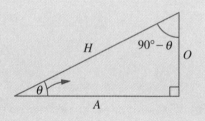

From the diagram, we can see that:

$$\sin(90° - \theta) = \frac{A}{H} = \cos \theta \quad \text{and} \quad \cos(90° - \theta) = \frac{O}{H} = \sin \theta$$

key
point

These ratios hold for all values of $\theta \in \mathbb{R}$, not just for $0° < \theta < 90°$.

Formulae for all triangles

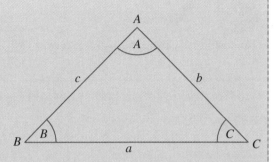

(see *booklet of formulae and tables, page 16*)

Sine rule

$$\frac{a}{\sin A} = \frac{b}{\sin B} = \frac{c}{\sin C}$$

or

$$\frac{\sin A}{a} = \frac{\sin B}{b} = \frac{\sin C}{c}$$

Cosine rule

$$a^2 = b^2 + c^2 - 2bc \cos A \quad \boxed{\text{or}} \quad b^2 = a^2 + c^2 - 2ac \cos B \quad \boxed{\text{or}} \quad c^2 = a^2 + b^2 - 2ab \cos C$$

Rearrange to find the angle:

$$\cos A = \frac{b^2 + c^2 - a^2}{2bc} \quad \boxed{\text{or}} \quad \cos B = \frac{a^2 + c^2 - b^2}{2ac} \quad \boxed{\text{or}} \quad \cos C = \frac{a^2 + b^2 - c^2}{2ab}$$

key point

- When using the **sine rule**, always place the unknown quantity on the top of the left fraction.
- If you need to use the **cosine rule** to find an angle, rearrange the rule first, then substitute the known values. This means that you can enter the solution directly into a calculator.

Use the following flowchart to work out which formula to use

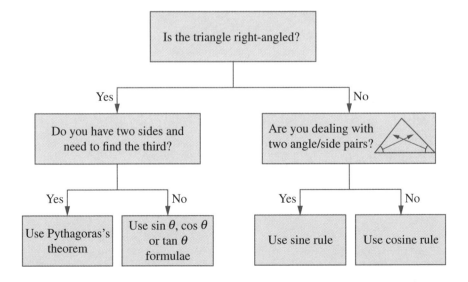

The cosine rule must be used in a non-right-angled triangle if:

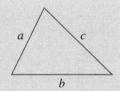

- You are given the three sides and need to find an angle.

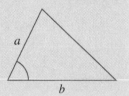

- You are given two sides and the included angle and need to find the third side.

Area of a triangle

(see *booklet of formulae and tables*, page 16)

Given two sides and the angle in between these sides:

$$\text{Area} = \frac{1}{2}ab \sin C = \frac{1}{2}ac \sin B = \frac{1}{2}bc \sin A$$

(see *booklet of formulae and tables*, page 9)

Given the three sides:

$$s = \frac{a + b + c}{2}$$

$$\text{Area} = \sqrt{s(s-a)(s-b)(s-c)}$$

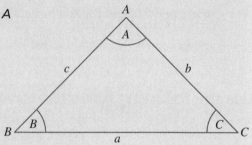

Example

In $\triangle PQR$, $|PR| = \sqrt{8}$ m, $|\angle RPQ| = 30°$ and $|\angle PQR| = 45°$.

(i) Find $|QR|$.

(ii) Show that the area of $\triangle PRQ = 2{\cdot}7$ m², correct to one decimal place.

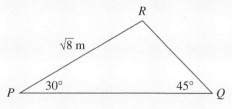

Solution

(i) Use the sine rule to find $|QR|$.

$$\frac{|QR|}{\sin P} = \frac{|PR|}{\sin Q}$$

$$\frac{|QR|}{\sin 30°} = \frac{\sqrt{8}}{\sin 45°}$$

$$|QR| = \frac{\sqrt{8}\sin 30°}{\sin 45°}$$

$$|QR| = \frac{2\sqrt{2}\left(\frac{1}{2}\right)}{\frac{1}{\sqrt{2}}}$$

$$|QR| = 2$$

(ii) Area of $\triangle PQR = \frac{1}{2}|PR| \times |QR| \sin R$.

We need angle R.

The three angles of the triangle sum to 180°.

$R = 180° - 45° - 30°$

$R = 105°$

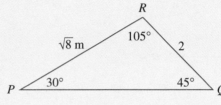

Thus, area $= \frac{1}{2}(\sqrt{8})(2) \sin 105°$

$= 2{\cdot}732050808$

$= 2{\cdot}7 \text{ m}^2$

(correct to one decimal place)

Example

A ball at P is 27 m from the nearer goalpost.

(i) Calculate its distance from the farther goalpost, to the nearest metre.

(ii) Find $|\angle RPQ|$.

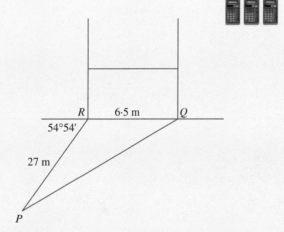

Solution

Draw a triangle by itself to represent the situation.

(i) Find $|PQ|$ (in the diagram, $|PQ| = r$).

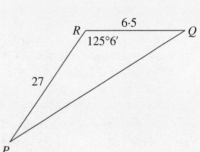

We have two sides and included angle,
∴ use the cosine rule.

$$r^2 = p^2 + q^2 - 2pq \cos R$$
$$= (6.5)^2 + (27)^2 - 2(6.5)(27) \cos 125°6'$$
$$r^2 = 42.25 + 729 - 2(6.5)(27)(-0.5750)$$
$$= 42.25 + 729 + 201.825$$
$$r^2 = 973.075$$
$$r = \sqrt{973.075}$$
$$= 31.1942$$

Thus, $|PQ| = 31$ m.   (correct to the nearest metre)

(ii) Find $|\angle RPQ|$ (from the diagram, $|\angle RPQ| = P$).
We have two sides and non-included angle,
∴ use the sine rule.

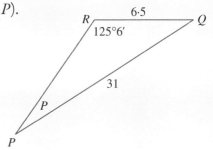

$$\frac{\sin P}{p} = \frac{\sin R}{r}$$
$$\frac{\sin P}{6.5} = \frac{\sin 125°6'}{31}$$
$$\sin P = \frac{6.5 \sin 125°6'}{31}$$
$$\sin P = 0.1715475214$$
$$P = \sin^{-1}(0.1715475214)$$
$$P = 9°53' \text{ or } P = 9.88°$$

(2017 Q.6)

(a) Take the earth as a sphere with radius 6371 km.

Jack is standing on the Cliffs of Moher at the point J which is 214 metres above sea level. He is looking out to sea at a point H on the horizon. Taking A as the centre of the earth, find $|JH|$, the distance from Jack to the horizon.

Give your answer correct to the nearest km.

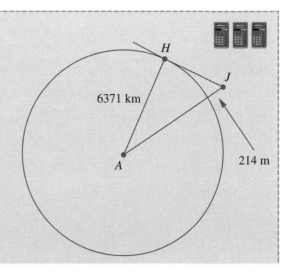

(b) The Cliffs of Moher, at point C, are at latitude 53° north of the equator. On the diagram, s_1 represents the circle that is at latitude 53°. s_2 represents the equator (which is at latitude 0°). A is the centre of the earth.

s_1 and s_2 are on parallel planes.

Find the length of the circle s_1.

Give your answer correct to the nearest km.

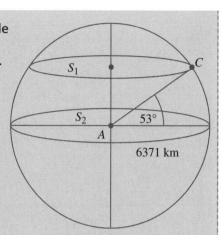

Solution

(a) AHJ is a right-angled triangle.

$|AJ| = 6371$ km $+ 214$ m $= 6371 \cdot 214$ km

Using Pythagoras's theorem:

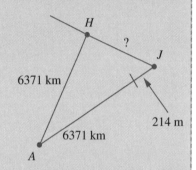

$$|AJ|^2 = |AH|^2 + |JH|^2$$
$$(6371\cdot214)^2 = (6371)^2 + |JH|^2$$
$$(6371\cdot214)^2 - (6371)^2 = |JH|^2$$
$$2726\cdot833796 = |JH|^2$$
$$52 \text{ km} = |JH|$$

(b) To find the length of s_1, we need to find its radius.

Observe the triangle with $[AC]$ as its hypotenuse.

The angle is $90° - 53° = 37°$

$|AC|$ = radius of the Earth = 6371 km

Find the radius of s_1, r:

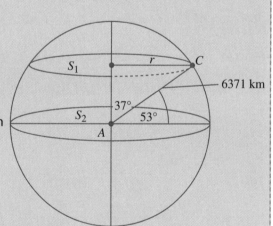

$$\sin 37° = \frac{r}{6371}$$
$$6371(\sin 37°) = r$$
$$3834\cdot16 \text{ km} = r$$
$$\text{Length of } s_1 = 2\pi r$$
$$= 2\pi(3834\cdot16)$$
$$= 24{,}090\cdot7 \implies L = 24{,}091 \text{ km}$$

In $\triangle ABC$, $|AB| = 3$, $|AC| = 5$ and $|BC| = 7$.

Calculate:

(i) The measure of the greatest angle of the triangle.

(ii) The area of $\triangle ABC$.

(iii) The distance from vertex A to the side $|BC|$.

Solution

(i) The largest angle is opposite the largest side.

Using the cosine rule:

$$a^2 = b^2 + c^2 - 2bc \cos A$$
$$7^2 = 5^2 + 3^2 - 2(5)(3) \cos A$$
$$49 = 25 + 9 - 30 \cos A$$
$$30 \cos A = 25 + 9 - 49$$
$$30 \cos A = -15$$
$$\cos A = -\frac{1}{2}$$
$$A = \cos^{-1}\left(-\frac{1}{2}\right) = 120°$$

(ii) Area of $\triangle ABC$ $= \frac{1}{2}bc \sin A$ $= \frac{1}{2}(5)(3) \sin 120°$ $= \frac{1}{2}(5)(3)\left(\dfrac{\sqrt{3}}{2}\right) = \dfrac{15\sqrt{3}}{4}$

(iii) Let d be the distance from A to $|BC|$.

Area of $\triangle ABC = \dfrac{1}{2}$base × perpendicular height

$$= \frac{1}{2}(7)(d) = \frac{7}{2}d$$

From (ii), area of $\triangle ABC = \dfrac{15\sqrt{3}}{4}$

$$\frac{7}{2}d = \frac{15\sqrt{3}}{4}$$

$14d = 15\sqrt{3}$ (multiplying both sides by 4)

$d = \dfrac{15\sqrt{3}}{14}$ (divide both sides by 14)

exam Q

(2015 Q.9 (a), (b) and (d))

(a) Joan is playing golf. She is 150 m from the centre of a circular green of diameter 30 m. The diagram shows the range of directions in which Joan can hit the ball so that it could land on the green. Find α, the measure of the angle of this range of directions. Give your answer, in degrees, correct to one decimal place.

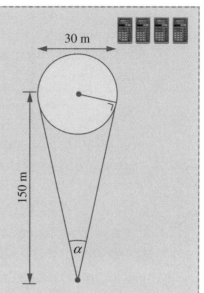

(b) At the next hole, Joan, at T, attempts to hit the ball in the direction of the hole H. Her shot is off target and the ball lands at A, a distance of 190 metres from T, where $|\angle ATH| = 18°$.

$|TH|$ is 385 metres.

Find $|AH|$, the distance from the ball to the hole, correct to the nearest metre.

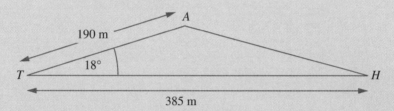

(d) At a later hole, Joan's first shot lands at the point G, on ground that is sloping downwards, as shown. A vertical tree, $[CE]$, 25 metres high, stands between G and the hole.

The distance, $|GC|$, from the ball to the bottom of the tree is also 25 metres.

The angle of elevation at G to the top of the tree, E, is θ, where

$$\theta = \tan^{-1}\frac{1}{2}.$$

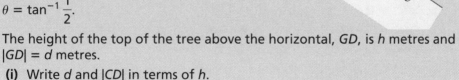

The height of the top of the tree above the horizontal, GD, is h metres and $|GD| = d$ metres.

   (i) Write d and $|CD|$ in terms of h.

   (ii) Hence, or otherwise, find h.

Solution

(a) Diameter is 30 m, so the radius is 15 m.

150 m from the centre of the circle to the vertex at the bottom, bisects the angle α.

$$\sin \beta = \frac{15}{150}$$

$$\beta = \sin^{-1}\left(\frac{15}{150}\right)$$

$$\beta = 5.739°$$

$$\alpha = 2(\beta) = 11.478° \implies \alpha = 11.5°$$

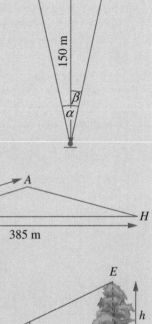

30 m

15 m

150 m

β

α

(b) To find $|AH|$, use the cosine rule:

$$a^2 = b^2 + c^2 - 2bc \cos A$$

$$|AH|^2 = (190)^2 + (385)^2 - 2(190)(385)\cos18°$$

$$|AH|^2 = 36{,}100 + 148{,}225 - 139{,}140$$

$$|AH|^2 = 45185$$

$$|AH| = 212.567 \implies |AH| = 213 \text{ m}$$

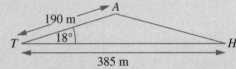

190 m   A

T   18°

385 m   H

(d) (i) $\tan\theta = \dfrac{h}{d}$ | $|CD| + h = 25$ m

$\dfrac{1}{2} = \dfrac{h}{d}$ ($\times 2d$) | $|CD| = 25 - h$

$d = 2h$

E

G θ

d D

h

(ii) Using Pythagoras's theorem on the lower triangle:

$$25^2 = (2h)^2 + (25 - h)^2$$

$$625 = 4h^2 + 625 - 50h + h^2$$

$$0 = 5h^2 - 50h + 625 - 625$$

$$0 = 5h^2 - 50h$$

$$0 = 5h(h - 10)$$

$$5h = 0 \quad \text{or} \quad h - 10 = 0$$

$$h = 0 \text{ (reject)} \qquad h = 10 \text{ m}$$

G θ

2h   D

25 m

25−h

C

(2010 Q.9B (b))

Roofs of buildings are often supported by frameworks of timber called roof trusses.

A quantity surveyor needs to find the total length of timber needed in order to make the triangular truss shown below.

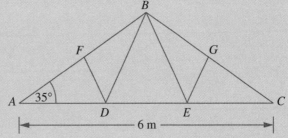

The length of [AC] is 6 metres and the pitch of the roof is 35°, as shown.

$$|AD|=|DE|=|EC| \text{ and } |AF|=|FB|=|BG|=|GC|$$

(i) Calculate the length of [AB], in metres, correct to two decimal places.

(ii) Calculate the total length of timber required to make the truss.

Solution

(i) Draw a line from B vertically down to [AC] this line meets [AC] at the midpoint, H, at right angles.

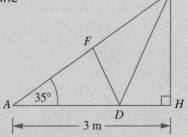

$$|AH| = 3 \text{ m}$$

$$\cos 35° = \frac{3}{|AB|}$$

$$|AB| = \frac{3}{\cos 35°} = 3\cdot66232$$

$$|AB| = 3\cdot66 \text{ m (to two decimal places)}$$

(ii) $|FD|^2 = 1\cdot83^2 + 2^2 - 2(1\cdot83)(2) \cos 35°$

$|FD|^2 = 1\cdot352707$

$|FD| = 1\cdot163 \text{ m}$

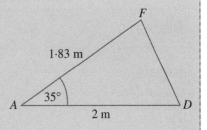

$|BD|^2 = 2^2 + 3\cdot66^2 - 2(2)(3\cdot66) \cos 35°$

$|BD|^2 = 5\cdot403214$

$|BD| = 2\cdot326 \text{ m}$

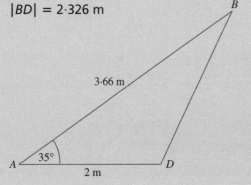

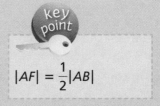

key point

$$|AF| = \frac{1}{2}|AB|$$

Putting all of the lengths together on the truss:

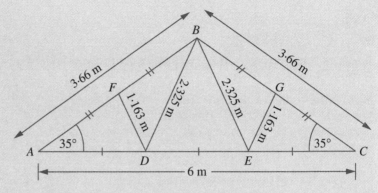

Total length required = 6 + 2(3·66) + 2(1·163) + 2(2·326)

$$= 20\cdot296$$
$$= 20\cdot3 \text{ m}$$

key point

In this question, $\triangle ADF$ and $\triangle AEB$ are similar triangles and so their sides are in proportion. This method could have been used instead of using the cosine rule to find $|BE|$, which is equal to $|BD|$.

Circular measure

Angles can be measured in either **degrees** or **radians**. $360° = 2\pi$ radians

Degrees	360°	270°	180°	90°	60°	45°	30°
Radians	2π	$\dfrac{3\pi}{2}$	π	$\dfrac{\pi}{2}$	$\dfrac{\pi}{3}$	$\dfrac{\pi}{4}$	$\dfrac{\pi}{6}$

key point

Throughout the course, you must be able to quickly and easily convert degrees to radians and radians to degrees.

- To **convert degrees to radians**, divide by 180 and multiply by π.
- To **convert radians to degrees**, divide by π and multiply by 180. Alternatively, replace π with 180°.

Sectors

(see booklet of formulae and tables, page 9)

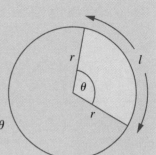

If θ is in degrees:

Length of arc: $l = \dfrac{\theta}{360°} \times 2\pi r$

Area of sector: $A = \dfrac{\theta}{360°} \times \pi r^2$

If θ is in radians:

Length of arc: $l = r\theta$

Area of sector: $A = \dfrac{1}{2}r^2\theta$

Example

(i) The radius of a circle is 10 cm. Find the angle subtended at the centre by an arc of length 4π cm.

(ii) Find the area of a sector of a circle of radius 4 cm if the arc of the sector subtended an angle of $\frac{\pi}{3}$ at the centre.

(iii) The area of a sector of a circle of radius r is 12π cm². If the angle subtended at the centre of the circle by this sector is $\frac{2\pi}{3}$, calculate r, the radius of the circle.

Solution

(i) $r = 10, l = 4\pi$. Find θ.
$$l = r\theta$$
$$4\pi = 10\theta$$
$$\theta = \frac{2\pi}{5} \text{ radians}$$

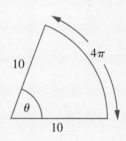

(ii) $r = 4, \theta = \frac{\pi}{3}$. Find A.
$$A = \frac{1}{2}r^2\theta$$
$$= \frac{1}{2}(4)^2\left(\frac{\pi}{3}\right)$$
$$A = \frac{8\pi}{3} \text{ cm}^2$$

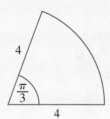

(iii) $A = 12\pi$, $\theta = \frac{2\pi}{3}$. Find r.

$$A = \frac{1}{2}r^2\theta$$

$$12\pi = \frac{1}{2}r^2\left(\frac{2\pi}{3}\right)$$

$$36 = r^2$$

$$r = 6 \text{ cm}$$

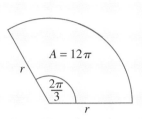

(2014 Q.2 (b))

The diagram shows part of the circular end of a running track with three running lanes shown. The centre of each of the circular boundaries of the lanes is at O.

Kate runs in the middle of lane 1, from A to B as shown. Helen runs in the middle of lane 2, from C to D as shown.

Helen runs 3 m further than Kate.

$|\angle AOB| = |\angle COD| = \theta$ radians.

If each lane is 1·2 m wide, find θ.

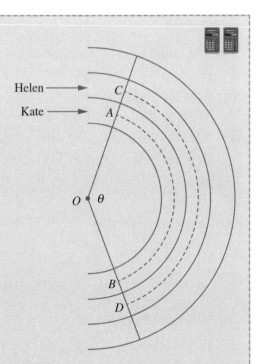

Solution

Let the radius from O to A be r	Arc CD − arc AB = 3
Length of arc $AB = \theta r$	$\theta(r + 1.2) - \theta r = 3$
Length of arc $CD = \theta(r + 1.2)$	$\theta r + 1.2\theta - \theta r = 3$
	$1.2\theta = 3 \quad (\div 1.2)$
	$\theta = 2.5$ rads

A chain passes around two circular wheels, as shown. One wheel has a radius of 75 cm and the other has a radius of 15 cm. The centres, *E* and *F*, of the wheels are 120 cm apart.

The chain consists of the common tangent [*AB*], the minor arc *BC*, the common tangent [*CD*] and the major arc *DA*.

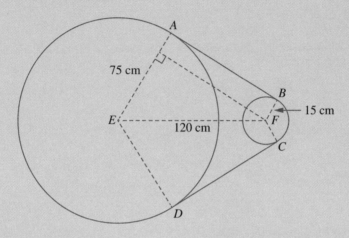

(i) Find the measure of $\angle AEF$.

(ii) Find |*AB*| in surd form.

(iii) Find the length of the chain, giving your answer in the form $k\pi + l\sqrt{3}$ where $k, l \in \mathbb{Z}$.

Solution

(i) Label the point *G*.

$$|GE| = |AE| - |AG|$$

$$|GE| = 75 - 15$$

$$|GE| = 60 \text{ cm}$$

In $\triangle GEF$:

$$\cos \angle AEF = \frac{|GE|}{|EF|} = \frac{60}{120} = \frac{1}{2}$$

$$\therefore \quad \angle AEF = \cos^{-1} \frac{1}{2}$$

$$\angle AEF = 60°$$

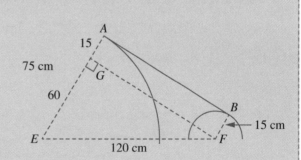

(ii) $|AB| = |GF|$

$$\sin \angle AEF = \frac{|GF|}{|EF|}$$

$$\sin 60° = \frac{|GF|}{120}$$

$$120 \sin 60° = |GF|$$

$$60\sqrt{3} = |GF|$$

$$\therefore \quad 60\sqrt{3} = |AB|$$

(iii) Length of chain $= |$major arc $AD| + |$minor arc $BC| + |AB| + |CD|$

Major arc $\angle AED = 240° = \dfrac{4\pi}{3}$ rad

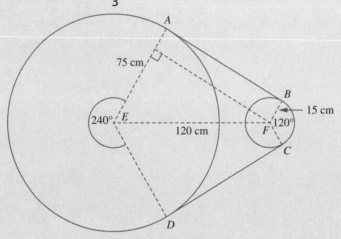

$|$Major arc $AD| = \theta r$	Minor arc $\angle BFC = 120° = \dfrac{2\pi}{3}$ rad
$= \left(\dfrac{4\pi}{3}\right)(75)$	$|$Minor arc $BC| = \theta r$
$= 100\pi$ cm	$= \left(\dfrac{2\pi}{3}\right)(15)$
	$= 10\pi$ cm

Length of chain $= 100\pi + 10\pi + 60\sqrt{3} + 60\sqrt{3}$

$= (110\pi + 120\sqrt{3})$ cm

Unit circle

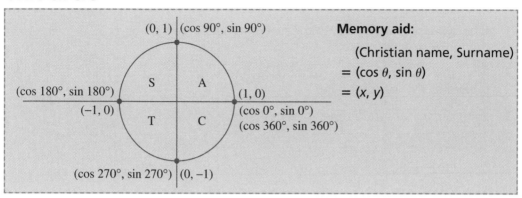

Angles between 0° and 360°

The trigonometric ratio of an angle between 0° and 360° can be found with the following steps.

1. Make a rough diagram of the angle on a unit circle.

2. Use [diagram: S+ A+ / T+ C+] to find whether this ratio is positive or negative.

3. Find its **reference** angle, the acute angle to the x-axis.

4. Use a calculator or the tables on page 13 of the *booklet of formulae and tables* to find the reference angle and use the sign in step 2.

Given the values of sin, cos and tan

Between 0° and 360° there may be two angles with the same trigonometric ratio,
e.g. $\cos 120° = -\frac{1}{2}$ and $\cos 240° = -\frac{1}{2}$.

To find the two values, we do the following:

1. Ignore the sign and evaluate the reference angle using the tables or a calculator.

2. From the sign of the given ratio, decide in which quadrants the angles can lie.

3. Using a diagram, state the angles between 0° and 360°.

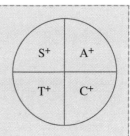

In a triangle PQR, $|\angle PQR| = 30°$, $|QR| = 15$ and $|RP| = 5\sqrt{3}$.
Find two values for $|\angle QPR|$ and sketch the two resulting triangles.

Solution

Draw a rough sketch of the triangle PQR.

Use the sine rule:

$$\frac{\sin \theta}{15} = \frac{\sin 30°}{5\sqrt{3}}$$

$$\sin \theta = \frac{15(\sin 30°)}{5\sqrt{3}}$$

$$\sin \theta = \frac{\sqrt{3}}{2}$$

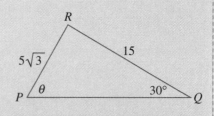

Solve for θ.

Reference angle $= \sin^{-1}\left(\frac{\sqrt{3}}{2}\right) = 60°$.

Sin is positive in the first and second quadrants.

So $\theta = 60°$ or $120°$.

Sketches:

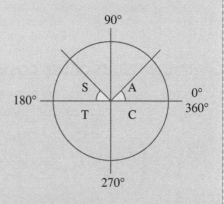

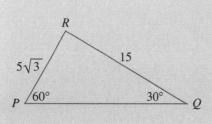

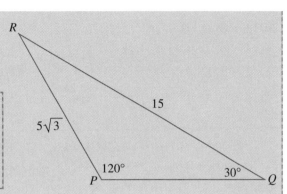

Candidates performed very badly on this exam question because they did not know how to get the second value for θ.

exam Q

(2018 Q.4 (a))

Find **all** the values of x for which $\cos(2x) = -\frac{\sqrt{3}}{2}$, where $0° \leq x \leq 360°$.

Solution

1. Find the reference angle by ignoring the negative sign.
   Reference angle $= \cos^{-1}(\frac{\sqrt{3}}{2}) = 30°$

2. Cos is negative in the second and third quadrants. Mark 30° from the horizontal into each of these quadrants.

3. We are told that
   $0° \leq x \leq 360°$, so $0° \leq 2x \leq 720°$.

   This means that when finding the actual values for x, we must go around the unit circle twice.

   $2x = 150°, 210°, 510°, 570°$

   $x = 75°, 105°, 255°, 285°$

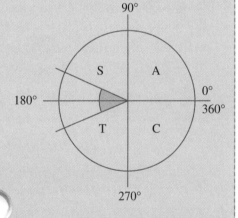

The part (b) for this question was badly answered, subsequently this part (a) was worth 20 marks out of the total 25 available for this question 4.

exam Q

(i) Show that the equation $15 \cos^2 x = 13 + \sin x$ may be written as a quadratic equation in $\sin x$.

(ii) Solve the quadratic equation for $\sin x$, and hence solve for all values of x where $0° \leq x \leq 360°$. Give your answer(s) correct to the nearest degree.

Solution

(i) $15 \cos^2 x = 13 + \sin x$

From the *booklet of formulae and tables*, page 13:

$$1 = \sin^2 x + \cos^2 x$$

$$1 - \sin^2 x = \cos^2 x \qquad \text{(substitute this into the original equation)}$$

$$15(1 - \sin^2 x) = 13 + \sin x$$

$$15 - 15 \sin^2 x = 13 + \sin x$$

$$15 \sin^2 x + \sin x - 2 = 0$$

(ii) Solve: $\qquad 15 \sin^2 x + \sin x - 2 = 0$

$$(5 \sin x + 2)(3 \sin x - 1) = 0$$

$\sin x = -\dfrac{2}{5}$	$\sin x = \dfrac{1}{3}$
Reference angle: $\sin^{-1}\left(\dfrac{2}{5}\right) = 24°$	Reference angle: $\sin^{-1}\left(\dfrac{1}{3}\right) = 19°$
(correct to the nearest degree)	(correct to the nearest degree)
Sin is negative in the 3rd and 4th quadrants.	Sin is positive in the 1st and 2nd quadrants.
Mark the reference angle into each quadrant.	Mark the reference angle into each quadrant.
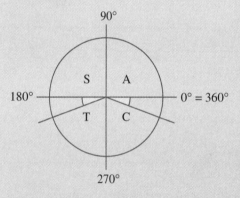	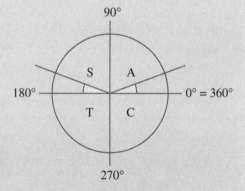
Read angle, x, from 0° to the marked positions:	Read angle, x, from 0° to the marked positions:
$x = 180° + 24° = 204°$	$x = 0° + 19° = 19°$
$x = 360° - 24° = 336°$	$x = 180° - 19° = 161°$

$$\therefore x = \{19°, 161°, 204°, 336°\}$$

exam focus

You should be very familiar with the trigonometric identities, which are in the *booklet of formulae and tables*. Knowing where these formulae are is a big advantage in an exam situation, where they can be used to simplify trigonometric expressions quickly and efficiently.

6 Trigonometry II

aims

☐ To graph any trigonometrical function of the form $a + b \sin c\theta$ and $a + b \cos c\theta$ and $b \tan c\theta$ for $a, b, c \in \mathbb{R}$

☐ To identify a trigonometrical graph, its period and range

☐ To model situations using a trigonometrical function

☐ To interpret graphs which model a situation

☐ To understand and simplify 3D situations

☐ To understand a compound angle and its associated formulae

☐ To manipulate the compound angle formulae

☐ To prove trigonometrical identities

Graph of trigonometric functions

The table shows values for $\sin \theta$, $\cos \theta$ and $\tan \theta$ for $0 \le \theta \le 2\pi$.

θ	0	$\dfrac{\pi}{4}$	$\dfrac{\pi}{2}$	$\dfrac{3\pi}{4}$	π	$\dfrac{5\pi}{4}$	$\dfrac{3\pi}{2}$	$\dfrac{7\pi}{4}$	2π
$\sin \theta$	0	0·7	1	0·7	0	−0·7	−1	−0·7	0
$\cos \theta$	1	0·7	0	−0·7	−1	−0·7	0	0·7	1
$\tan \theta$	0	1	undefined	−1	0	1	undefined	−1	0

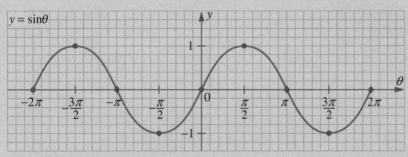

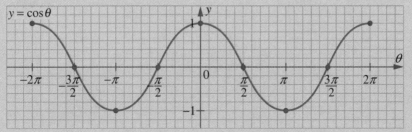

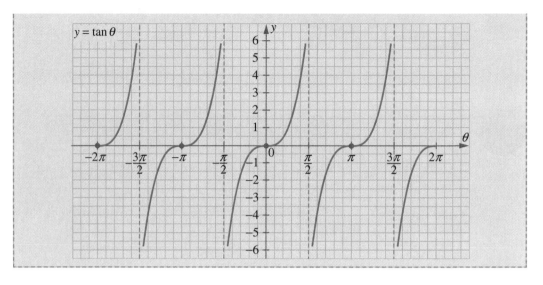

Period and range

The **period** is the minimum horizontal distance over which the graph repeats indefinitely.

The **range** is a set of values from the lowest to the highest that the function can produce.

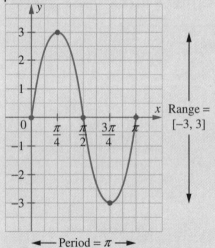

Range = [−3, 3]

Period = π

	Period	Range
sin θ	2π	[−1, 1]
cos θ	2π	[−1, 1]
tan θ	π	$\mathbb{R}$

key point

a = y-value at midway line
b = difference between midway line and maximum height
c = 360°/period or 2π/period

Variations on the basic trigonometric functions:

	Period	Range
b sin cθ	$\dfrac{2\pi}{c}$	[−b, b]
b cos cθ	$\dfrac{2\pi}{c}$	[−b, b]
b tan cθ	$\dfrac{\pi}{c}$	$\mathbb{R}$

	Period	Range
a + b sin cθ	$\dfrac{2\pi}{c}$	[−b + a, b + a]
a + b cos cθ	$\dfrac{2\pi}{c}$	[−b + a, b + a]

- Sin and cos have the same values for period and range, while tan is very different.
- Multiplying the function by a value multiplies the range by the same value. For example, the range for 2 sin θ is [−2, 2].
- Increasing the angle reduces the period. For example, the period for cos 3θ is $\frac{2\pi}{3}$.
- Adding or subtracting a value to the entire function shifts the graph up or down the y-axis. For example, the range for 4 + sin θ is [3, 5].

exam focus

You must be able to recognise the period, range and vertical position of a graph and use it to identify the exact trigonometric function, in the form:

$$a + b\sin c\theta, \ a + b\cos c\theta \text{ for } a, b, c \in \mathbb{R}.$$

Example

The diagram shows the graph of a function of the form $y = a\cos bx$ for $0 \le x \le 2\pi$.

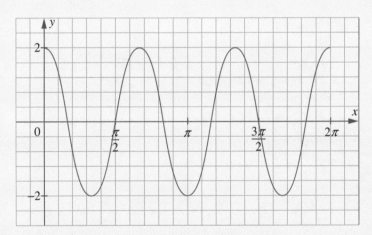

(i) What is the period and range of this function?

(ii) What is the value of a and the value of b?

Solution

(i) The range is $[-2, 2]$ from the graph.

Between 0 and 2π there are three complete U-shaped segments to this curve.

This means that the curve repeats itself three times in 2π and so the period is $\frac{2\pi}{3}$.

(ii) As the range is $[-2, 2]$ and the graph looks like the usual cosine graph, the value of a is 2.

As the graph has three repeated segments, the value of b must be 3.

The equation of the graph is $y = 2 \cos 3x$.

The function $f : x \rightarrow 3 \sin(2x)$ is defined for $x \in \mathbb{R}$.

(i) Complete the table.

x	0	$\dfrac{\pi}{4}$	$\dfrac{\pi}{2}$	$\dfrac{3\pi}{4}$	π
$2x$					
$\sin(2x)$					
$3\sin(2x)$					

(ii) Draw the graph of $y = f(x)$ in the domain $0 \leq x \leq \pi$, $x \in \mathbb{R}$.

(iii) Write down the period and range of f.

Solution

(i) The table:

x	0	$\dfrac{\pi}{4}$	$\dfrac{\pi}{2}$	$\dfrac{3\pi}{4}$	π
$2x$	0	$\dfrac{\pi}{2}$	π	$\dfrac{3\pi}{2}$	2π
$\sin(2x)$	0	1	0	-1	0
$3\sin(2x)$	0	3	0	-3	0

(ii) The graph:

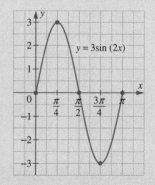

$y = 3\sin(2x)$

key point

It is vital that you do not join the dots with a straight line. You must know that the expected shape is a curve.

(iii) The period is π.

The range is $[-3, 3]$.

(2010 Q.5 (b))

The graphs of three functions are shown on the diagram below.

The scales on the axes are not labelled. The three functions are:

$$x \to \cos 3x \quad x \to 2 \cos 3x \quad x \to 3 \cos 2x$$

Identify which function is which and label the scales on the axes

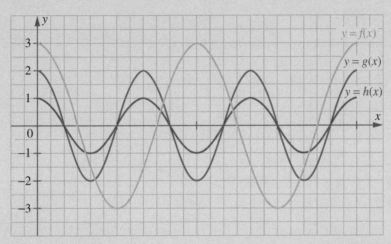

Solution

The range of each wave is determined by the number in front of the cos function. So, a function in the form $a \cos bx$ will have a range of $[-a, a]$.

This tells us that: $h(x) \to \cos 3x \quad g(x) \to 2 \cos 3x \quad f(x) \to 3 \cos 2x$

The period of each wave is determined by the number in front of the variable (x).

So, a function in the form $a \cos bx$ will have a period of $\frac{360°}{b}$ degrees or $\frac{2\pi}{b}$ radians

So, $h(x)$ has a period of 120°, $g(x)$ has a period of 120° and $f(x)$ has a period of 180°.

Using this information, we can scale the axes as follows:

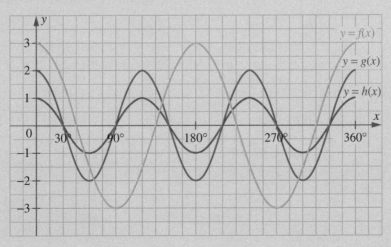

The diagram shows the graph of the function $f : x \rightarrow \sin 2x$.
The line $2y = 1$ is also shown.

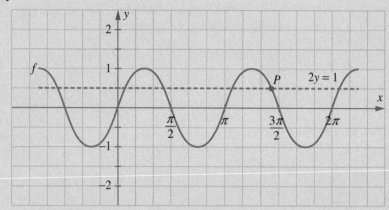

(i) On the same diagram, sketch the graphs of $g : x \rightarrow \sin x$ and $h : x \rightarrow 3\sin 2x$.
Indicate clearly which is g and which is h.

(ii) Find the coordinates of the point P in the diagram.

Solution

(i) Make sure to identify each graph. Using colour is an option. Labelling them on
the left side where the graphs begin is another option.

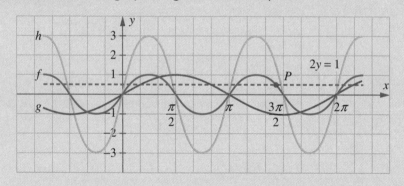

(ii) The point P is where the $2y = 1$ line intersects the $\sin 2x$ curve.

$$2y = 1 \Rightarrow y = \frac{1}{2}$$

$$\sin 2x = \frac{1}{2}$$

$$2x = \sin^{-1}\frac{1}{2}$$

$$2x = \frac{\pi}{6} \text{ or } \frac{5\pi}{6} \text{ or } \frac{13\pi}{6} \text{ or } \frac{17\pi}{6} \text{ or } \ldots$$

$$x = \frac{\pi}{12} \text{ or } \frac{5\pi}{12} \text{ or } \frac{13\pi}{12} \text{ or } \frac{17\pi}{12} \text{ or } \ldots$$

We need the 4th point of intersection, from the right of the y-axis, so P is $\left(\frac{17\pi}{12}, \frac{1}{2}\right)$.

(2016 Q.8 (a), (b), (d), (e) and (f))

The height of the water in a port was measured over a period of time. The average height was found to be 1·6 m. The height measured in metres, $h(t)$, was modelled using the function

$$h(t) = 1\cdot6 + 1\cdot5 \cos\left(\frac{\pi}{6}t\right)$$

where t represents the number of hours since the last recorded high tide and $\left(\frac{\pi}{6}t\right)$ is expressed in radians.

(a) Find the period and range of $h(t)$

(b) Find the maximum height of the water in the port.

(d) (i) On a particular day the high tide occurred at midnight (i.e. $t = 0$). Use the function to complete the table and show the height, $h(t)$, (of the water between midnight and the following midnight.

$h(t) = 1\cdot6 + 1\cdot5 \cos\left(\dfrac{\pi}{6}t\right)$								
Time	Midnight	3 a.m.	6 a.m.	9 a.m.	12 noon	3 p.m.	6 p.m.	9 p.m.	Midnight
t (hours)	0	3							
$h(t)$ (m)									

(ii) Sketch the graph of $h(t)$ between midnight and the following midnight.

(e) Find, from your sketch, the difference in water height between low tide and high tide.

(f) A fully loaded barge enters the port, unloads its cargo and departs some time later. The fully loaded barge requires a minimum water level of 2 m. When the barge is unloaded it only requires 1·5 m. Use your graph to estimate the **maximum** amount of time that the barge can spend in port, without resting on the sea-bed.

Solution

(a) Period = $\dfrac{2\pi}{\left(\dfrac{\pi}{6}\right)}$ = 12 hours

For: $h(t) = 1\cdot6 + 1\cdot5 \cos\left(\frac{\pi}{6}t\right)$

The lowest point will be when cos $\left(\frac{\pi}{6}t\right) = -1$ (smallest possible value for cos A)

The highest point will be when cos $\left(\frac{\pi}{6}t\right) = +1$ (largest possible value for cos A)

Range: $[1\cdot6 + 1\cdot5(-1), \ 1\cdot6 + 1\cdot5(+1)] = [0\cdot1\ m, 3\cdot1\ m]$

(b) Maximum height = $3\cdot1$ m (from the range above)

(d) (i) Using a calculator, we can find each value for the height for each value of t:

$h(t) = 1\cdot6 + 1\cdot5 \cos\left(\dfrac{\pi}{6}t\right)$								
Time	Midnight	3 a.m.	6 a.m.	9 a.m.	12 noon	3 p.m.	6 p.m.	9 p.m.	Midnight
t (hours)	0	3	6	9	12	15	18	21	24
$h(t)$ (m)	3·1	1·6	0·1	1·6	3·1	1·6	0·1	1·6	3·1

(ii) Graph:

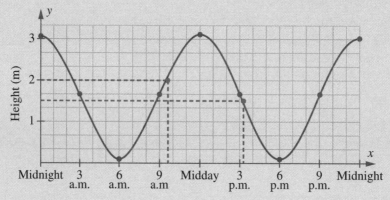

(e) Low tide = $0\cdot1$ m

High tide = $3\cdot1$ m

Difference = $3\cdot1 - 0\cdot1 = 3$ m

(f) To find the maximum time, the water must be at 2 m and rising when the barge enters the port. It must then leave before the water gets down to 1·5 m.

Enters at: 09:30

Leaves at: 15:15

Time in port: 15:15 − 09:30

     = 5 hrs 45 mins

exam
Q

A local authority is analysing its water usage during a period of time in history. They discovered that it was possible to represent the approximate amount of water, $W(t)$, in millions of litres, stored in a reservoir t months after 1 May 1946 by the formula

$$W(t) = 1 \cdot 1 - \sin \frac{\pi t}{6}.$$

(i) Draw and label the sketches of the graphs of $y = \sin \frac{\pi t}{6}$ and $y = -\sin \frac{\pi t}{6}$, for $0 \leq t \leq 36$, on the same diagram.

(ii) On a separate diagram and using the same scale on the t-axis as you used in part **(i)**, draw a sketch of the graph of $W(t) = 1 \cdot 1 - \sin \frac{\pi t}{6}$.

(iii) With further research, the local authority discovered that on 1 April 1948, there was a serious fire in the area. This fire required an extra $\frac{1}{4}$ million litres of water from the reservoir to bring the fire under control.

Assuming that the previous trend continued and that water rationing was not imposed to compensate for the loss of this additional water, when did the reservoir run dry?

Solution

(i) Sketches:

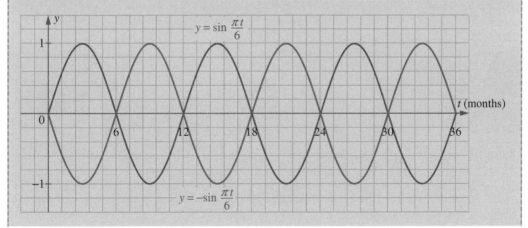

(ii) and **(iii)** Diagram of $W(t)$:

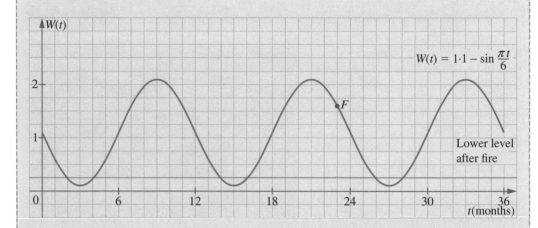

$$W(t) = 1 \cdot 1 - \sin \frac{\pi t}{6}$$

The red curve shows that the water will go to a very low level during the summer months of each year.

The fire occurred when $t = 23$ (23 months after 1 May 1946), marked F on the diagram. Given that the fire required the use of an extra 0·25 million litres of water, if rationing was not imposed, the reservoir would be empty at the time when it would usually have had 0·25 million litres in reserve.

The green line on the diagram shows the lower level raised to 0·25 million litres to account for this loss in water.

After $t = 23$ months, the red curve first hits this green line at $t = 26$, so the reservoir is most likely to have run dry when $t = 26$, 1 July 1948.

(2017 Paper 1 Q.9)

The depth of water, in metres, at a certain point in a harbour varies with the tide and can be modelled by a function of the form $f(t) = a + b \cos ct$

Where t is the time in hours from the first high tide on a particular Saturday and a, b, and c are constants. (Note: ct is expressed in radians.)

On that Saturday, the following were noted:

• The depth of the water in the harbour at high tide was 5·5 m
• The depth of the water in the harbour at low tide was 1·7 m
• High tide occurred at 02:00 and again at 14:34.

(a) Use the information you are given to add, as accurately as you can, labelled and scaled axes to the diagram below to show the graph of f over a portion of that Saturday. The point P should represent the depth of the water in the harbour at high tide on that Saturday morning.

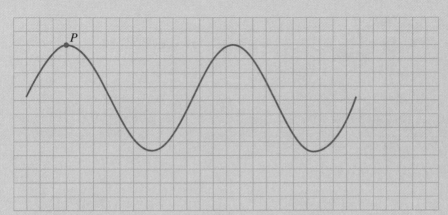

(b) (i) Find the value of a and the value of b.

(ii) Show that c = 0·5, correct to 1 decimal place.

(c) Use the equation $f(t) = a + b \cos ct$ to find the times on that Saturday **afternoon** when the depth of the water in the harbour was exactly 5·2 m.

Give each answer correct to the nearest minute.

Solution

(a) • The point P is the high tide at 02:00. So the coordinates are (2, 5·5)

• This high tide of 5·5 m occurs again at 14:34

• The low tide of 1·7 m occurs midway between the high tides, at 08:17

Use this information to scale the axes as shown below:

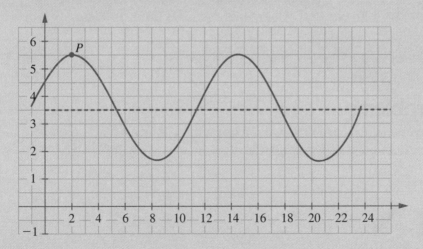

(b) (i) Max height = 5·5, Min height = 1·7 m, therefore the midway height, a = 3·6

Amplitude = b = distance from midway line to max height = 5·5 − 3·6

= 1·9

(ii) Period for the graph = 12:34 = $12\frac{34}{60} = \frac{754}{60}$

Period = $\frac{2\pi}{c}$

$$c = \frac{2\pi}{\text{period}} = \frac{2\pi}{\left(\frac{754}{60}\right)} = 0{\cdot}4999 \quad \Rightarrow \quad c = 0{\cdot}5$$

(c) $f(t) = a + b \cos ct$

$5{\cdot}2 = 3{\cdot}6 + 1{\cdot}9 \cos 0{\cdot}5t$

$1{\cdot}6 = 1{\cdot}9 \cos 0{\cdot}5t$

$\dfrac{1{\cdot}6}{1{\cdot}9} = \cos 0{\cdot}5t$

$\cos^{-1}\left(\dfrac{1{\cdot}6}{1{\cdot}9}\right) = 0{\cdot}5t$

$0{\cdot}5696 = 0{\cdot}5t$

$t = 1{\cdot}139$ hour = 1 hr 8 min before and after high tide

The two times are: 14:34 − 1:08 = 13:26   and   14:34 + 1:08 = 15:42

This question came up on **Paper 1** under the topic of functions. Candidates found it challenging and so part (a) was awarded 20 marks, with 10 of those for correctly drawing **one** of the axes and 18 marks if it was correctly scaled. Part (b)(i) was worth 10 marks and parts (b)(ii) and (c) were worth 5 marks each.

3D problems

Some trigonometrical problems will involve a three-dimensional situation. In these questions, it is a good idea to break the diagram up into small flat pieces.

Many 3D problems will involve right angles. This is because a vertical plane (e.g. a wall) meets a horizontal plane (e.g. the ground) at right angles.

Example

[SP] and [TQ] are vertical poles, each of height 10 m.
P, Q and R are points on level ground.
Two wires of equal length join S and T to
R, i.e. $|SR| = |TR|$.

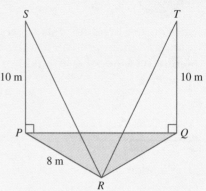

If $|PR| = 8$ m and $|\angle PRQ| = 120°$, calculate:

(i) $|SR|$ in the form $c\sqrt{d}$, where d is prime.

(ii) $|PQ|$ in the form $a\sqrt{b}$, where b is prime.

(iii) $|\angle SRT|$ to the nearest degree.

Solution

Redraw the triangles separately.

(i)

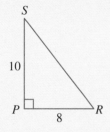

Using Pythagoras's theorem:

$$|SR|^2 = |SP|^2 + |PR|^2$$
$$= 10^2 + 8^2$$

$$|SR|^2 = 164$$
$$|SR| = \sqrt{164}$$
$$|SR| = 2\sqrt{41}$$

(ii)

$$|SP| = |TQ| = 10 \text{ m} \quad \text{(given)}$$
$$|\angle SPR| = |\angle TQR| = 90°$$
$$|SR| = |TR| \quad \text{(given)}$$
$$\therefore \triangle SPR \equiv \triangle TQR \quad \text{(RHS)}$$
$$\therefore |PR| = |QR| = 8 \text{ m}$$

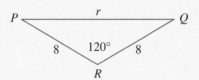

Let $|PQ| = r$.

Using the cosine rule:

$$r^2 = p^2 + q^2 - 2pq \cos R$$
$$r^2 = 8^2 + 8^2 - 2(8)(8) \cos 120°$$
$$r^2 = 192$$
$$r = \sqrt{192} = 8\sqrt{3}$$

(iii)
$$r^2 = s^2 + t^2 - 2st \cos R$$
$$(8\sqrt{3})^2 = (2\sqrt{41})^2 + (2\sqrt{41})^2 - 2(2\sqrt{41})(2\sqrt{41}) \cos R$$
$$192 = 164 + 164 - 328 \cos R$$
$$328 \cos R = 136$$
$$\cos R = \frac{136}{328} = \frac{17}{41}$$
$$R = \cos^{-1}\frac{17}{41} = 65.50372095°$$
$$|\angle SRT| = 66° \text{ to the nearest degree}$$

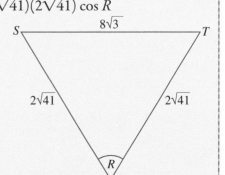

Example

The diagram shows a crystal pyramid of rectangular base 12 mm by 7 mm and slant height of 28 mm.

Calculate the vertical height of the crystal, correct to one decimal place.

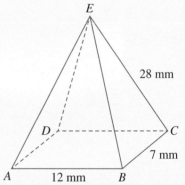

Solution

Redraw the diagram, marking in the vertical height with base point P.

Construct a right-angled triangle involving the vertical height and the slant height.

The third side of the triangle is along the base of the triangle, from the centre of the rectangular base to one of the corners.

By considering the rectangular base, we can calculate $|AC|$ and therefore the base of our new triangle.

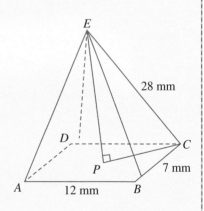

$$|AC|^2 = 12^2 + 7^2$$
$$|AC|^2 = 193$$
$$|AC| = \sqrt{193}$$
$$\therefore |PC| = \frac{\sqrt{193}}{2}$$

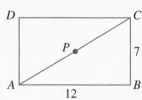

Back to the triangle *EPC* to find $|EP|$, the vertical height.

$$|EP|^2 + \left(\frac{\sqrt{193}}{2}\right)^2 = 28^2$$

$$|EP|^2 = 28^2 - \left(\frac{\sqrt{193}}{2}\right)^2$$

$$|EP|^2 = \frac{2,943}{4}$$

$$\therefore |EP| = \frac{3\sqrt{327}}{2} = 27.12471198$$

Thus, the vertical height is 27·1 mm, correct to one decimal place.

(2017 Q.9)

Conor's property is bounded by the straight bank of a river, as shown in **Figure 1**. *T* is the base of a vertical tree that is growing near the opposite bank of the river.

$|TE|$ is the height of the tree, as shown in **Figure 2**. From the point C, which is due west of the tree, the angle of elevation of *E*, the top of the tree, is 60°.

From the point *D*, which is 15 m due north of *C*, the angle of elevation of *E* is 30° (see **Figure 2**). The land on both sides of the river is flat and at the same level.

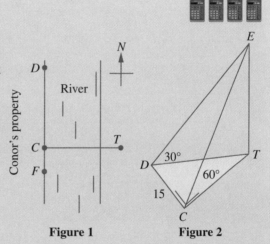

Figure 1

Figure 2

(a) Use triangle *ECT*, to express $|TE|$ in the form $\sqrt{a}|CT|$ metres, where $a \in \mathbb{N}$.

(b) Show that $|TE|$ may also be expressed as $\sqrt{\dfrac{225 + |CT|^2}{3}}$ metres

(c) Hence find $|CT|$, the distance from the base of the tree to the bank of the river at Conor's side. Give your answer correct to 1 decimal place.

(d) Find $|TE|$, the height of the tree. Give your answer correct to 1 decimal place.

(e) The tree falls across the river and hits the bank at Conor's side at the point *F*. Find the maximum size of the angle *FTC*. Give your answer in degrees, correct to 1 decimal place.

(f) If the tree was equally likely to fall in any direction, find the probability that it would hit the bank at Conor's side, when it falls. Give your answer as a percentage, correct to 1 decimal place.

Solution

(a) In $\triangle CET$: $\tan 60° = \dfrac{|TE|}{|CT|}$

$$\sqrt{3} = \dfrac{|TE|}{|CT|}$$

$$\sqrt{3}|CT| = |TE|$$

(b) In $\triangle DET$:

$$\tan 30° = \dfrac{|TE|}{|DT|}$$

$$\dfrac{1}{\sqrt{3}} = \dfrac{|TE|}{|DT|}$$

$$|DT| = \sqrt{3}|TE|$$

In $\triangle DCT$:

$$|DT|^2 = 15^2 + |CT|^2$$

$$|DT|^2 = 225 + |CT|^2$$

$$|DT| = \sqrt{225 + |CT|^2}$$

Let $|DT| = |DT|$

$$\sqrt{3}|TE| = \sqrt{225 + |CT|^2}$$

$$|TE| = \sqrt{\dfrac{225 + |CT|^2}{3}}$$

(c) Let $|TE|$ from part (a) equal to $|TE|$ from part (b)

$$\sqrt{3}|CT| = \sqrt{\dfrac{225 + |CT|^2}{3}} \qquad \text{(square both sides)}$$

$$3|CT|^2 = \dfrac{225 + |CT|^2}{3} \qquad \text{(multiply both sides by 3)}$$

$$9|CT|^2 = 225 + |CT|^2$$

$$8|CT|^2 = 225$$

$$|CT| = \sqrt{\dfrac{225}{8}} \Rightarrow |CT| = 5.3 \text{ m}$$

(d) $|TE| = \sqrt{3}|CT|$

$$|TE| = \sqrt{3}(5.3)$$

$$|TE| = 9.17987$$

$$|TE| = 9.2 \text{ m}$$

(e) $|FT| = |TE|$

$$\cos|\angle FTC| = \dfrac{|CT|}{|FT|} = \dfrac{|CT|}{\sqrt{3}|CT|}$$

$$|\angle FTC| = \cos^{-1}\left(\dfrac{1}{\sqrt{3}}\right)$$

$$|\angle FTC| = 54.7°$$

(f) F could be up to 54·7° above or below the point C.
So, the tree could fall anywhere within a 109·4° range of 360°.

$$P(\text{Landing on Conor's side}) = \frac{109{\cdot}4°}{360°} = 30{\cdot}4\%$$

exam Q

$QRST$ is a vertical rectangular wall of height h on level ground. P is a point on the ground in front of the wall. The angle of elevation of R from P is θ and the angle of elevation of S from P is 2θ.

$|PQ| = 3|PT|$.

Find θ.

Solution

Using the nearer triangle, we find a relationship between θ, x and h.

$$\tan\theta = \frac{h}{3x}$$

$$3x\tan\theta = h$$

Using the farther triangle, we find another relationship between θ, x and h.

$$\tan 2\theta = \frac{h}{x}$$

$$x\tan 2\theta = h$$

$$3x\tan\theta = x\tan 2\theta \quad \text{(as both equal } h\text{)}$$

$$3\tan\theta = \tan 2\theta \quad \text{(divide both sides by non-zero } x\text{)}$$

$$3\tan\theta = \frac{2\tan\theta}{1-\tan^2\theta} \quad \left(\text{from formula } \tan 2\theta = \frac{2\tan\theta}{1-\tan^2\theta}\right)$$

$$3t = \frac{2t}{1-t^2} \quad \text{(abbreviating } \tan\theta \text{ as } t\text{)}$$

$$3t(1-t^2) = 2t$$

$$3t - 3t^3 - 2t = 0$$

$$t - 3t^3 = 0$$

$$3t^3 - t = 0$$

$$t(3t^2 - 1) = 0$$

$$t = 0 \text{ or } t = \frac{1}{\sqrt{3}} \text{ or } t = -\frac{1}{\sqrt{3}}$$

$$\tan \theta = 0 \text{ or } \tan \theta = \frac{1}{\sqrt{3}} \text{ or } \tan \theta = -\frac{1}{\sqrt{3}}$$

Rejecting 0 (θ cannot be 0) and $-\frac{1}{\sqrt{3}}$ (θ cannot be obtuse), we are left with $\tan \theta = \frac{1}{\sqrt{3}} \Rightarrow \theta = 30°$ or $\frac{\pi}{6}$ rads.

Trigonometric formulae

You must be able to apply the trigonometric formulae 1–24, listed in the table below. These formulae are in your *booklet of formulae and tables*.

Of these formulae, you must be able to derive the trigonometric formulae 1, 2, 3, 4, 5, 6, 7 and 9, which are **marked with an asterisk (*)** in the table below.

1.* $\cos^2 A + \sin^2 A = 1$	13. $\cos 2A = \dfrac{1 - \tan^2 A}{1 + \tan^2 A}$
2.* Sine formula: $\dfrac{a}{\sin A} = \dfrac{b}{\sin B} = \dfrac{c}{\sin C}$	14. $\tan 2A = \dfrac{2 \tan A}{1 - \tan^2 A}$
3.* Cosine formula: $a^2 = b^2 + c^2 - 2bc \cos A$	15. $\cos^2 A = \frac{1}{2}(1 + \cos 2A)$
4.* $\cos (A - B) = \cos A \cos B + \sin A \sin B$	16. $\sin^2 A = \frac{1}{2}(1 - \cos 2A)$
5.* $\cos (A + B) = \cos A \cos B - \sin A \sin B$	17. $2 \cos A \cos B = \cos (A + B) + \cos (A - B)$
6.* $\cos 2A = \cos^2 A - \sin^2 A$	18. $2 \sin A \cos B = \sin (A + B) + \sin (A - B)$
7.* $\sin (A + B) = \sin A \cos B + \cos A \sin B$	19. $2 \sin A \sin B = \cos (A - B) - \cos (A + B)$
8. $\sin (A - B) = \sin A \cos B - \cos A \sin B$	20. $2 \cos A \sin B = \sin (A + B) - \sin (A - B)$
9.* $\tan(A + B) = \dfrac{\tan A + \tan B}{1 - \tan A \tan B}$	21. $\cos A + \cos B = 2 \cos \dfrac{A + B}{2} \cos \dfrac{A - B}{2}$
10. $\tan(A - B) = \dfrac{\tan A - \tan B}{1 + \tan A \tan B}$	22. $\cos A - \cos B = -2 \sin \dfrac{A + B}{2} \sin \dfrac{A - B}{2}$
11. $\sin 2A = 2 \sin A \cos A$	23. $\sin A + \sin B = 2 \sin \dfrac{A + B}{2} \cos \dfrac{A - B}{2}$
12. $\sin 2A = \dfrac{2 \tan A}{1 + \tan^2 A}$	24. $\sin A - \sin B = 2 \cos \dfrac{A + B}{2} \sin \dfrac{A - B}{2}$

Compound angles

This deals will angles such as $A + B$ and $2B$. There are many formulae available to convert from compound angles to single angles.

Example

(i) Express cos 75° in surd form and, hence, cos 255°.

(ii) Express the following in surd form: (a) $\tan\left(-\dfrac{7\pi}{12}\right)$ (b) sin 195°.

Solution

First express each angle as a combination of 30°, 45° or 60° and then use the compound angle formulae from the *booklet of formulae and tables*, pages 14 and 15.

(i)
$$\cos 75°$$
$$= \cos(45° + 30°)$$
$$= \cos 45° \cos 30° - \sin 45° \sin 30°$$
$$= \frac{1}{\sqrt{2}} \times \frac{\sqrt{3}}{2} - \frac{1}{\sqrt{2}} \times \frac{1}{2}$$
$$= \frac{\sqrt{3}}{2\sqrt{2}} - \frac{1}{2\sqrt{2}} = \frac{\sqrt{3}-1}{2\sqrt{2}}$$
$$= \frac{\sqrt{6}-\sqrt{2}}{4}$$

$$\cos 255°$$
$$= -\cos 75°$$
$$= -\frac{\sqrt{3}-1}{2\sqrt{2}}$$
$$= \frac{1-\sqrt{3}}{2\sqrt{2}}$$
$$= \frac{\sqrt{2}-\sqrt{6}}{4}$$

(ii) (a)
$$\tan\left(-\frac{7\pi}{12}\right) = \tan(-105°) = -\tan 105°$$
$$= -\tan(60° + 45°)$$
$$= -\frac{\tan 60° + \tan 45°}{1 - \tan 60° \tan 45°}$$
$$= -\frac{\sqrt{3}+1}{1-\sqrt{3}(1)} = -\frac{\sqrt{3}+1}{1-\sqrt{3}} = \frac{\sqrt{3}+1}{\sqrt{3}-1} = 2 + \sqrt{3}$$

(b)
$$\sin 195° = -\sin 15°$$
$$= -\sin(45° - 30°)$$
$$= -(\sin 45° \cos 30° - \cos 45° \sin 30°)$$
$$= -\left(\frac{1}{\sqrt{2}} \times \frac{\sqrt{3}}{2} - \frac{1}{\sqrt{2}} \times \frac{1}{2}\right)$$
$$= -\left(\frac{\sqrt{3}-1}{2\sqrt{2}}\right) = \frac{1-\sqrt{3}}{2\sqrt{2}} = \frac{\sqrt{2}-\sqrt{6}}{4}$$

key point

You need to be very familiar with the unit circle and be able to manipulate it to find the values you need.

In the last example, **(ii) (b)**, the value of 195° on the sine axis is the same value as 15° on the sine axis, but on the negative side of the sine axis. Therefore, sin 195° = −sin 15°.

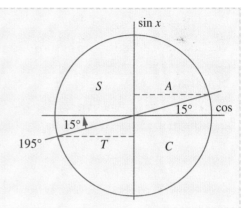

exam Q

(2016 Q.3 (b))

Given that $\cos 2\theta = \dfrac{1}{9}$, find $\cos \theta$ in the form $\pm\dfrac{\sqrt{a}}{b}$, where $a, b \in \mathbb{N}$.

Solution

$\dfrac{1}{2}(1 + \cos 2\theta) = \cos^2\theta$ (from the *booklet of formulae and tables*, page 14)

$\dfrac{1}{2}\left(1 + \dfrac{1}{9}\right) = \cos^2\theta$

exam focus

$\dfrac{5}{9} = \cos^2\theta$

$\pm\sqrt{\dfrac{5}{9}} = \cos\theta$

$\pm\dfrac{\sqrt{5}}{3} = \cos\theta$

Remember, there can often be more than one way to solve a problem. If you try several different methods in the exam, **never erase or Tipp-Ex any of your attempts**. All attempts will be corrected by the examiner.

exam Q

(2018 Q.4 (b))

Let $\cos A = \dfrac{y}{2}$, where $0° < A < 90°$. Write sin (2A) in terms of y.

Solution

Since, sin 2A = 2 sin A cos A, we need to find an expression for sin A.

$\cos A = \dfrac{y}{2} = \dfrac{\text{Adjacent side}}{\text{Hypotenuse}}$

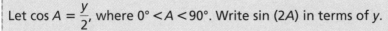

Use Pythagoras's theorem to find the opposite side:

$$2^2 = y^2 + \text{opposite}^2$$
$$4 = y^2 + \text{opposite}^2$$
$$4 - y^2 = \text{opposite}^2$$
$$\sqrt{4 - y^2} = \text{opposite}$$

$$\sin A = \frac{\text{Opposite side}}{\text{Hypotenuse}} = \frac{\sqrt{4 - y^2}}{2}$$

$$\sin 2A = 2 \sin A \cos A$$

$$\sin 2A = 2\left(\frac{\sqrt{4 - y^2}}{2}\right)\left(\frac{y}{2}\right)$$

$$\sin 2A = \frac{y\sqrt{4 - y^2}}{2}$$

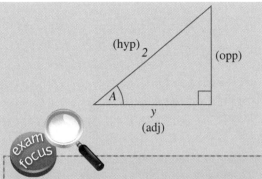

(hyp) 2   (opp)

A

y
(adj)

exam focus

This (b) part was very poorly answered by candidates. With the result that it was only awarded 5 marks. 2 of the 5 marks were awarded for writing the formula for sin 2A and if a candidate correctly substituted in the given value for cos A (without finding sin A) they were awarded 4 of the 5 marks.

The lesson here is to not let a difficult question put you off. Attempt all questions. There are no marks for blanks!

exam Q

If $\sin \alpha = \dfrac{5}{13}$ and $\cos \beta = \dfrac{4}{5}$, $0 < \alpha < \dfrac{\pi}{2}$, $0 < \beta < \dfrac{\pi}{2}$, express

$\sin(\alpha + \beta)$ in the form $\dfrac{a}{b}$, $a, b \in N$.

Hence or otherwise, show that $\cos(45° - \alpha - \beta) = \dfrac{89\sqrt{2}}{130}$.

Solution

We represent each given angle with a right-angled triangle and use Pythagoras' theorem to find the third side and the other ratios.

Given: $\sin \alpha = \dfrac{5}{13}$

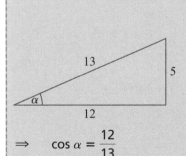

13   5

α

12

$$\Rightarrow \quad \cos \alpha = \frac{12}{13}$$

Given: $\cos \beta = \dfrac{4}{5}$

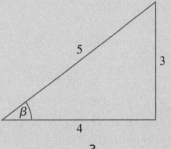

5   3

β

4

$$\Rightarrow \quad \sin \beta = \frac{3}{5}$$

$$\sin(\alpha + \beta) = \sin \alpha \cos \beta + \cos \alpha \sin \beta$$

$$= \frac{5}{13} \times \frac{4}{5} + \frac{12}{13} \times \frac{3}{5} = \frac{20}{65} + \frac{36}{65} = \frac{56}{65}$$

$$\cos(45° - \alpha - \beta) = \cos[45° - (\alpha + \beta)]$$

$$= \cos 45° \cos(\alpha + \beta) + \sin 45° \sin(\alpha + \beta)$$

$$= \cos 45° \left[\cos \alpha \cos \beta - \sin \alpha \sin \beta\right] + \sin 45° \sin(\alpha + \beta)$$

$$= \frac{1}{\sqrt{2}}\left[\frac{12}{13} \times \frac{4}{5} - \frac{5}{13} \times \frac{3}{5}\right] + \frac{1}{\sqrt{2}} \times \frac{56}{65}$$

$$= \frac{1}{\sqrt{2}} \times \frac{33}{65} + \frac{1}{\sqrt{2}} \times \frac{56}{65}$$

$$= \frac{33}{65\sqrt{2}} + \frac{56}{65\sqrt{2}}$$

$$= \frac{89}{65\sqrt{2}} = \frac{89}{65\sqrt{2}} \times \frac{\sqrt{2}}{\sqrt{2}} = \frac{89\sqrt{2}}{65(2)} = \frac{89\sqrt{2}}{130}$$

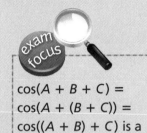

exam focus

$\cos(A + B + C) =$
$\cos(A + (B + C)) =$
$\cos((A + B) + C)$ is a
very useful technique
to known.

---

exam Q

(i) If $A + B = \dfrac{\pi}{4}$, write $\tan A$ in terms of $\tan B$, and hence
prove that $(1 + \tan A)(1 + \tan B) = 2$.

(ii) Show that $\tan 22\frac{1}{2}° = \sqrt{2} - 1$.

Solution

(i) $A + B = \dfrac{\pi}{4}$ (given)

$$\Rightarrow \quad A = \frac{\pi}{4} - B$$

$$\Rightarrow \tan A = \tan\left(\frac{\pi}{4} - B\right)$$

$$\tan A = \frac{\tan\dfrac{\pi}{4} - \tan B}{1 + \tan\dfrac{\pi}{4}\tan B}$$

$$\Rightarrow \tan A = \frac{1 - \tan B}{1 + \tan B}$$

$$\left(\text{as } \tan \frac{\pi}{4} = 1\right)$$

$(1 + \tan A)(1 + \tan B)$

$$= \left(1 + \frac{1 - \tan B}{1 + \tan B}\right)(1 + \tan B)$$

$$= \left(\frac{1 + \tan B + 1 - \tan B}{1 + \tan B}\right)(1 + \tan B)$$

$$= \left(\frac{2}{1 + \tan B}\right)(1 + \tan B)$$

$$= 2$$

$$\therefore (1 + \tan A)(1 + \tan B) = 2$$

(ii) Let $A = B = 22\frac{1}{2}°$ (as $A + B = \dfrac{\pi}{4} = 45°$).

$$(1 + \tan A)(1 + \tan B) = 2 \quad \text{(from above)}$$

$$(1 + \tan 22\tfrac{1}{2}°)(1 + \tan 22\tfrac{1}{2}°) = 2$$

$$(1 + \tan 22\tfrac{1}{2}°)^2 = 2$$

$$1 + \tan 22\tfrac{1}{2}° = \sqrt{2}$$

$$\tan 22\tfrac{1}{2}° = \sqrt{2} - 1$$

$\tan 22\frac{1}{2}°$ has appeared several times on exams. Watch out for it!

Trigonometric identities

Trigonometric identities are equations which involve trigonometric functions and are true for all values of the variables.

key point

When proving a trigonometric identity, start with the more complicated side of the equation. Then, using the trigonometric formulae from your *booklet of formulae and tables*, manipulate the expression until it equals the opposite side of the equation. **That is, take one side (e.g. RHS) and manipulate it until it equals the other side (LHS).**

Example

Prove that $\sqrt{\dfrac{1 - \cos 2A}{1 + \cos 2A}} = \tan A$.

Solution

$$\sqrt{\frac{1 - \cos 2A}{1 + \cos 2A}} = \tan A$$

$$\text{LHS} = \sqrt{\frac{1 - \cos 2A}{1 + \cos 2A}} \qquad (\cos 2A = \cos^2 A - \sin^2 A)$$

$$= \sqrt{\frac{1 - (\cos^2 A - \sin^2 A)}{1 + (\cos^2 A - \sin^2 A)}}$$

$$= \sqrt{\frac{(1 - \cos^2 A) + \sin^2 A}{(1 - \sin^2 A) + \cos^2 A}} \qquad (1 = \cos^2 A + \sin^2 A)$$

$$= \sqrt{\frac{\sin^2 A + \sin^2 A}{\cos^2 A + \cos^2 A}}$$

$$= \sqrt{\frac{2 \sin^2 A}{2 \cos^2 A}} \qquad \left(\frac{\sin A}{\cos A} = \tan A\right)$$

$$= \sqrt{\tan^2 A} = \tan A = \text{RHS}$$

(i) Prove that $\sin\left(\theta + \dfrac{\pi}{4}\right) - \cos\left(\theta + \dfrac{\pi}{4}\right) = \sqrt{2}\,\sin\theta$.

(ii) Prove that $\cos\left(\dfrac{\pi}{3} + \theta\right) + \sin\left(\dfrac{\pi}{6} + \theta\right) = \cos\theta$.

Solution

In both questions, the compound angles formulae are used:

$\sin(A + B) = \sin A\cos B + \cos A\sin B$ and $\cos(A + B) = \cos A\cos B - \sin A\sin B$

(i) $\text{LHS} = \sin\left(\theta + \dfrac{\pi}{4}\right) - \cos\left(\theta + \dfrac{\pi}{4}\right)$

$= \left(\sin\theta\cos\dfrac{\pi}{4} + \cos\theta\sin\dfrac{\pi}{4}\right) - \left(\cos\theta\cos\dfrac{\pi}{4} - \sin\theta\sin\dfrac{\pi}{4}\right)$

$= \sin\theta \times \dfrac{1}{\sqrt{2}} + \cancel{\cos\theta} \times \dfrac{1}{\sqrt{2}} - \cancel{\cos\theta} \times \dfrac{1}{\sqrt{2}} + \sin\theta \times \dfrac{1}{\sqrt{2}}$

$= 2\left(\sin\theta \times \dfrac{1}{\sqrt{2}}\right)$

$= \dfrac{2}{\sqrt{2}}\sin\theta$

$= \sqrt{2}\,\sin\theta \quad \left(\dfrac{2}{\sqrt{2}} = \sqrt{2}\right)$

(ii) $\text{LHS} = \cos\left(\dfrac{\pi}{3} + \theta\right) + \sin\left(\dfrac{\pi}{6} + \theta\right)$

$= \cos\dfrac{\pi}{3}\cos\theta - \sin\dfrac{\pi}{3}\sin\theta + \sin\dfrac{\pi}{6}\cos\theta + \cos\dfrac{\pi}{6}\sin\theta$

$= \dfrac{1}{2}\cos\theta - \cancel{\dfrac{\sqrt{3}}{2}\sin\theta} + \dfrac{1}{2}\cos\theta + \cancel{\dfrac{\sqrt{3}}{2}\sin\theta}$

$= 2 \times \dfrac{1}{2}\cos\theta = \cos\theta$

exam Q

(2016 Q.3 (a))

Show that $\dfrac{\cos 7A + \cos A}{\sin 7A - \sin A} = \cot 3A$

Solution

LHS: $\dfrac{\cos 7A + \cos A}{\sin 7A - \sin A}$

From the *booklet of formulae and tables:*

$$\dfrac{2\cos\left(\dfrac{7A + A}{2}\right)\cos\left(\dfrac{7A - A}{2}\right)}{2\cos\left(\dfrac{7A + A}{2}\right)\sin\left(\dfrac{7A - A}{2}\right)}$$

$$\cos A + \cos B = 2\cos\left(\dfrac{A + B}{2}\right)\cos\left(\dfrac{A - B}{2}\right)$$

$$\sin A - \sin B = 2\cos\left(\dfrac{A + B}{2}\right)\sin\left(\dfrac{A - B}{2}\right)$$

$$\dfrac{2\cos 4A \cos 3A}{2\cos 4A \sin 3A}$$

key point

$$\dfrac{\cos 3A}{\sin 3A} = \dfrac{1}{\tan 3A} = \cot 3A = \text{RHS}$$

You need to know that $\dfrac{1}{\tan \theta} = \cot \theta$.

---

exam Q

Prove that $\sin 2\theta = \dfrac{2 \tan \theta}{1 + \tan^2 \theta}$

Solution

$\sin 2\theta = \dfrac{2 \tan \theta}{1 + \tan^2 \theta}$

$\text{RHS} = \dfrac{2 \tan \theta}{1 + \tan^2 \theta}$

$= \dfrac{2\dfrac{\sin \theta}{\cos \theta}}{1 + \dfrac{\sin^2 \theta}{\cos^2 \theta}}$ (Multiply top and bottom by $\cos^2 \theta$)

$= \dfrac{2 \sin \theta \cos \theta}{\cos^2 \theta + \sin^2 \theta}$

$= \dfrac{\sin 2\theta}{1} = \sin 2\theta = \text{LHS}$

7 Perimeter, Area, Volume and Nets

Perimeter and area

- When using $\pi = \dfrac{22}{7}$, it is good practice to write the radius as a fraction $\left(\text{for example, } 21 = \dfrac{21}{1} \text{ or } 4\cdot5 = \dfrac{9}{2}\right)$.

- If a question says 'give your answer in terms of π', then leave π in the answer: do not use $3\cdot14$ or $\dfrac{22}{7}$ for π.

- Your calculator leaves the answer in terms of π. This can be very useful.

- If you are not given an approximate value for π, then you must use the value given by the calculator.

- It is vital to know the whereabouts of the relevant information in the *booklet of formulae and tables*.

The diagram represents the frame of a photograph in the shape of a regular hexagon of side-length 30 cm.

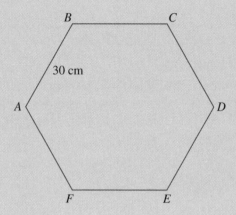

(i)   Find the perimeter of the frame.

(ii) Find the area of the frame.

(iii) Hence or otherwise, derive a formula for:

   (a) the perimeter

   (b) the area of a similar hexagonal-shaped frame of side-length k cm.

Solution

(i) A hexagon has six sides, so its perimeter = 6 × 30 cm = 180 cm.

(ii)

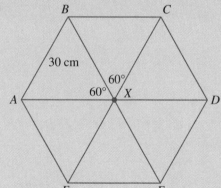

Notes:

1. All the angles at the centre, X, equal 60°.

2. $|AX| = |BX| = |CX| = |DX| = |EX| = |FX|$ = radius

$\triangle ABX$ is isosceles because $|AX| = |BX|$.

This means the base angles of $\triangle ABX$ are equal. In fact, $|\angle ABX| = |\angle BAX| = 60°$.

Hence, $\triangle ABX$ is equilateral, all sides = 30 cm.

Area $\triangle ABX = \dfrac{1}{2}ab \sin C$ (see *booklet of formulae and tables*, page 9)

$\qquad = \dfrac{1}{2}(30)(30) \sin 60°$

$\qquad = 450\dfrac{\sqrt{3}}{2} = 225\sqrt{3}$ cm^2

Area of frame $= 6$ Area $\triangle ABX = 6[225\sqrt{3}] = 1{,}350\sqrt{3}$ cm^2

(iii) (a) If each side has length k cm,

then the perimeter of the frame $= 6 \times k$ cm $= 6k$ cm.

(b)

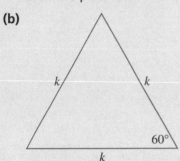

If each side has length k cm,

then area $\triangle = \dfrac{1}{2}(k)(k) \sin 60° = \dfrac{1}{2}k^2\dfrac{\sqrt{3}}{2}$.

Hence, area of frame $= 6\left[\dfrac{1}{2}k^2\dfrac{\sqrt{3}}{2}\right]$

$\qquad = \dfrac{3\sqrt{3}}{2}k^2$ cm^2.

(2014 Q.9 (b))

The triangle ABC is right-angled at C.

The circle s has a diameter $[AC]$ and the circle t has diameter $[CB]$.

(i) Draw the circle u which has diameter $[AB]$.

(ii) Prove that in any right-angles triangle ABC, the area of the circle u equals the sum of the areas of the circles s and t.

(iii) The diagram shows the right-angled triangles ABC and arcs of the circles s, t and u.

Each of the shaded areas in the diagram is called a lune, a crescent-shaped area bounded by arcs of the circles.

Prove that the sum of the areas of the two shaded lunes is equal to the area of the triangle ABC.

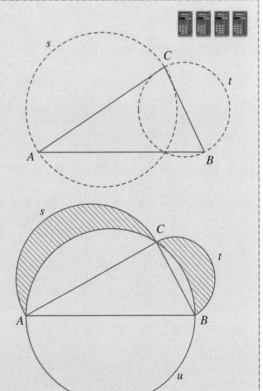

Solution

(i)

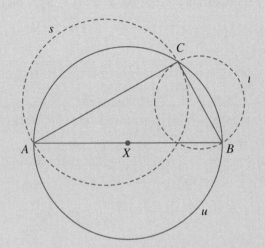

Bisect $[AB]$ to find X. With X as centre and $|XA|$ or $|XB|$ as radius, draw the circle u. This works because $|\angle ACB| = 90°$ and the angle in a semi-circle is always 90°.

(ii) Is area circle u = Area circle s + Area of circle A

Is $\pi\left(\frac{1}{2}|AB|\right)^2 = \pi\left(\frac{1}{2}|AC|\right)^2 + \pi\left(\frac{1}{2}|CB|\right)^2$

Use area of circle $= \pi r^2$ three times

Is $\frac{1}{4}|AB|^2 = \frac{1}{4}|AC|^2 + \frac{1}{4}|CB|^2$?

Is $|AB|^2 = |AC|^2 + |CB|^2$ True because the triangle ABC is right-angled.

(iii) Mark areas ①, ②, ③, ④, and ⑤ as in diagram.

Asked to prove ③ = ① + ⑤

From part (ii) we know

$$\frac{1}{2}\text{ Area } u = \frac{1}{2}\text{ Area } s + \frac{1}{2}\text{ Area } t$$

$$② + ③ + ④ = (① + ②) + (④ + ⑤)$$

$$③ = ① + ⑤$$

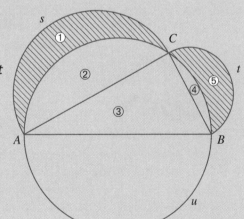

Volume of cylinders, cones and spheres

exam
Q (2012 Paper 1 Q.8)

A solid cone has a slant height of $2\sqrt{13}$ cm.

(i) Express r^2 in terms of h, where r is the radius and h is the vertical height of the cone.

(ii) If the volume of the cone is found to be 32π cm^3, calculate the height, h, where $h \in \mathbb{N}$ and $h < 6$.

Solution

(i)

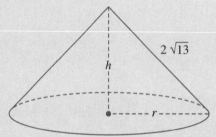

$$l^2 = h^2 + r^2 \quad \text{(Pythagoras's theorem)}$$
$$(2\sqrt{13})^2 = h^2 + r^2$$
$$52 = h^2 + r^2$$
$$52 - h^2 = r^2$$

(ii) Volume of cone $= \dfrac{1}{3}\pi r^2 h$ (see *booklet of formulae and tables*, page 10)

$$32\pi = \frac{1}{3}\pi(52 - h^2)h \quad \text{since from (i) } r^2 = 52 - h^2$$
$$96 = 52h - h^3$$
$$h^3 - 52h + 96 = 0$$

exam
focus

- To solve a cubic equation, we usually have to guess a solution.
- The exam syllabus promises at least one solution in a cubic equation is a factor of the constant term.

Here we consider $h = \pm1, \pm2, \pm3, \pm4$ because $h < 6$ in the question and h will divide into 96, the constant term in our cubic equation. In addition, height h cannot be negative.

By 'trial and improvement', we find $h = 2$.

Substituting $h = 2$ into $h^3 - 52h + 96 = 0$

          to get $(2)^3 - 52(2) + 96 = 0$

                  $8 - 104 + 96 = 0$

$\therefore h = 2$ is the solution.

(i) In Turlough Hill, a pumped storage electric power station, water issues from a cylindrical pipe of internal diameter 2·4 m at a rate of 29,000 l per second. At what speed is the water flowing through the pipe?

Give your answers:

(a) in m/sec correct to one decimal place

(b) in km/h correct to the nearest km.

(ii) Hence or otherwise, if the diameter of the pipe was 1·2 m, find, correct to one decimal place, the new speed of the water in m/sec given that the rate of flow remained 29,000 l per second.

(iii)

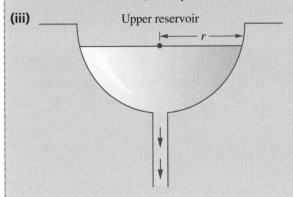

Upper reservoir

The cylindrical pipe drains water from an upper reservoir of hemispherical shape. It takes 4 hours at a constant flow rate of 29,000 l per second to empty the upper reservoir. Find, correct to the nearest integer, the depth in m of the water in the upper reservoir before the water began to flow.

Solution

(i)

- Diameter 2·4 m $\Rightarrow$ Radius = 1·2 m
- 29,000 l = 29 m³, as 1,000 l = 1 m³
- Flow in pipe should be considered at 1-second intervals.

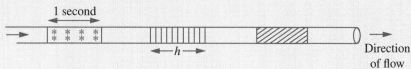

Then speed is h m/sec.

Rate of flow is 29 m³/sec.

Volume of water per second = Volume of cylinder = $\pi r^2 h$

$$29 = \pi(1·2)^2 h$$

$$6·4104 = h$$

(a) Speed = 6·4 m/sec

(b) Speed = $\dfrac{6·4 \times 60 \times 60}{1,000}$ = 23 km/h

Diameter halved (to 1·2 m) then radius = 0·6 m

Flow rate unchanged means $29 = \pi(0·6)^2 h$

$$25·6 = h \Rightarrow \text{speed } 25·6 \text{ m/sec}$$

Radius halved means r^2 decreases by a factor of $\left(\frac{1}{2}\right)^2 = \frac{1}{4}$.

(ii) Hence, to compensate for this decrease $\left(\text{of } \frac{1}{4}\right)$, the speed must increase by a factor of 4 if the rate of flow is unchanged.

(iii)

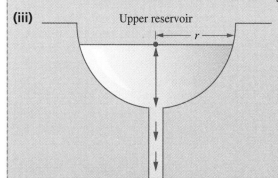

Upper reservoir

Flow rate of 29 m³/sec means

$$29 \times 60 \times 60 \times 4 = 417,600 \text{ m}^3$$
in 4 hours.

$\therefore$ Vol. hemisphere reservoir = $\dfrac{2}{3}\pi r^3$

$$417,600 = \dfrac{2}{3}\pi r^3$$

$$58·420 = r$$

Depth = 58 m to nearest integer

(2018 Q.7)

A section of a garden railing is shown below. This section consists of nine cylindrical bars, labelled *A* to *I*, with a solid sphere attached to the centre of the top of each bar.

The **volume** of each sphere from *B* to *E* is 1·75 times the volume of the previous sphere.

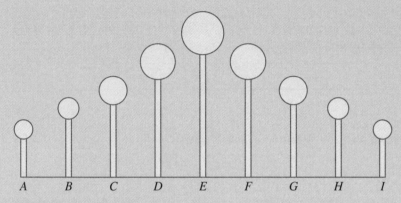

(a) The radius of sphere *A* is 3 cm. Find the **sum** of the volumes of the five spheres *A, B, C, D* and *E*. Give your answer correct to the nearest cm³.

Solution

The five volumes are in geometric sequence with $r = 1{\cdot}75$

First term $= a =$ Vol sphere $A = \dfrac{4}{3}\pi(3)^3 = 36\pi$

Volume of 5 spheres $= S_5 = \dfrac{a(1 - r^5)}{1 - r}$ (see *booklet of formulae and tables, page 22*)

Do not confuse radius $= r = 3$ with common ratio $r = 1{\cdot}75$

$$S_5 = \frac{36\pi(1 - 1{\cdot}75^5)}{1 - 1{\cdot}75} = \frac{36\pi(-15{\cdot}413)}{-0{\cdot}75} = 2324 \text{ cm}^3$$

(b) (i) The **surface area** of sphere *E* can be taken to be 503 cm². The height of the railing at *E* (i.e the sum of the heights of bar *E* and sphere *E*) is 1·2 metres.

Find the height of bar *E*, in cm, correct to 1 decimal place.

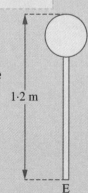

Solution

(b) (i) Surface area = $4\pi r^2$ (see *booklet of formulae and tables*, page 10)

$$503 = 4\pi r^2$$

$$\sqrt{\frac{503}{4\pi}} = r^2$$

$$6{\cdot}33 = r$$

Height of bar $= 120 - 2r = 120 - 2(6{\cdot}33) = 107{\cdot}3$ cm

(b) (ii) The radius of each bar is 1 cm. The volume of bar A is $71{\cdot}3\pi$ cm³. The heights of the bars A, B, C, D and E form an arithmetic sequence. Find, in cm, the height of each bar.

A =	B =	C =	D =	E =

Solution

(b) (ii) Volume bar A = Volume cylinder = $\pi r^2 h$

$$71{\cdot}3\pi = \pi(1)^2 h$$

$$71{\cdot}3 = h$$

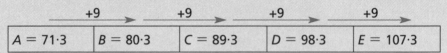

A = 71·3	B =	C =	D =	E = 107·3

$E - A = 107{\cdot}3 - 71{\cdot}3 = 36 = 4$ equal height differences

$9 =$ each height difference

+9	+9	+9	+9

A = 71·3	B = 80·3	C = 89·3	D = 98·3	E = 107·3

(c) There is a wall on each side of the section of railing, as shown in the diagram below which is not drawn to scale. The distance from wall to wall is 1·5 m. The distance from the wall to bar A is 20 cm and similarly from the other wall to bar I is 20 cm.

The radius of each bar is 1 cm. The gap between each bar is identical. Find the size of this gap.

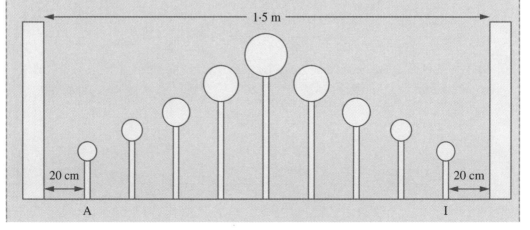

Solution

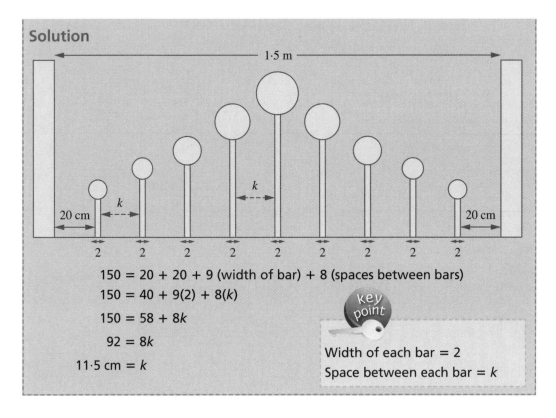

150 = 20 + 20 + 9 (width of bar) + 8 (spaces between bars)

150 = 40 + 9(2) + 8(k)

150 = 58 + 8k

92 = 8k

11·5 cm = k

key point

Width of each bar = 2

Space between each bar = k

Nets of 3D shapes

- When a 3D shape is opened out, the flat shape is called the **net**.

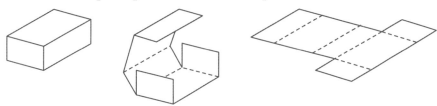

- This is how the net folds up to make a cuboid.

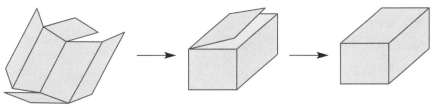

- **Naming parts of a 3D shape**

  Each flat surface is called a **face**. Two faces meet at an **edge**. Edges of a shape meet at a corner, or point, called a **vertex**. The plural of vertex is **vertices**.

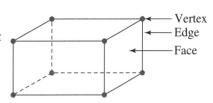

Vertex
Edge
Face

- This is how the net folds up to make a cylinder.

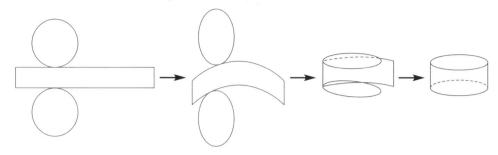

Note: There can be different nets for one solid cylinder.

(i) Express 165° in radians.

(ii) The diagram is a drawing of the net of a cone with vertex *O*.

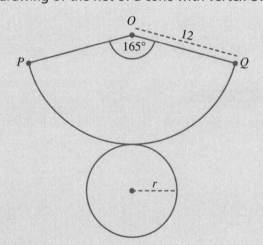

Show that the length of the minor arc *PQ* is 11π cm.

(iii) Hence or otherwise, find:

(a) the total surface area of the cone

(b) the volume of the cone.

Give your answers correct to the nearest integer.

Solution

(i) $165° = \dfrac{165}{180}\pi = \dfrac{11}{12}\pi$ radians

(ii)

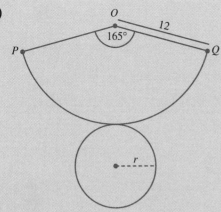

Length of minor arc PQ = (radius)(θ)

$$= (12)\left(\frac{11}{12}\pi\right)$$

$$= 11\pi \text{ cm}$$

(iii) (a) To find the total surface area, we require the radius, r, of the circle.

The circumference of the base of the cone = length of minor arc PQ.

$$2\pi r = 11\pi$$
$$r = 5.5 \text{ cm}$$

Total surface area of cone = area sector OPQ + area circle

$$= \frac{1}{2}(\text{radius})^2\theta + \pi r^2$$

$$= \frac{1}{2}(12)^2\left(\frac{11}{12}\pi\right) + \pi(5.5)^2$$

$$= 66\pi + 30.25\pi$$

$$= 302 \text{ cm}^2$$

(b) To find the volume of the cone, we require h, the height of the cone.

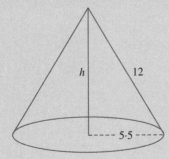

$$(12)^2 = h^2 + (5.5)^2 \text{ (by Pythagoras' theorem)}$$
$$144 = h^2 + 30.25$$
$$113.75 = h^2$$
$$10.66 = h$$

$$\text{Volume of cone} = \frac{1}{3}\pi r^2 h = \frac{1}{3}\pi(5.5)^2(10.66) = 338 \text{ cm}^3$$

The above procedural area and volume question can easily convert into an in-context exam question, as follows:

A company uses waterproof paper to make disposable conical (with a lid) drinking cups. To make each cup, a sector *POQ* and a circle, as shown in the diagram, are cut from a waterproof sheet of paper. The edges *PO* and *QO* are joined to form the cup, as shown.

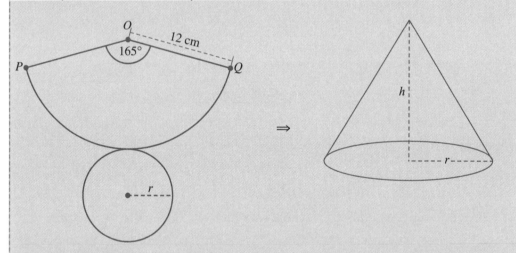

Find the radius, height and volume of such a conical cup.

In practice, would these dimensions be suitable for a drinking cup? Justify your answer.

Solution

We found radius = 5·5 cm

        Height = 10·66 cm

           Volume = 338 cm^3 = 0·338 l in the previous example

Overall, the radius and height are a bit bigger than a traditional cup, but acceptable.

Volume = 0·338 l = 338 ml is a suitable quantity for drinking.

Not sure about the lid. The pointed base of the cup is not very practical.

Conclusion: Dimensions are good but the design needs work!

8 The Trapezoidal Rule and its Applications

aims

☐ To know where to find the general form of the formula for the trapezoidal rule in the *booklet of formulae and tables*

☐ To develop the skill of applying the trapezoidal rule for specific cases, e.g. when the number of strips is 5 or when we are given an equation in disguise

☐ To know we can be asked to take measurements from a drawing (either in cm or using a scale) and apply the trapezoidal rule with the numbers we have found

☐ To acquire the skill necessary to apply the trapezoidal rule to in-context and procedural exam questions

Trapezoidal rule

The trapezoidal rule gives a concise formula to enable us to make a good approximation of the area of an irregular shape.

This formula, shown below, is to be found on page 12 of the *booklet of formulae and tables*.

A represents the area of the shape.

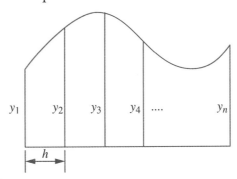

$$A = \frac{h}{2}[y_1 + y_n + 2(y_2 + y_3 + y_4 + \cdots + y_{n-1})]$$

- The greater the number of strips taken, the greater the accuracy
- The trapezoidal rule lends itself very well to real-life in-context questions, e.g. area of a lake or area under a curve.

(2015 Paper 1 Q.3)

Let $f(x) = -x^2 + 12x - 27$, $x \in \mathbb{R}$.

(a) (i) Complete Table 1 below.

Table 1						
x	3	4	5	6	7	8	9
$f(x)$	0	5			8		

(ii) Use Table 1 and the trapezoidal rule to find the approximate area of the region bounded by the graph of f and the x-axis.

(b) (i) Find $\displaystyle\int_{3}^{9} f(x)dx$

(ii) Use your answers above to find the percentage error in your approximate of the area, correct to one decimal place.

Solution

(a) (i)

Table 1						
x	3	4	5	6	7	8	9
$f(x)$	0	5	8	9	8	5	0

(ii) e.g. $f(5) = -(5)^2 + 12(5) - 27 = -25 + 60 - 27 = 8$

h = width of each strip = 1

$y_1 = 0 \qquad y_2 = 5 \qquad y_3 = 8 \qquad y_4 = 9$

$y_5 = 8 \qquad y_6 = 5 \qquad y_7 = 0$

$\text{Area} = \dfrac{h}{2}[y_1 + y_7 + 2(y_2 + y_3 + y_4 + y_5 + y_6)]$

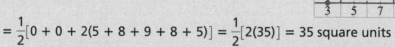

$= \dfrac{1}{2}[0 + 0 + 2(5 + 8 + 9 + 8 + 5)] = \dfrac{1}{2}[2(35)] = 35$ square units

(b) (i) $\displaystyle\int_{3}^{9}(-x^2 + 12x - 27)dx$

$= \left[\dfrac{-x^3}{3} + \dfrac{12x^2}{2} - 27x\right]_{3}^{9}$ 	 (see integral calculus in *LSMS Maths HL Paper 1*)

$= (-243 + 486 - 243) - (-9 + 54 - 81) = 36$

(ii) Error = 36 − 35 = 1

Percentage error = $\dfrac{1}{36}$ × 100 = 2·8%

Trapezoidal rule gives an approximation for the area, whereas integration gives the exact value for the area.

The trapezoidal rule often appears on Paper 1 because of the link to integration and area.

Example

A sketch of a piece of land is shown. Using the trapezoidal rule, the area of the piece of land is estimated to be 141 m². Calculate the value of k.

All units given in the diagram are in metres.

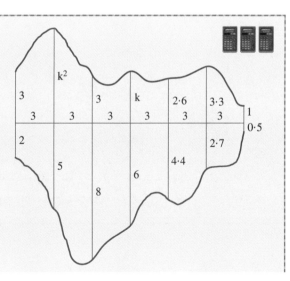

Solution

Width $= h = 3$

$y_1 = 5$

$y_2 = k^2 + 5$ $\qquad\qquad\qquad y_5 = 7$

$y_3 = 11$ $\qquad\qquad\qquad\quad y_6 = 6$

$y_4 = k + 6$ $\qquad\qquad\qquad y_7 = 1\cdot5$

key point

Add the heights above and below the horizontal line to get each value for y.

Equation given in disguise:

$$\text{Area} = \frac{h}{2}[y_1 + y_7 + 2(y_2 + y_3 + y_4 + y_5 + y_6)]$$

$$141 = \frac{3}{2}[5 + 1\cdot5 + 2(k^2 + 5 + 11 + k + 6 + 7 + 6)]$$

$$282 = 3[6\cdot5 + 2(k^2 + k + 35)] \qquad \text{(multiply both sides by 2)}$$

$$282 = 19\cdot5 + 6k^2 + 6k + 210$$

$$0 = 6k^2 + 6k - 52\cdot5$$

$$0 = 12k^2 + 12k - 105 \qquad \text{(multiply both sides by 2)}$$

$$0 = 4k^2 + 4k - 35$$

$$0 = (2k + 7)(2k - 5)$$

$$\therefore 2k + 7 = 0 \qquad \text{or} \qquad 2k - 5 = 0$$

$$k = -\frac{7}{2} \quad \text{or} \qquad k = \frac{5}{2}$$

$$\text{Reject} \qquad\qquad\qquad \text{Answer}$$

key point

This example shows how we can merge two irregular shapes together and apply one application of the trapezoidal rule (instead of two applications).

exam Q

The rate at which flashbulbs give off light varies during the flash.

For some bulbs, the light, measured in lumens, reaches a peak and fades quickly, as shown in Figure 1.

For other bulbs, the light, instead of reaching a peak, stays at a moderate level for a relatively longer period of time, as shown in Figure 2.

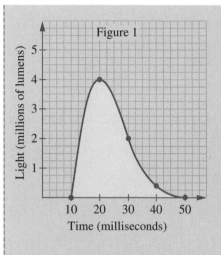

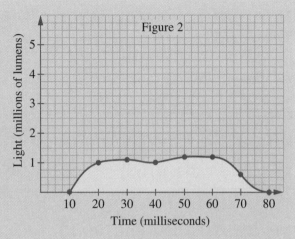

To calculate how much light reaches the film in a camera, we must know when the shutter opens and closes. A typical shutter opens after 10 milliseconds and closes approximately 60 milliseconds after the button is pressed.

The amount, A, in lumen–milliseconds of light emitted by the flash bulb is given by the shaded area under the curve.

Use the trapezoidal rule and the numerical data from Figure 1 and Figure 2 to estimate A for each of the given bulbs. State which bulb gets more light to the film. Justify your answer.

Solution

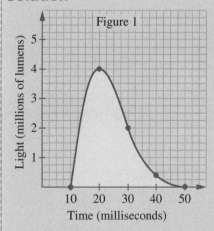

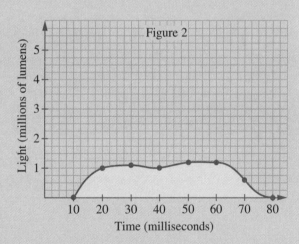

The question gives no instruction/suggestion for the interval widths. Here, each interval width is taken as 10 milliseconds. An interval width of 5 milliseconds would give a more accurate answer.

Given values:

Width = h = 10

$y_1 = 0$
$y_2 = 4$
$y_3 = 2$
$y_4 = 0.4$
$y_5 = 0$

Area = $\frac{h}{2}[y_1 + y_5 + 2(y_2 + y_3 + y_4)]$

Area = $\frac{10}{2}[0 + 0 + 2(4 + 2 + 0.4)]$

Area = 5[0 + 12.8]

Area = 64 lumen–milliseconds

Given values:

Width = h = 10

$y_1 = 0$
$y_2 = 1$
$y_3 = 1.1$
$y_4 = 1$
$y_5 = 1.2$
$y_6 = 1.2$
$y_7 = 0.6$
$y_8 = 0$

Area = $\frac{h}{2}[y_1 + y_8 + 2(y_2 + y_3 + y_4$
$+ y_5 + y_6 + y_7)]$

Area = $\frac{10}{2}[0 + 0 + 2(1 + 1.1 + 1 + 1.2$
$+ 1.2 + 0.6)]$

Area = 5[0 + 12.2]

Area = 61 lumen–milliseconds

Hence, we conclude the bulb from Figure 1 gets more light to the film.

The flash bulb problem is a question where you use the numbers from the graphs and the paragraphs of text to solve the question. Do not be thrown by the language, (e.g. lumens), but look for the numbers that will be useful.

- ☐ To understand the two versions of the fundamental principle of counting
- ☐ To be able to calculate the number of arrangements (permutations) of objects
- ☐ To learn how to calculate the number of selections (combinations) of objects
- ☐ Solving equations involving $n!$ and $\binom{n}{r}$

Outcomes

The result of an operation is called an outcome. For example, if we throw a die, one possible outcome is 2. If we throw a die there are six possible outcomes: 1, 2, 3, 4, 5 or 6.

Fundamental principle of counting 1

> Suppose one operation has m possible outcomes and that a second operation has n outcomes. The number of possible outcomes when performing the first operation **followed by** the second operation is $m \times n$.

Performing one operation **and** another operation means we **multiply** the number of possible outcomes.

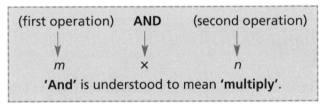

(first operation)   **AND**   (second operation)

m $\times$ n

'And' is understood to mean 'multiply'.

Note: We assume that the outcome of one operation does not affect the number of possible outcomes of the other operation.

The fundamental principle of counting 1 can be extended to three or more operations.

Fundamental principle of counting 2

> Suppose one operation has m possible outcomes and that a second operation has n outcomes. Then the number of possible outcomes of the first operation **or** the second operation is given by $m + n$.

Performing one operation **or** another operation means we **add** the number of possible outcomes.

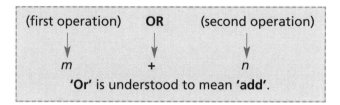

(first operation)	OR	(second operation)
↓	↓	↓
m	+	*n*

'**Or**' is understood to mean '**add**'.

Note: We assume it is not possible for both operations to occur. In other words, there is no overlap of the two operations.

The fundamental principle of counting 2 can be extended to three or more operations, as long as none of the operations overlap.

There are two key words when applying the fundamental principles of counting:
- '**And**' is understood to mean '**multiply**'. Thus, and means ×.
- '**Or**' is understood to mean '**add**'. Thus, or means +.

Permutations (arrangements)

A **permutation** is an arrangement of a number of objects in a definite order.

Look out for the word '**arranged**' or '**arrangements**'. This indicates that the question is about **permutations**.

Example

A number-plate is to consist of three letters of the English alphabet followed by two digits. If no letter or digit can be repeated and 0 can never be used as the first digit, how many different plates can be manufactured?

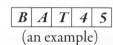
(an example)

Solution

Represent each choice with a box.

no 0

$26 \times 25 \times 24 \times 9 \times 9 = 26 \times 25 \times 24 \times 9 \times 9 = 1,263,600$

exam focus

There are very few calculations involved with some of these questions, so it is very important that you show the method you used to solve the problem. **In general, the answer alone, with no workings, will not be awarded full marks.**

exam Q

At the Olympic Games, eight lanes are marked on the running track. Each runner is allocated to a different lane. Find the number of ways in which the runners in a heat can be allocated to these lanes when there are

(i) eight runners in the heat

(ii) five runners in the heat and any five lanes may be used.

Solution

(i) Number of ways lanes can be allocated

$= 8 \times 7 \times 6 \times 5 \times 4 \times 3 \times 2 \times 1 = 8! = 40,320$

(ii) Five runners. Any of the eight lanes can be used by the five runners. Number of ways lanes can be allocated

$= 8 \times 7 \times 6 \times 5 \times 4 = 6,720$ or $^8P_5 = 6,720$

Factorial function (!)

A function on your calculator that instantly multiplies a number by all the numbers which come before it, down as far as 1.

$5 \times 4 \times 3 \times 2 \times 1 = 5! = 120$

$7 \times 6 \times 5 \times 4 \times 3 \times 2 \times 1 = 7! = 5,040$

> **key point**
>
> **Permutation function (^nP_r)**
> A function on your calculator that calculates the number of ways r objects can be arranged from n distinct objects.
> Six objects permuted in three ways: $^6P_3 = 120$
> Eight objects permuted in four ways: $^8P_4 = 1{,}680$

Restrictions

If there is a restriction on the arrangement (for example, the arrangement must begin with a D), put this restriction in first.

Example

The password for a mobile phone consists of five digits.

(i) How many passwords are possible?

(ii) How many of these passwords start with a 2 and finish with an odd digit?

Solution

(i) There are 10 digits: 0, 1, 2, 3, 4, 5, 6, 7, 8, 9.
Number of possible passwords = $\boxed{10} \times \boxed{10} \times \boxed{10} \times \boxed{10} \times \boxed{10} = 10^5 = 100{,}000$

(ii) The first position can be filled in only one way (2).
The fifth position can be filled in five ways (1 or 3 or 5 or 7 or 9).
The middle three positions can each be filled in 10 ways.

$\quad\quad\quad\quad\quad\quad\quad\quad\quad\quad\quad\quad\quad$**2**$\quad\quad\quad\quad\quad\quad\quad\quad\quad$**odd**

Thus, the number of possible passwords = $\boxed{1} \times \boxed{10} \times \boxed{10} \times \boxed{10} \times \boxed{5} = 5{,}000$

> **exam focus**
>
> It is good practice to draw the boxes and **put the restriction above the box.** This makes it very clear to the examiner where your figures are coming from and the steps you took in reaching your solution.

Example

Two adults and four children stand in a row for a photograph.
How many different arrangements are possible if the four children are between the two adults?

Solution

The four children can stand in the middle in $\boxed{4} \times \boxed{3} \times \boxed{2} \times \boxed{1} = 4! = 24$ ways.

The two adults can stand on each side in $\boxed{2} \times \boxed{1} = 2! = 2$ ways.

Thus, the number of arrangements $= 2! \times 4! = 2 \times 24 = 48$.

Alternatively, the number of arrangements $= \boxed{2} \times \boxed{4} \times \boxed{3} \times \boxed{2} \times \boxed{1} \times \boxed{1} = 48$.

Example

P, Q, R, S, T, U and V are seven students. In how many ways can they stand in a row if:

  (i) there are no restrictions

 (ii) P and Q must sit beside each other

(iii) P and Q must **not** sit beside each other

(iv) T, U and V must sit beside each other

 (v) P or V must never sit at the end of each row.

Solution

  (i) **No restrictions**

Number of arrangements $= \boxed{7} \times \boxed{6} \times \boxed{5} \times \boxed{4} \times \boxed{3} \times \boxed{2} \times \boxed{1} =$

$7! = 5,040$

 (ii) ***P* and *Q* must sit beside each other**

Consider P and Q as one person.

$\boxed{P, Q}, R, S, T, U, V$

The seven students (six objects) can be arranged in

$\boxed{6} \times \boxed{5} \times \boxed{4} \times \boxed{3} \times \boxed{2} \times \boxed{1} = 6! = 720$ ways.

But P and Q can be arranged in $\boxed{2} \times \boxed{1} = 2! = 2$ ways while seated together.

Thus, the number of arrangements $= 2! \times 6! = 2 \times 720 = 1,440$.

(iii) ***P* and *Q* must not sit beside each other**

$$\begin{pmatrix} \text{Number of arrangements with} \\ P \text{ and } Q \text{ not together} \end{pmatrix} = \begin{pmatrix} \text{Total number} \\ \text{of arrangements} \end{pmatrix} - \begin{pmatrix} \text{Number of arrangements with} \\ P \text{ and } Q \text{ together} \end{pmatrix}$$

$$= 5{,}040 \qquad\quad - 1{,}440$$

$$= 3{,}600$$

(iv) ***T*, *U* and *V* must sit beside each other**

Consider *T*, *U* and *V* as one person.

$$P, Q, R, S, \boxed{T, U, V}$$

The seven students (5 objects) can be arranged in

$$\boxed{5} \times \boxed{4} \times \boxed{3} \times \boxed{2} \times \boxed{1} = 5! = 120 \text{ ways.}$$

But *T*, *U* and *V* can be arranged in $\boxed{3} \times \boxed{2} \times \boxed{1} = 3! = 6$ ways while seated together.

Thus, the number of arrangements $= 3! \times 5! = 6 \times 120 = 720$.

(v) ***P* or *V* must never sit at the end of a row**

The first position can be filled in five ways **and then** the last position in four ways.

Then the middle five positions can be filled in

$$\boxed{5} \times \boxed{4} \times \boxed{3} \times \boxed{2} \times \boxed{1} = 5! = 120 \text{ ways.}$$

Number of arrangements $= \boxed{5} \times \boxed{5} \times \boxed{4} \times \boxed{3} \times \boxed{2} \times \boxed{1} \times \boxed{4} = 2{,}400$

This next example uses both fundamental principles of counting.

A bag contains nine discs, numbered from 1 to 9. A disc is drawn from the bag. If the number is prime, then a die is thrown. If the number is non-prime, then a coin is tossed. How many outcomes are possible?

Solution

Break the experiment into two different experiments and work out the number of outcomes separately. Then add the results.

Prime numbers: 2, 3, 5, 7   **Non-prime numbers: 1, 4, 6, 8, 9**
(4 outcomes)   (5 outcomes)
Die: 1, 2, 3, 4, 5, 6 (6 outcomes)   **Coin: H, T (2 outcomes)**

First experiment   Second experiment

$$\left[\begin{pmatrix} \text{Prime} \\ \text{number} \end{pmatrix} \text{and} \begin{pmatrix} \text{Throw} \\ \text{a die} \end{pmatrix} \right] \text{ or } \left[\begin{pmatrix} \text{Non-prime} \\ \text{number} \end{pmatrix} \text{and} \begin{pmatrix} \text{Toss a} \\ \text{coin} \end{pmatrix} \right]$$

$$= \quad \boxed{4} \quad \times \quad \boxed{6} \qquad + \qquad \boxed{5} \quad \times \quad \boxed{2}$$

$$= \qquad\qquad 24 \qquad\qquad\quad + \qquad\qquad 10$$

$$= \qquad 34$$

key point

1 is not a prime number.

exam
Q

(2018 Q.3 (a))

A security code consists of six digits chosen at random from the digits 0 to 9. The code may begin with zero and digits may be repeated.

For example, $\boxed{0}\,\boxed{7}\,\boxed{1}\,\boxed{7}\,\boxed{3}\,\boxed{7}$ is a valid code.

(i) Find how many of the possible codes will end with a zero.

(ii) Find how many of the possible codes will contain the digits 2 0 1 8 together and in this order.

Solution

(i)
$\qquad\qquad\qquad\qquad\qquad\qquad\qquad\qquad$ zero

$\boxed{10} \times \boxed{10} \times \boxed{10} \times \boxed{10} \times \boxed{10} \times \boxed{1} = 100{,}000$

(ii) $\quad$ 2 $\qquad$ 0 $\qquad$ 1 $\qquad$ 8

$\boxed{1} \times \boxed{1} \times \boxed{1} \times \boxed{1} \times \boxed{10} \times \boxed{10} = 100$

$\qquad\qquad$ 2 $\qquad$ 0 $\qquad$ 1 $\qquad$ 8 $\qquad\qquad$ +

$\boxed{10} \times \boxed{1} \times \boxed{1} \times \boxed{1} \times \boxed{1} \times \boxed{10} = 100$

$\qquad\qquad\qquad\qquad$ 2 $\qquad$ 0 $\qquad$ 1 $\qquad$ 8 $\quad$ +

$\boxed{10} \times \boxed{10} \times \boxed{1} \times \boxed{1} \times \boxed{1} \times \boxed{1} = \underline{100}$

$\qquad\qquad\qquad\qquad$ Total number of ways = 300

Combinations (selections)

A **combination** is a selection of a number of objects in any order.

key
point

Combinations function $(^{n}C_{r}) = \dbinom{n}{r}$

A function on your calculator that calculates the number of ways r objects can be selected from n distinct objects.

Four objects selected from seven objects: $^{7}C_{4} = 35$

Three objects selected from nine objects: $^{9}C_{3} = 84$

Example

A committee of five is to be selected from six students and three teachers.

(i) How many different committees of five are possible?

(ii) How many of these possible committees have three students and two teachers?

(iii) How many of these possible committees have more students than teachers?

Solution

6 students and 3 teachers = 9 people

(i) **No restrictions**

Number of committees $= \binom{9}{5} = 126$

(ii) **3 students and 2 teachers**

We have to choose three students from the six students **and** two teachers from the three teachers.

Number of committees $= \binom{6}{3} \times \binom{3}{2} = 20 \times 3 = 60$

(iii) **We need more students, S, than teachers, T**

Let S = the number of students and T = the number of teachers.

Possibilities are:

$5\,S$ and $0\,T$ or $4\,S$ and $1\,T$ or $3\,S$ and $2\,T$

Number of committees

$$= \binom{6}{5} \times \binom{3}{0} \quad + \quad \binom{6}{4} \times \binom{3}{1} \quad + \quad \binom{6}{3} \times \binom{3}{2}$$

$$= 6 \times 1 \quad\quad\quad\quad + \quad\quad 15 \times 3 \quad\quad\quad + \quad\quad 20 \times 3$$

$$= 6 + 45 + 60 = 111$$

Example

A team of four is selected from a group of seven girls and five boys.

(i) How many different selections are possible?

(ii) How many of these selections include at least one girl?

Solution

7 girls + 5 boys = 12 people

(i) **No restrictions**

$$\text{Number of selections} = \binom{12}{4} = 495$$

(ii) In this case it is easier to calculate the number of selections with no girls and then subtract this from the total number of selections.
No girls means having exactly four boys on the team:

$$\text{Number of selections} = \binom{5}{4} = 5$$

$$\binom{\text{Number of selections}}{\text{with at least one girl}} = \binom{\text{Total number}}{\text{of selections}} - \binom{\text{Number of selections}}{\text{with no girls}}$$

$$= 495 - 5 = 490$$

'At least one girl' means one girl or more. In this example: 1 girl and 3 boys or 2 girls and 2 boys or 3 girls and 1 boy or 4 girls and 0 boys.

Ten distinct points are taken on the circumference of a circle (as shown).

(i) (a) Calculate the number of different chords that can be formed using these points as end points.

   (b) How many different triangles can be formed using these points as vertices?

(ii) (a) Calculate the number of different quadrilaterals that can be formed using these points as vertices.

   (b) Two of the 10 points are labelled x and y, respectively. How many of the above quadrilaterals have x and y as vertices?

   (c) How many of the quadrilaterals do not have x and y as vertices?

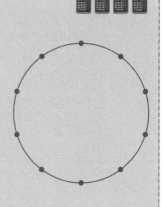

Solution

(i) (a) Number of chords

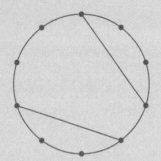

We have 10 points.
Each chord uses two points.

∴ Number of chords

$$= \binom{10}{2} = 45$$

(b) Number of triangles

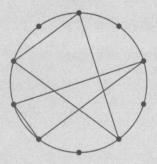

We have 10 points.
Each triangle uses three points.

∴ Number of triangles

$$= \binom{10}{3} = 120$$

(ii) (a) Number of quadrilaterals

We have 10 points.

Each quadrilateral uses four points.

∴ Number of quadrilaterals

$$= \binom{10}{4} = 210$$

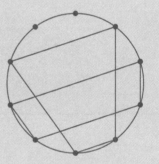

(b) Number of quadrilaterals with x and y as vertices.

We have 10 points.

Each quadrilateral uses four points.

But two of these, x and y, are fixed.

Thus, we have eight points from which we can choose two.

∴ Number of quadrilaterals with x and y as

$$\text{vertices} = \binom{8}{2} = 28$$

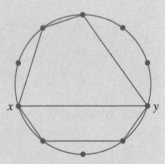

(c) $\left(\begin{array}{c} \text{Number of quadrilaterals} \\ \text{with } [xy] \text{ as vertices} \end{array} \right) = \left(\begin{array}{c} \text{Total number of} \\ \text{quadrilaterals} \end{array} \right) - \left(\begin{array}{c} \text{Number of quadrilaterals} \\ \text{with } [xy] \text{ as vertices} \end{array} \right)$

$$= 210 - 28 = 182$$

Equations involving $n!$ and $\binom{n}{r}$

Sometimes we have to solve equations involving $\binom{n}{r}$.

In these questions, we make use of the following:

$$\binom{n}{1} = \frac{n}{1} = n \qquad \binom{n}{2} = \frac{n(n-1)}{(2)(1)} = \frac{n^2 - n}{2} \qquad \binom{n}{3} = \frac{n(n-1)(n-2)}{(3)(2)(1)}$$

$$\frac{(n+1)!}{n!} = \frac{(n+1)n!}{n!} = n + 1$$

- $\binom{n}{0} = \binom{n}{n} = 1$
- n and r must be positive whole numbers, where r can be zero, but n can't.
- $n \geq r$

Example

Solve: (i) $\binom{n}{2} = 36$ $\qquad$ (ii) $\binom{n+1}{2} = 10\binom{n}{1}$, where $n \in \mathbb{N}$

Solution

(i) $\qquad \binom{n}{2} = 36$

$$\frac{n(n-1)}{2} = 36$$

$$n(n-1) = 72$$

$$n^2 - n = 72$$

$$n^2 - n - 72 = 0$$

$$(n+8)(n-9) = 0$$

$$n = -8 \quad \text{or} \quad n = 9$$

Reject $n = -8$, as $-8 \notin \mathbb{N}$.

$$\therefore n = 9$$

Check: $\binom{9}{2} = 36$ (correct)

(ii) $\qquad \binom{n+1}{2} = 10\binom{n}{1}$

$$\frac{n(n+1)}{2} = 10(n)$$

$$n(n+1) = 20(n)$$

$$n^2 + n = 20n$$

$$n^2 - 19n = 0$$

$$n(n-19) = 0$$

$$n = 0 \quad \text{or} \quad n = 19$$

Reject $n = 0$, as $0 \notin \mathbb{N}$.

$$\therefore n = 19$$

Check: $\binom{20}{2} = 190$

$$10\binom{19}{1} = 190 \quad \text{(correct)}$$

exam Q

(2018 Q.3 (b))

Find a, b, c, and d, if $\dfrac{(n + 3)!(n + 2)!}{(n + 1)!(n + 1)!} = an^3 + bn^2 + cn + d$,

where a, b, c, and $d \in \mathbb{N}$.

Solution

$\dfrac{(n + 3)!(n + 2)!}{(n + 1)!(n + 1)!}$

Remember: $(n + 3)! = (n + 3)(n + 2)(n + 1)(n) \ldots (2)(1)$

So, $(n + 3)! = (n + 3)(n + 2)(n + 1)!$

$\dfrac{(n + 3)(n + 2)(n + 1)!(n + 2)(n + 1)!}{(n + 1)!(n + 1)!}$

(divide top and bottom by $(n + 1)!\,(n + 1)!$)

$(n + 3)(n + 2)(n + 2)$

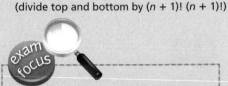

exam focus

$(n + 3)(n^2 + 4n + 4)$

$n^3 + 7n^2 + 16n + 12$

So, $a = 1$, $b = 7$, $c = 16$ and $d = 12$

Many candidates found part **(b)** very challenging in this question. Subsequently, **(a) (i)** was awarded 15 marks, **(a) (ii)** and **(b)** were awarded 5 marks each.

Example

Solve $\dfrac{n!}{(n - 2)!} = 90$, when $n \in \mathbb{N}$ and $n \geq 2$.

Solution

$$\frac{n!}{(n - 2)!} = 90$$

$$\frac{n(n - 1)(n - 2)!}{(n - 2)!} = 90$$

$\left(\dfrac{n!}{(n - 2)!} = \dfrac{n(n - 1)(n - 2)!}{(n - 2)!} \right)$

(divide top and bottom by $(n - 2)!$)

$$n(n - 1) = 90$$

$$n^2 - n = 90$$

$$n^2 - n - 90 = 0$$

$$(n + 9)(n - 10) = 0$$

$$n = -9 \quad \text{or} \quad n = 10$$

Reject $n = -9$, as $-9 \notin \mathbb{N}$.

$\therefore n = 10$

Check: $\dfrac{10!}{8!} = \dfrac{10 \times 9 \times 8!}{8!} = 10 \times 9 = 90$ (correct)

10 Probability

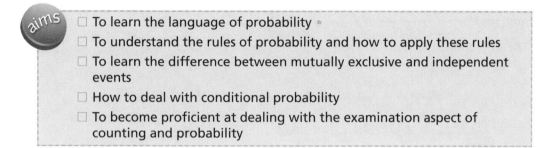

aims

- ☐ To learn the language of probability
- ☐ To understand the rules of probability and how to apply these rules
- ☐ To learn the difference between mutually exclusive and independent events
- ☐ How to deal with conditional probability
- ☐ To become proficient at dealing with the examination aspect of counting and probability

Introduction

Probability involves the study of the laws of chance. It is a measure of the chance, or likelihood, of something happening.

If you carry out an operation, or experiment, using coins, dice, spinners or cards, then each toss, throw, spin or draw is called a **trial**.

The possible things that can happen from a trial are called **outcomes**. The outcomes of interest are called an **event**. In other words, an event is the set of successful outcomes.

If E is an event, then $P(E)$ stands for the probability that the event occurs. $P(E)$ is read as 'the probability of E'.

The probability of an event is a number between 0 and 1, including 0 and 1.

$$0 \leq P(E) \leq 1$$

The value of $P(E)$ can be given as a fraction, decimal or percentage.

Note: $P(E) = 0$ means that an event is **impossible**.
$P(E) = 1$ means that an event is **certain**.

Formulae:

The measure of the probability of an event, E, is given by:

$$P(E) = \frac{\text{Number of successful outcomes}}{\text{Number of possible outcomes}}$$

$$P(E) + P(\text{not } E) = 1$$

or

$$P(\text{not } E) = 1 - P(E)$$

key point

$P(\text{not } E)$ is sometimes written $P(\bar{E})$ or $P(E')$.

exam Q

(2016 Q.5 (a))

In an archery competition, the team consisting of John, David, and Mike will win 1st prize if at least two of them hit the bullseye with their last arrows. From past experience, they know that the probability that John, David, and Mike will hit the bullseye on their last arrow is $\frac{1}{5}$, $\frac{1}{6}$, and $\frac{1}{4}$ respectively.

(i) Complete the table below to show all the ways in which they could win 1st prize.

	Way 1	Way 2	Way 3	Way 4
John	✓			
David	✓			
Mike	✕			

✓ = Hit
✕ = Miss

(ii) Hence or otherwise find the probability that they will win the competition.

Solution

(i) 'At least' two hits means that we can have two hits and one miss or three hits.

	Way 1	Way 2	Way 3	Way 4
John	✓	✓	✕	✓
David	✓	✕	✓	✓
Mike	✕	✓	✓	✓

(ii) To find the probability of each way: $P(\text{John}) \times P(\text{David}) \times P(\text{Mike})$

Way 1: $\dfrac{1}{5} \times \dfrac{1}{6} \times \dfrac{3}{4} = \dfrac{3}{120}$

Way 2: $\dfrac{1}{5} \times \dfrac{5}{6} \times \dfrac{1}{4} = \dfrac{5}{120}$

Way 3: $\dfrac{4}{5} \times \dfrac{1}{6} \times \dfrac{1}{4} = \dfrac{4}{120}$

Way 4: $\dfrac{1}{5} \times \dfrac{1}{6} \times \dfrac{1}{4} = \dfrac{1}{120}$

Total probability $= \dfrac{3}{120} + \dfrac{5}{120} + \dfrac{4}{120} + \dfrac{1}{120} = \dfrac{13}{120}$

key point

$P(\text{Miss}) = 1 - P(\text{Hit})$

The probability that two events, A or B, can happen is given by:

$$P(A \text{ or } B) = P(A) + P(B) - P(A \text{ and } B)$$

(removes double counting)

Mutually exclusive events

$P(A \cap B) = 0$ (no double counting)

Conditional probability

$$P(A|B) = \frac{P(A \cap B)}{P(B)}$$

Independent events

1. $P(A|B) = P(A)$ **2.** $P(B|A) = P(B)$ **3.** $P(A \cap B) = P(A) \times P(B)$

Any one of 1, 2 or 3 is sufficient to prove independence.

General multiplication rule: $P(A \text{ and } B) = P(A) \times P(B|A)$

Note: If A and B are independent events, then $P(A \text{ and } B) = P(A) \times P(B)$.

Do not confuse mutually exclusive events and independent events.

Mutually exclusive events are events that cannot happen together.
For mutually exclusive events A and B: **P(A and B) = 0.**   (no double counting)

Independent events are events that can happen at the same time or can happen one after the other. For independent events A and B:

P(A and B) = P(A) × P(B) or **P(A|B) = P(A)** or **P(B|A) = P(B)**

Independent events cannot be mutually exclusive and mutually exclusive events cannot be independent.

Example

A and B are two events such that $P(A) = 0.6$ and $P(B) = 0.2$.
What is $P(A \cup B)$ if:

(i) A and B are mutually exclusive
(ii) A and B are independent.

Solution

(i) A and B are mutually exclusive.

$$\therefore P(A \cap B) = 0$$

$$P(A \cup B) = P(A) + P(B)$$
$$- P(A \cap B)$$
$$= 0{\cdot}6 + 0{\cdot}2 - 0$$
$$= 0{\cdot}8$$

(ii) A and B are independent.

$$\therefore P(A \cap B) = P(A) \times P(B)$$
$$= 0{\cdot}6 \times 0{\cdot}2 = 0{\cdot}12$$

$$P(A \cup B) = P(A) + P(B)$$
$$- P(A \cap B)$$
$$= 0{\cdot}6 + 0{\cdot}2 - 0{\cdot}12$$
$$= 0{\cdot}68$$

Give an example of:

(i) two mutually exclusive events

(ii) two non-mutually exclusive events.

Solution

(i) If you throw a die once, it is impossible to obtain an odd number and an even number.

P(odd number and a even number on one throw of a normal die) = 0

(no double counting)

∴ Obtaining an odd number and an even on one throw of a normal die are mutually exclusive events.

(ii) If you draw one card from a normal 52-card deck of cards, it is possible to obtain an ace and a diamond.

P(drawing an ace and a diamond) ≠ 0. (It is actually equal to $\frac{1}{52}$.)

∴ Obtaining an ace and a diamond from a normal 52-card deck of cards are non-mutually exclusive events.

(2016 Q.5 (b))

Two events, A and B, are represented in the diagram.
$P(A \cap B) = 0{\cdot}1$, $P(B \backslash A) = 0{\cdot}3$ and $P(A \backslash B) = x$.

Write $P(A)$ in terms of x and hence, or otherwise, find the value of x for which the events A and B are independent.

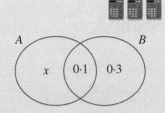

Solution

$$P(A) = x + 0·1$$

If independent, then $P(A \cap B) = P(A) \times P(B)$

$$0·1 = (x + 0·1) \times (0·4)$$
$$0·1 = 0·4x + 0·04$$
$$0·1 - 0·04 = 0·4x$$
$$0·06 = 0·4x$$
$$\frac{0·06}{0·4} = x$$
$$0·15 = x$$

(2010 Q.1)

Two events, A and B, are such that $P(A) = 0·2$, $P(A \cap B) = 0·15$ and $P(A' \cap B) = 0·6$.

(i)   Complete this Venn diagram.

(ii) Find the probability that neither A nor B happens.

(iii) Find the conditional probability $P(A|B)$.

(iv) State whether A and B are independent events and justify your answer.

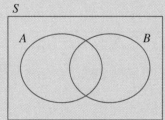

Solution

(i) $A' \cap B$ is the region B only or $B \backslash A$.

$$P(A' \cap B) = P(B \backslash A) = P(B \text{ only}) = 0·6$$
$$P(A \cap B) = 0·15$$
$$P(A \backslash B) = P(A) - P(A \cap B) = 0·2 - 0·15 = 0·05$$

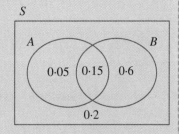

(ii) $P[S \backslash (A \cup B)] = P(\text{neither } A \text{ nor } B)$
$$= 1 - 0·05 - 0·15 - 0·6 = 0·2$$

(iii) $P(A|B) = \dfrac{P(A \cap B)}{P(B)} = \dfrac{0·15}{0·75} = 0·2$ [$P(B) = 0·15 + 0·6 = 0·75$]

(iv) $P(A|B) = 0·2$ $P(A) = 0·2$

$P(A|B) = P(A)$ $\therefore$ A and B are independent events.

or

$P(B|A) = 0·75$ $P(B) = 0·75$

$P(B|A) = P(B)$ $\therefore$ A and B are independent events.

or

$P(A) \times P(B) = 0·2 \times 0·75 = 0·15$ $P(A \cap B) = 0·15$

$P(A) \times P(B) = P(A \cap B)$ $\therefore$ A and B are independent events.

exam Q

Four students work separately on a mathematical problem. The probability that the four students have of solving the problem is as follows: $\frac{7}{8}, \frac{3}{4}, \frac{1}{3}$ and $\frac{2}{7}$.

Show the probability that the problem will be solved by at least one of the four students is $\frac{331}{336}$.

Solution

Let the students be A, B, C and D.

Let $P(S)$ = probability of solving the problem and $P(F)$ = probability of failing to solve the problem.

	A	B	C	D
P(S)	$\frac{7}{8}$	$\frac{3}{4}$	$\frac{1}{3}$	$\frac{2}{7}$
P(F)	$\frac{1}{8}$	$\frac{1}{4}$	$\frac{2}{3}$	$\frac{5}{7}$

P(all four fail to solve the problem)
$= P(A_F$ and B_F and C_F and $D_F)$
$= P(A_F) \times P(B_F) \times P(C_F) \times P(D_F)$
$= \frac{1}{8} \times \frac{1}{4} \times \frac{2}{3} \times \frac{5}{7} = \frac{5}{336}$

P(at least one will solve the problem) $= 1 - P$(all four fail to solve the problem)

$$= 1 - \frac{5}{336} = \frac{331}{336}$$

Note: $P(A_F)$ = probability that A fails to solve the problem and so on.

key point

The phrase 'at least one' occurs in many probability problems. 'At least one' means 'one or more'. In the above problem it means one or two or three or four students solve the problem.

exam focus

TREE DIAGRAMS
- If a question says 'using a tree diagram', then you **must** use a tree diagram.
- If a question says 'using a tree diagram or otherwise', then other methods are accepted.
- Tree diagrams display all possible mutually exclusive events.
- The sum of the probabilities on **any set** of branches always adds up to 1.
- Multiply the probabilities along the branches to get the end result.

- If more than one set of end results are required, simply add the end results together.
- It is good practice to check that the sum of all the probabilities is 1.

exam Q

If Mr Smith has a good week at work (which happens 70% of the time), there's a 0·8 probability that he will take the family out to a restaurant on Friday evening, otherwise they'll eat at home. If he's had a bad week there is only a 0·3 probability of eating in a restaurant on Friday evening.

(i) By making a tree diagram or otherwise, calculate:

    (a) the probability that the family eat at a restaurant on a Friday.

    (b) the probability that Mr Smith had a good week at work, given that they ate at a restaurant on a certain Friday.

(ii) A restaurant meal will cost the family €100, while a meal at home will only cost €20. Find the expected cost of their Friday evening meal.

Solution

Let $G = P$(good day), $B = P$(bad day), $M = P$(meal out) and $H = P$(meal at home).

(i) (a)

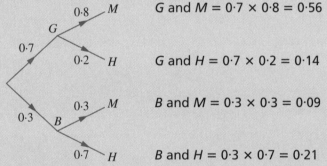

G and $M = 0·7 \times 0·8 = 0·56$

G and $H = 0·7 \times 0·2 = 0·14$

B and $M = 0·3 \times 0·3 = 0·09$

B and $H = 0·3 \times 0·7 = 0·21$

(Check: Sum of the probabilities = 0·56 + 0·14 + 0·09 + 0·21 = 1)

P(meal out)

$$= P(M) = P(G \text{ and } M) + P(B \text{ and } M) = 0·56 + 0·09 = 0·65 \text{ or } \frac{13}{20}$$

(b) P(Mr Smith had a good week at work, given that the family ate out)

$$= P(G|M) = \frac{P(G \text{ and } M)}{P(M)} = \frac{0·56}{0·65} = \frac{56}{65}$$

(ii)

	Meal out (M)	Meal home (H)
x	€100	€20
P(x)	0·65	0·35

Expected cost

$= E(x)$

$= \Sigma x P(x)$

$= 100(0·65) + 20(0·35)$

$= 65 + 7 = 72$

∴ The expected cost = €72.

exam
Q

(2017 Q.8 (b))

In Galway, rain falls in the morning on $\frac{1}{3}$ of the school days in the year.

When it is raining the probability of heavy traffic is $\frac{1}{2}$.

When it is not raining the probability of heavy traffic is $\frac{1}{4}$.

When it is raining and there is heavy traffic, the probability of being late for school is $\frac{1}{2}$.

When it is not raining and there is no heavy traffic, the probability of being late for school is $\frac{1}{8}$. In any other situation the probability of being late for school is $\frac{1}{5}$.

(i) Draw a tree diagram to represent this information and write the probability of each outcome at the end of each branch. Give each answer in the form $\frac{a}{b}$ where $a, b \in \mathbb{N}$.

(ii) On a random school day in Galway, find the probability of being late for school.

(iii) On a random school day in Galway, find the probability that it rained in the morning, given that you were late for school.

Solution

(i)

Key	Rain = R	Heavy traffic = T	Late = L
	No rain = no R	Not heavy traffic = no T	Not late = no L

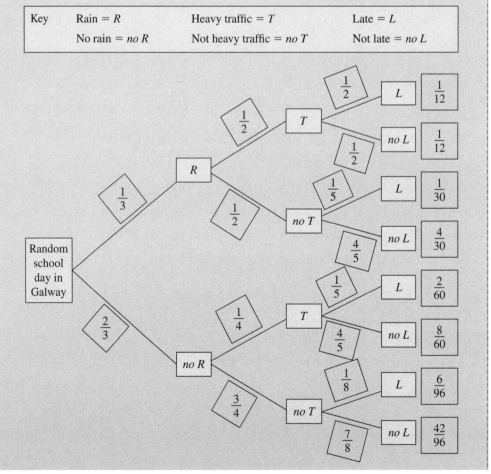

(ii) P(Late) = All outcomes that end in L

$$P(\text{Late}) = \frac{1}{12} + \frac{1}{30} + \frac{2}{60} + \frac{6}{96}$$

$$P(\text{Late}) = \frac{17}{80}$$

(iii) $P(\text{Rain}|\text{Late}) = \dfrac{P(\text{Rain} \cap \text{Late})}{P(\text{Late})}$

$$P(\text{Rain}|\text{Late}) = \frac{\dfrac{1}{12} + \dfrac{1}{30}}{\left(\dfrac{17}{80}\right)}$$

$$P(\text{Rain}|\text{Late}) = \frac{28}{51}$$

key point

The word "given" in the question indicates that the formula for conditional probability is needed here.

exam Q

A bag contains discs of three different colours. There are five red discs, one white disc and x black discs. Three discs are picked together at random.

(i) Write down an expression in x for the probability that the three discs are all different colours.

(ii) If the probability that the three discs are all different colours is equal to the probability that they are all black, find x.

Solution

$5R, 1W, xB$ Total $(x + 6)$

(i) P(discs are all different colours)

$$= P(R) \times P(W) \times P(B)$$

$$= \frac{5}{x + 6} \times \frac{1}{x + 5} \times \frac{x}{x + 4} = \frac{5x}{(x + 6)(x + 5)(x + 4)}$$

But this can occur 3! or six different ways.

$\therefore$ P(discs are all different colours)

$$= 6\left(\frac{5x}{(x + 6)(x + 5)(x + 4)}\right) = \frac{30x}{(x + 6)(x + 5)(x + 4)}$$

(ii) P(all three are black) $= P(B_1) \times P(B_2) \times P(B_3)$

$$= \frac{x}{x + 6} \times \frac{x - 1}{x + 5} \times \frac{x - 2}{x + 4} = \frac{x(x - 1)(x - 2)}{(x + 6)(x + 5)(x + 4)}$$

Given:

P(discs are all different colours) $= P$(all three are black)

$$\frac{30x}{(x + 6)(x + 5)(x + 4)} = \frac{x(x - 1)(x - 2)}{(x + 6)(x + 5)(x + 4)}$$

$$30 = (x - 1)(x - 2)$$

$$x^2 - 3x - 28 = 0$$

$$(x + 4)(x - 7) = 0$$

$$x = -4 \quad \text{or} \quad x = 7$$

$$\text{Reject } x = -4$$

$$\therefore x = 7$$

Estimating probabilities from experiments

Often a probability can only be found by carrying out a series of experiments and recording the results. For example, if you drop a drawing pin and you want to find the probability that it lands point up, there is no obvious method except by dropping a lot of drawing pins and recording the results. The probability of the event can then be **estimated** from these results. A probability found in this way is known as **experimental probability** or **relative frequency** of an event. Each separate experiment carried out is called a **trial**. To find the relative frequency, the experiment has to be repeated a number of times. It is important to remember that if an experiment is repeated, there will be different outcomes and that increasing the number of times an experiment is repeated generally leads to better estimates of probability.

Estimating probabilities using relative frequency

The relative frequency of an event in an experiment is given by:

$$P(E) = \text{Relative frequency of an event} = \frac{\text{Number of successful trials}}{\text{Number of trials}}$$

Relative frequency can be used to estimate how many times you would **expect** a particular outcome to happen in an experiment.

The expected number of outcomes (or expected value) is calculated as follows.

> Expected number of outcomes = (relative frequency) × (number of trials)
>
> or
>
> Expected number of outcomes = P(event) × (number of trials)

Note: To estimate the probability of some events, it is necessary to carry out a survey or look at historical data (past data).

Three casino managers, A, B and C, meet to consider a new type of four-sided die with numbers 1, 2, 3 and 4. To use the die in their casino it must be fair. At the meeting they each throw the die a number of times. The results are recorded in the table below.

Casino	Number of throws	1	2	3	4
A	30	5	8	10	7
B	45	8	13	15	9
C	61	9	14	22	16

(i) Which manager's results are more likely to give the best estimate of the probability of obtaining each number occuring? Justify your answer.

(ii) Calculate the relative frequency of manager A obtaining a score of 3.

(iii) If the die is fair, write down the probability of obtaining each number.

(iv) Calculate the relative frequency for each number on this die for all three managers' results.

(v) In your opinion, should the casinos use this die? Justify your answer.

Solution

(i) Manager C. He has thrown the die more times. The more times you throw the die, the more accurate the estimate of the probability of each number occuring.

(ii)   Relative frequency of Manager A obtaining a 3 $= \dfrac{\text{Number of successful trials}}{\text{Number of trials}} = \dfrac{10}{30} = \dfrac{1}{3}$

(iii) If the die was fair, the probability of obtaining each number would be $\frac{1}{4}$.

(iv)

Number	1	2	3	4
Frequency	22	35	47	32
Relative frequency	$\dfrac{22}{136}$	$\dfrac{35}{136}$	$\dfrac{47}{136}$	$\dfrac{32}{136}$

(v) If the die was fair, each number should occur about the same number of times. In other words, each number should occur about $\dfrac{136}{4} = 34$ times.

Also, the relative frequency of each number should be close to $\dfrac{34}{136}$. The result of this experiment is that the relative frequency of 2 and 4 is close to $\dfrac{34}{136}$.

However, the relative frequency of 3, $\dfrac{47}{136}$, is well above $\dfrac{34}{136}$ and the relative frequency of 1, $\dfrac{22}{136}$, is well below $\dfrac{34}{136}$.

The result of this experiment appears to show that the die is biased in favour of 3 and biased against 1. Thus, I would recommend that the casinos do **not** use this die. However, the die was only thrown 136 times. The accuracy of the estimate of the probability of each number occuring could be improved if the die was thrown, and the results recorded, many more times. I would suggest about 1,000 times to improve the accuracy of the results.

Normal distribution and probability

One reason the normal distribution is so important is that the measurement of many natural phenomena are normally distributed (or nearly so), such as heights, weights, IQ scores and examination results. (See Chapter on Statistics IV for more on the normal distribution.)

key point

- The z-score tells us how many standard deviations a value is from the mean. It is given by $z = \dfrac{x - \mu}{\sigma}$.

- The area under the curve of **any** normal curve is **always** equal to 1.

Finding areas under the normal curves

The mathematical tables give us the area to the left of a specified value of z. The table can be used to obtain a required area. The three graphs below summarise how to use the tables from the *booklet of formulae and tables*. **A copy of this table can also be found at the end of this book.**

Working with the normal curve is a vital skill in both probability and statistics.

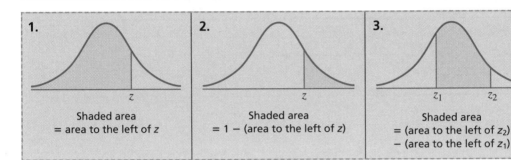

1.

Shaded area
= area to the left of z

2.

Shaded area
= 1 − (area to the left of z)

3.

Shaded area
= (area to the left of z_2)
− (area to the left of z_1)

Note: Alternative to graph 3: Find the area to the left of z_1 and the area to the right of z_2 and subtract both from 1.

Some questions require that the table for normal distribution probabilities is read in reverse.

Example

A random variable, x, follows a normal distribution with mean 20 and standard deviation 5. Find $P(16 \leq x \leq 26)$.

Solution

Given: $\mu = 20$, $\sigma = 5$, $x_1 = 16$ and $x_2 = 26$. Find $P(16 \leq x \leq 26)$.

We first convert the x-values into z-values using $z = \frac{x - \mu}{\sigma}$.

$$z_1 = \frac{x_1 - \mu}{\sigma}$$

$$= \frac{16 - 20}{5} = \frac{-4}{5} = -0.8$$

$$z_2 = \frac{x_2 - \mu}{\sigma}$$

$$= \frac{26 - 20}{5} = \frac{6}{5} = 1.2$$

Use the normal distribution tables from your *booklet of formulae and tables* to find the area corresponding to these z-scores

Area under the curve between

$z_1 = -0.8$ and $z_2 = 1.2$

$= 1 - 0.1151 - 0.2119$

$= 0.673$

$P(16 \leq x \leq 26) = 0.673$

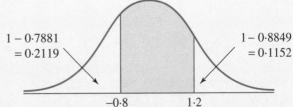

1 − 0·7881
= 0·2119

1 − 0·8849
= 0·1152

−0·8   1·2

In a normal distribution, a raw score of 56 corresponds to a z-score of 1 and a raw score of 60 corresponds to a z-score of 2. Find
(i) the standard deviation and **(ii)** the mean of this distribution.

Solution

Given: $x_1 = 56$ and $z_1 = 1$ and $x_2 = 60$ and $z_2 = 2$. Find σ and μ.

$$\frac{x_1 - \mu}{\sigma} = z_1$$

$$\frac{56 - \mu}{\sigma} = 1$$

$$56 - \mu = \sigma$$

$$\mu + \sigma = 56 \quad ①$$

$$\frac{x_2 - \mu}{\sigma} = z_2$$

$$\frac{60 - \mu}{\sigma} = 2$$

$$60 - \mu = 2\sigma$$

$$\mu + 2\sigma = 60 \quad ②$$

Solving the simultaneous equations ① and ② gives $\sigma = 4$ and $\mu = 52$.

∴ **(i)** Standard deviation = 4 and **(ii)** mean = 52.

Notice the ability to solve linear simultaneous equations from algebra is essential to finish the above question on the normal curve.

Example

The heights of students in a certain class are normally distributed with a mean of 165 cm and a standard deviation of 10 cm. If 90% of the students in this class have a height of less than or equal to x cm, find the value of x.

Solution

$$\frac{x - \mu}{\sigma} = z$$

> Reading the tables in reverse, the closest to 0·9 is 0·8997. This gives a z-value of 1·28.

Given: $\mu = 165, \sigma = 10$ and $z = 1\cdot28$. Find x.

$$\frac{x - 165}{10} = 1\cdot28$$

$$x - 165 = 12\cdot8$$

$$x = 177\cdot8$$

Thus, we conclude that 90% of these students have a height of 177·8 cm or less.

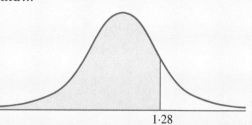

In the next example, the x values are not obvious.

(2018 Q.2)

(a) The diagram shows the standard normal curve. The shaded area represents 67% of the data.
Find the value of z_1.

(b) The percentage results in a Maths exam for a class had a mean mark of 70 with a standard deviation of 15. The percentage results in an English exam for the same class had a

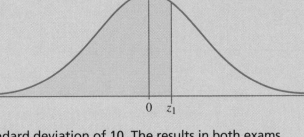

mean mark of 72 with a standard deviation of 10. The results in both exams were normally distributed.

(i) Mary got 65 in Maths and 68 in English. In which exam did Mary do better relative to the other students in the class? Justify your answer.

(ii) In English the top 15% of students were awarded an A grade. Find the least whole number mark that merited the award of an A grade in English.

(iii) Using the empirical rule, or otherwise, estimate the percentage of students in the class who scored between 52 and 82 in the English test.

Solution

(a) We need to read the normal distribution tables backwards. The area is 0·67 and this corresponds to a z-score of 0·44.

Therefore, $z_1 = 0.44$

z	0·00	0·01	0·02	0·03	0·04	0·05
0·0	0·5000	0·5040	0·5080	0·5120	0·5160	0·5199
0·1	0·5398	0·5438	0·5478	0·5517	0·5557	0·5596
0·2	0·5793	0·5832	0·5871	0·5910	0·5948	0·5987
0·3	0·6179	0·6217	0·6255	0·6293	0·6331	0·6368
0·4	0·6554	0·6591	0·6628	0·6664	0·6700	0·6736
0·5	0·6915	0·6950	0·6985	0·7019	0·7054	0·7088
0·6	0·7257	0·7291	0·7324	0·7357	0·7389	0·7422
0·7	0·7580	0·7611	0·7642	0·7673	0·7704	0·7734
0·8	0·7881	0·7910	0·7939	0·7967	0·7995	0·8023

(b) (i) Find the z-score for Mary for each exam:

Maths:

$$z_{maths} = \frac{x - \mu}{\sigma}$$

$$z_{maths} = \frac{65 - 70}{15} = -\frac{1}{3}$$

English:

$$z_{English} = \frac{x - \mu}{\sigma}$$

$$z_{English} = \frac{68 - 72}{10} = -\frac{2}{5} = -0.4$$

$$-\frac{1}{3} > -\frac{2}{5}$$

Therefore, Mary did better in her Maths exam than her English exam.

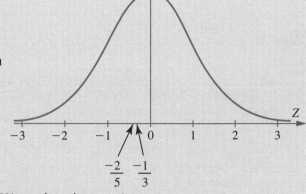

(ii) Top 15% got an A, so 85% got less than an A.
We need to read the normal distribution tables backwards.
The area is 0·85 and this corresponds to a z-score of 1·04.

$$z = \frac{x - \mu}{\sigma}$$

$$1.04 = \frac{x - 72}{10}$$

$$10.4 = x - 72$$

$$10.4 + 72 = x$$

$$82.4 = x$$

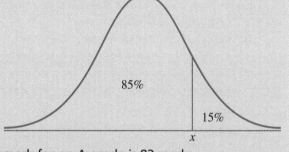

So, the least whole number mark for an A grade is 83 marks.

(iii) Applying the empirical rule, we can see that the percentage of students who scored between 52 and 82 in the English test was:

47·5% + 34%

= 81·5%

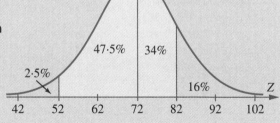

The empirical rule is covered in detail in Chapter 14 - Statistics IV

Binomial distribution (Bernoulli trials)

An experiment that satisfies the following four conditions is called a binomial distribution or a Bernoulli trial.

1. A fixed number, n, of repeated trials
2. Only two possible outcomes in each trial: success or failure
3. The trials are independent
4. The probability of a success in each trial is constant

In this situation, we let:

$p = P(\text{success})$ and $q = P(\text{failure})$, where $(p + q) = 1$.

$$P(r \text{ successes}) = \binom{n}{r}p^r q^{n-r}$$

Method

1. Write down n, the number of trials.
2. Calculate p and q ($q = 1 - p$).
3. Let r = number of successes required.
4. Use the formula above.

Examples of Bernoulli trials are:

1. Tossing coins   **2.** Shots in a competition   **3.** A search for defective products

Example

A factory manufactures light bulbs. Over a long period of time it was found that 5% of the bulbs were defective. An inspector randomly selects 10 bulbs. Find, correct to three decimal places, the probability that:

(i) exactly four bulbs are defective

(ii) at least three bulbs are defective.

Solution

(i) $P(\text{exactly four defective bulbs})$

$$= \binom{10}{4}(0{\cdot}05)^4(0{\cdot}95)^6 = 0{\cdot}001 \qquad \text{(correct to three decimal places)}$$

(ii) We first calculate the probability of obtaining no defective bulbs, one defective bulb and two defective bulbs and then subtract this from 1.

$P(\text{no defective}) + P(\text{one defective}) + P(\text{two defective})$

$$= \binom{10}{0}(0{\cdot}05)^0(0{\cdot}95)^{10} + \binom{10}{1}(0{\cdot}05)^1(0{\cdot}95)^9 + \binom{10}{2}(0{\cdot}05)^2(0{\cdot}95)^8$$

$$= 0{\cdot}598736939 + 0{\cdot}315124704 + 0{\cdot}074634798$$

$$= 0{\cdot}988 \qquad \text{(correct to three decimal places)}$$

$\therefore \ P(\text{at least three defective bulbs}) = 1 - 0{\cdot}988 = 0{\cdot}012$

exam Q

(2015 Q.1)

An experiment consists of throwing two fair, standard, six-sided dice and noting the sum of the two numbers thrown. If the sum is 9 or greater it is recorded as a 'win' (W). If the sum is 8 or less it is recorded as a 'loss' (L).

(a) Draw a two-way table to show all possible outcomes of the experiment.

(b) (i) Find the probability of a win on one throw of the two dice.

   (ii) Find the probability that each of 3 successive throws of the two dice results in a loss. Give your answer correct to four decimal places.

(c) The experiment is repeated until a total of 3 wins occur. Find the probability that the third win occurs on the tenth throw of the two dice. Give your answer correct to four decimal places.

Solution

(a) Completed two-way table:

				Die 2			
		1	**2**	**3**	**4**	**5**	**6**
Die 1	**1**	L	L	L	L	L	L
	2	L	L	L	L	L	L
	3	L	L	L	L	L	W
	4	L	L	L	L	W	W
	5	L	L	L	W	W	W
	6	L	L	W	W	W	W

(b) (i) $P(\text{win}) = \dfrac{10}{36} = \dfrac{5}{18}$

   (ii) $P(\text{loss}) \times P(\text{loss}) \times P(\text{loss}) = \dfrac{26}{36} \times \dfrac{26}{36} \times \dfrac{26}{36} = \left(\dfrac{26}{36}\right)^3 = 0.3767$

(c)

Throw	1	2	3	4	5	6	7	8	9	10
Result				Wins 2 out of 9						win

$P(\text{3rd win on 10th throw}) = \left[\binom{9}{2}\left(\dfrac{10}{36}\right)^2\left(\dfrac{26}{36}\right)^7\right] \times \dfrac{10}{36}$

$P(\text{3rd win on10th throw}) = 0.0791$

(2017 Q.1)

When Conor rings Ciara's house, the probability that Ciara answers the phone is $\frac{1}{5}$.

(a) Conor rings Ciara's house once every day for 7 consecutive days. Find the probability that she will answer the phone on the 2nd, 4th, and 6th days but not on the other days.

(b) Find the probability that she will answer the phone for the 4th time on the 7th day.

(c) Conor rings her house once every day for n days. Write, in terms of *n*, the probability that Ciara will answer the phone at least once.

(d) Find the minimum value of n for which the probability that Ciara will answer the phone at least once is greater than 99%.

Solution

(a)

Day	1	2	3	4	5	6	7
Answer	No	Yes	No	Yes	No	Yes	No

$$P\text{(answer on 2, 4 and 6)} = \frac{4}{5} \times \frac{1}{5} \times \frac{4}{5} \times \frac{1}{5} \times \frac{4}{5} \times \frac{1}{5} \times \frac{4}{5}$$

$$P\text{(answer on 2, 4 and 6)} = \frac{256}{78125}$$

(b) For Ciara to answer the phone for the 4th time on the 7th call means that she must have answered exactly 3 of the first 6 calls and then she also answers the 7th call.

Day	1	2	3	4	5	6	7
Answer		Answers 3 and misses 3					Yes

$$P\text{(4th answer on 7th call)} = \left[\binom{6}{3}\left(\frac{1}{5}\right)^3 \left(\frac{4}{5}\right)^3 \right] \times \frac{1}{5}$$

$$P\text{(4th answer on 7th call)} = \left[\frac{256}{3125} \right] \times \frac{1}{5}$$

$$P\text{(4th answer on 7th call)} = \frac{256}{15625}$$

(c) $P\text{(Answer at least once)} = 1 - P\text{(answers none of the } n \text{ calls)}$

$$P\text{(Answer at least once)} = 1 - \left(\frac{4}{5}\right)^n$$

(d) $P\text{(Answer at least once)} > 0\cdot99$

$$1 - \left(\frac{4}{5}\right)^n > 0\cdot99$$

Find the value for n for which the probability is equal to 0.99 and then interpret your answer:

$$1 - \left(\frac{4}{5}\right)^n = 0.99$$

$$1 - 0.99 = \left(\frac{4}{5}\right)^n$$

$$0.01 = \left(\frac{4}{5}\right)^n$$

$$\log_{\frac{4}{5}} 0.01 = n$$

$$20.63770 = n \qquad \qquad \text{Therefore, minimum value of } n = 21$$

Probability distributions

Expected value and standard deviation of a discrete random variable x

The mean value, μ, of the random variable x is called the **expected value** of x and is written as $E(x)$. The standard deviation is denoted by $\sigma(x)$.

$$\Sigma P(x) = 1$$

$$\boxed{\text{Mean} = \mu = E(x) = \Sigma x P(x)}$$

A game is considered fair if $E(x) = 0$.   (expected value = 0)

(2018 Q.1)

In a competition, Mary has a probability of $\frac{1}{20}$ of winning, a probability of $\frac{1}{10}$ of finishing in second place, and a probability of $\frac{1}{4}$ of finishing in third place. If she wins the competition, she gets €9,000. If she comes second she gets €7,000 and if she comes third she gets €3,000. In all other cases she gets nothing. Each participant in the competition must pay €2,000 to enter.

(a) Find the expected value of Mary's loss if she enters the competition

(b) Each of the 3 prizes in the competition above is increased by the same amount (€x) but the entry fee is unchanged. For example, if Mary wins the competition now, she would get €(9000 + x). Mary now expects to break even. Find the value of x.

Solution

(a) Expected pay out = $\frac{1}{20}(9000) + \frac{1}{10}(7000) + \frac{1}{4}(3000)$

Expected pay out = 450 + 700 + 750

Expected pay out = €1,900

Expected loss = Pay out − Pay in

Expected loss = €1,900 − €2,000

Expected loss = −€100

This means that, on average, each person playing would lose €100 and so the competition organisers would expect to gain €100 from each person playing.

(b) For Mary to break even, the expected pay out = pay in = €2000

Expected pay out = $\frac{1}{20}(9000 + x) + \frac{1}{10}(7000 + x) + \frac{1}{4}(3000 + x)$

$2000 = 450 + \frac{1}{20}(x) + 700 + \frac{1}{10}(x) + 750 + \frac{1}{4}(x)$

$2000 = 1900 + \frac{1}{20}(x) + \frac{1}{10}(x) + \frac{1}{4}(x)$

$100 = \frac{2}{5}(x)$

€250 = x

(2016 Q.6)

A local sports club is planning to run a weekly lotto. To win the jackpot of €1,000, contestants must match one letter chosen from the 26 letters in the alphabet and two numbers chosen, in the correct order, from the numbers 0 to 9. In this lottery, repetition of numbers is allowed (e.g. M, 3, 3 is an outcome).

(a) Calculate the probability that M, 3, 3 would be the winning outcome in a particular week.

(b) If a contestant matches the letter only, or the letter and one number (but not both numbers), they will win €50. Using the table below, or otherwise, find how much the club should expect to make or lose on each play, correct to the nearest cent, if they charge €2 per play.

Event	Payout (x) €	Probability (P(x))	x.P(x)
Win jackpot			
Match letter and first number only			
Match letter and second number only			
Match letter and neither number			
Fail to win			

(c) The club estimates that the average number of plays per week will be 845. If the club wants to make an average profit of €600 per week from the lotto, how much should the club charge per play, correct to the nearest cent?

Solution

(a) $P(M) \times P(3) \times P(3) = \dfrac{1}{26} \times \dfrac{1}{10} \times \dfrac{1}{10} = \dfrac{1}{2600}$

(b) Win jackpot has a payout of €1,000.

If the contestant does not match the correct letter, they fail to win and has a a payout of €0.

$P(\text{letter}) \times P(\text{number}) \times P(\text{wrong number}) = \dfrac{1}{26} \times \dfrac{1}{10} \times \dfrac{9}{10} = \dfrac{9}{2600}$

$P(\text{letter}) \times P(\text{wrong number}) \times P(\text{number}) = \dfrac{1}{26} \times \dfrac{9}{10} \times \dfrac{1}{10} = \dfrac{9}{2600}$

$P(\text{letter}) \times P(\text{wrong number}) \times P(\text{wrong number}) = \dfrac{1}{26} \times \dfrac{9}{10} \times \dfrac{9}{10} = \dfrac{81}{2600}$

Event	Payout (x) €	Probability (P(x))	x.P(x)
Win jackpot	1000	$\dfrac{1}{2600}$	$\dfrac{1000}{2600}$
Match letter and first number only	50	$\dfrac{9}{2600}$	$\dfrac{450}{2600}$
Match letter and second number only	50	$\dfrac{9}{2600}$	$\dfrac{450}{2600}$
Match letter and neither number	50	$\dfrac{81}{2600}$	$\dfrac{4050}{2600}$
Fail to win	0	$\dfrac{2500}{2600}$	0

$$\text{Estimated payout} = \sum x.P(x) = \frac{1000}{2600} + \frac{450}{2600} + \frac{450}{2600} + \frac{4050}{2600} + 0$$

$$= \frac{5950}{2600}$$

$$= €2·29$$

This means that on average, for each person that plays, the club will take in €2 (the cost to play) but payout €2·29. So they will, on average, lose 29c per play.

(c) Desired profit per play $= \dfrac{\text{Desired income}}{\text{Number of players}}$

Desired profit per play $= \dfrac{€600}{845} = €0·71$

The club are currently losing 29c per play. They want to gain 71c per play, so they need to increase the price of a play by €1.

So, the new price per play = €3.

11

Statistics I:
Statistical Investigations

- ☐ To know the types of statistical data
- ☐ To be clear on the differences between populations and samples
- ☐ To learn about some sampling methods and random sampling
- ☐ To know and be able to accurately describe the various ways of selecting a sample

Introduction to statistics

Statistics deals with the collection, presentation, analysis and interpretation of data. Insurance (of people and property), which now dominates many aspects of our lives, utilises statistical methodology. Social scientists, psychologists, pollsters, medical researchers, governments and many others use statistical methodology to study behaviours of populations.

Statistics deals with events which have more than one possible outcome. If you buy a sandwich in the school canteen priced at €2·20 and offer the cashier a €5 note, you should receive €2·80 in change. This is not statistics, as there is (or should be) only one amount of change possible.

If the school canteen manager wishes to know how much students spend when visiting the canteen, this is statistics because different customers spend different amounts.

The quantity which varies (in this case, the amount of money) is called a **variable**.

A collection of variables are referred to as **data** in statistics.

An **observation** is the value of a variable for one particular element of the sample or population, for example your sandwich purchase.

A **data set** is all the observations of a particular variable for the elements of the sample, for example a complete list of the canteen transactions of all students from your class on a certain day.

Types of data

Data are a collection of facts. It can be numbers, measurements, descriptions or observations. On our course we consider **two** types of data: quantitative and qualitative.

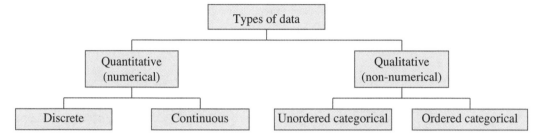

Quantitative data (numerical)

Discrete numerical data	Continuous numerical data
Discrete numerical data are data which can only have certain values.	Continuous data are data which can take any numerical value within a certain range.
Examples are the number of students in a school, number of goals scored in a match and shoe sizes (including half-sizes).	Examples are time, weight, height, temperature, pressure and area. (Accuracy depends on the measuring device used.)

Qualitative data (non-numerical)

Unordered categorical data	Ordered categorical data
Unordered categorical data are data that can be counted but only described in words without any order or ranking.	Ordered categorical data are data that can be counted but only described in words and have an order or ranking.
Examples are colours, names, type of car and gender (male or female).	Examples are examination grades, football divisions and income groups.

Note: Ordered categorical data are sometimes called **ordinal data**.

If a code is used to put data into a category, the data is called **nominal data**. The data are assigned a code in the form of a number or letter. The numbers or letters are simply labels. For example, males could be coded as 1 and females as 2. Marital status can be coded as M if married or S if single. Nominal data can be counted but not measured or ordered.

Primary and secondary data

Primary data (first-hand data) are data that you collect yourself or are collected by someone under your direct supervision.

Secondary data (second-hand data) is data that have already been collected and made available from an external source such as newspapers, government departments, organisations or the Internet.

Primary and secondary data have their advantages and disadvantages.

Data	Advantages	Disadvantages
Primary	Know how it was obtained Accuracy is also known	Time consuming Can be expensive
Secondary	Easy and cheap to obtain	Could be out of date May have mistakes and be biased Unknown source of collection

Example

Classify each of the following variables in terms of data type (qualitative/quantitative, etc.).

 (i) Colours of flowers
 (ii) Number of bicycles owned by students in your school
 (iii) Ages of students in a primary school
 (iv) Volumes of contents of water bottles
 (v) Countries of birth of Irish citizens
 (vi) Number of strokes to complete a round of golf
 (vii) Proportions of faulty fridges in samples of size 50
 (viii) Diameter of tennis balls
 (ix) Examination grades
 (x) Makes of TV in a salesroom

Solution

 (i) Qualitative – unordered categorical
 (ii) Quantitative – discrete numerical
 (iii) Quantitative – continuous numerical (but age in years is discrete)
 (iv) Quantitative – continuous numerical
 (v) Qualitative – unordered categorical
 (vi) Quantitative – discrete numerical
 (vii) Quantitative – discrete numerical
 (viii) Quantitative – continuous numerical
 (ix) Qualitative – ordered categorical (ordinal)
 (x) Qualitative – unordered categorical

Populations and samples

To find out the average weight of men in Ireland we could, in theory, measure them all. In practice this would be almost impossible. Instead we can measure the weights of a sample.

Provided the sample is carefully chosen, we can obtain almost as much information from the sample as from measuring the weight of every man in Ireland.

In statistics we distinguish between a population and a sample.

A **population** is all the possible data and a **sample** is part of the data.

The population is all the possible data

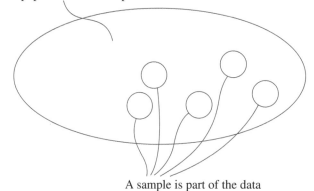

A sample is part of the data

The difference between a population and a sample is of great importance.

Sampling is useful because it reduces the amount of data you need to collect and process. It also allows you to carry out a test without affecting all the population. For example, the contents of a sample of tubs of margarine, from a large batch, might be weighed to ensure that the actual contents matched that claimed on the label. Emptying the tubs to weigh the margarine makes them unsaleable, so it would be ridiculous to weigh the contents of the whole population of tubs.

Samples

A sample is a small part of the population selected for surveying. A random sample is a sample in which every member of the population has an equal chance of being selected and the selections are made independently. Notice this is sampling with replacement. When a population is very large compared with the size of the sample, the difference between sampling with and without replacement is negligible. Random sampling without replacement is considered to be a modification to random sampling with replacement.

Sampling methods

There are various ways of actually selecting a sample.

1. **Simple random sampling:** Sometimes called the lottery method, this is the best method (from a theoretical viewpoint) of selecting a truly random sample. All the

items in a population are given a number and pieces of paper, each with one number on it, are placed in a drum or hat. The numbers are selected one at a time until the required sample size is reached. This method is very tedious, particularly for very large populations. You must bear in mind that although the method of selection is free from personal bias, there is no guarantee that the resulting sample is unbiased. Sometimes a computer simulation may be used instead.

2. **Stratified sampling:** This method uses the natural divisions of a population, such as gender, age, weight, occupation or colour. These are the strata and they can be used to ensure all sections of the population are adequately represented in any sample. It is essential when using this method to know in advance the proportion of the population in each natural stratum and to take account of this when selecting the sample. The strata chosen must be readily determinable. They should be exhaustive and mutually exclusive (that is, covering the whole population and each item in the population belongs to one and only one stratum).

3. **Cluster sampling:** This consists of a list of groups of individuals rather than individuals themselves. A random sample of these groups or clusters is taken and then observations are made on every individual within these selected groups. Cluster samples are popular with biologists, agricultural scientists and geographers. Their technique is to cover the survey area with a grid of numbered squares. A random sample of the squares is taken and a complete study/investigation is made of the selected squares, whether it be plant species, incidence of disease or number of bacteria. It is preferable to divide the population/area into a large number of small clusters rather than a small number of large clusters.

4. **Quota sampling:** This method allows the interviewer a certain amount of discretion when collecting the data. Quotas for different sections of the population are set and the interviewer is allowed to select the sample according to these quotas, for example 30 teenagers, 15 female pensioners, 20 farmers, etc. Quota sampling is used to ensure that the sample contains members of the population in the desired proportions. As a result, the interviewer can be a source of bias, as only the views of those chosen by the interviewer are recorded. Quota sampling is an example of non-random sampling. Its main advantage is that it reduces survey time and cost.

exam focus

Candidates are expected to learn by rote the sampling methods described above.

exam Q

Q7 (a) (i) 2013 asked: Explain what is meant by a stratified random sample.
Awarded 5 marks = $1\frac{2}{3}$% of the exam.

An Irish sports journalist intends to write a book about the English football premiership. She will analyse all premiership matches in the season. For each match she records whether it is a home win, an away win or a draw. She also records, for each match, the total number of goals scored and the amount of time played before a goal is scored. Reference books showed that in the previous season the mean number of goals per game was 2·345. On the first weekend of the season she recorded the number of goals scored in each match and calculated the mean number of goals per match as 2·6.

After carefully reading the above passage, identify an example of:

(i) a population
(ii) a sample
(iii) a qualitative variable
(iv) a discrete variable
(v) a continuous variable
(vi) primary data
(vii) secondary data.

Solution

(i) Populations mentioned in the passage will relate to all premiership matches played in the season and are either the results, the total number of goals or the amounts of time played before a goal is scored.

(ii) A sample would be the total number of goals scored in each match played, for example on the fourth weekend of the season.

(iii) A qualitative variable would be the result of matches: home win (H), away win (A), draw (D).

(iv) A discrete variable would be the number of goals scored in each match.

(v) A continuous variable would be the amount of time played before a goal is scored.

(vi) Primary data would be the data the journalist collected in that season.

(vii) Secondary data (obtained from a reference book) would be the mean number of goals per game in the previous season.

Sampling without bias

When you are selecting a sample, you need to avoid bias (anything which makes the sample unrepresentative). For example, if you want to estimate how often residents of Waterford visit the cinema in a year, it would be foolish to stand outside a cinema as the audience is coming out and ask people as they pass. This would give a biased sample, as all the people you ask would have been to the cinema at least once that year. You can avoid bias by taking a random sample.

Random sampling

> - For a sample to be random, every member of the population must have an equal chance of being selected.
> - A random sample chosen without replacement is called a simple random sample.

Suppose the population consists of the heights of 100 students in a college and you wish to take a sample of size 5. The students' names are arranged in alphabetical order and numbered 00 to 99. A number between 00 and 19 is selected by lottery methods. For example, place 20 equally sized balls numbered 00 to 19 in a bag and ask a blindfolded assistant to pick one out. This student and every 20th one thereafter are chosen and their heights measured. That is, if the number 13 is selected, then the students numbered 13, 33, 53, 73 and 93 are chosen. Every student would have an equal chance of being chosen. However, a sister and brother who were next to each other in the alphabetical list could never both be included in the same sample, so this is **not** a random sample.

Usually, if you decide to choose five students at random you intend to choose five different students and would not consider choosing the same student twice. This is known as sampling without replacement.

Example

An inspector tests every 80th assembly coming off a production line. Is this a good random sample of the assemblies? Justify your answer.

Solution

It is not a good random sample because, for example, two adjacent assemblies could not both be sampled.

However, it is a commonly used system in quality control.

It is vital in the exam to have the ability and confidence to make a statement and back it up with a reason. The above example shows a system of selecting samples that is not strictly random but works very well in practice.

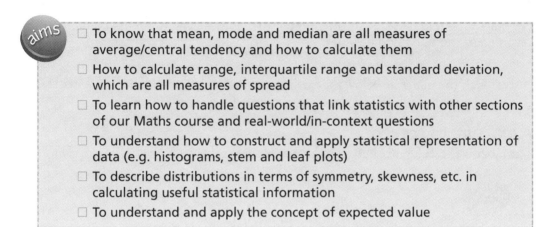

Averages

There are many types of averages. Three that we meet initially are called the mean, the mode and median. They are also known as measures of central tendency.

Mean

The mean is the proper name for what most people call the average.

key point

The mean of a set of values is defined as the sum of all the values divided by the number of values.

That is:

$$\text{Mean} = \frac{\text{Sum of all the values}}{\text{Number of values}}$$

The formula is often written as: $\mu = \dfrac{\Sigma x}{n}$ (see *booklet of formulae and tables*, page 33)

Mode

key point

The mode of a set of items is the item that occurs most often. If there are no repeated items, then the mode does not exist.

Median

When the values are arranged in ascending or descending order of size, then the median is the middle value. If the number of values is even, then the median is the average of the two middle values.

Note: Half the values lie below the median and half the values lie above the median. The median is also called the second quartile (Q_2).

A measure of spread

The range is the difference between the highest data value and the lowest data value.

Range = highest value − lowest value

The interquartile range is more useful than the range, but is more complicated to calculate.

Here is a diagram to help clarify the situation.

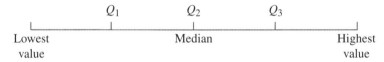

Q_1 Q_2 Q_3

Lowest value   Median   Highest value

The median (Q_2) is the value that subdivides the ordered data into two halves.

The quartiles (Q_1 and Q_3) subdivide the data into quarters.

The interquartile range is upper quartile minus lower quartile = $Q_3 − Q_1$.

Example

Four numbers are:
$$2, 13, x, 5$$

(i) If their mode is 13, find the value of x.

(ii) If their mean is 7, find the value of x.

(iii) If their range is 12, find the possible values of x.

(iv) If their median is 7, find the value of x.

Solution

(i) Mode = 13 $\Rightarrow$ the most common number in the list 2, 13, x, 5 is 13.

$\Rightarrow x = 13$

(ii) Mean $= \mu = \dfrac{2 + 13 + x + 5}{4} = 7$

$$20 + x = 28$$
$$x = 8$$

(iii) If x is not an end value, then the range $= 13 - 2 = 11 \neq 12$. Hence, we need to consider two (ascending) cases.

2, 5, 13, x	x, 2, 5, 13
Range $= x - 2$	Range $= 13 - x$
$12 = x - 2$	$12 = 13 - x$
$14 = x$	$x = 1$

(iv) The median of four numbers is the average of the two middle numbers when the numbers are arranged in ascending (or descending) order.

Now x cannot be the smallest number because x, 2, 5, 13 has

median $= \dfrac{2 + 5}{2} = 3\dfrac{1}{2} \neq 7.$

Similarly, x cannot be the largest number because 2, 5, 13, x has

median $= \dfrac{5 + 13}{2} = 9 \neq 7.$

Thus, either 2, x, 5, 13 $\boxed{\text{or}}$ 2, 5, x, 13 is possible.

Then $\dfrac{5 + x}{2} = 7$

$$5 + x = 14$$
$$x = 9$$

(2014, Q7 (a) and (b))

Table 1 below gives details of the number of males (M) and females (F) aged 15 years and over at work, unemployed, or not in the labour force for each year in the period 2004 to 2013.

Table 1									
Labour Force Statistics 2004 to 2013 – Persons aged 15 years and over (000s)									
Year	At work			Unemployed			Not in labour force			Total
	M	F	Total	M	F	Total	M	F	Total	
2004	1045·9	738·9	1784·8	79·6	31·6	111·2	457·1	854·2	1311·3	3207·3
2005	1087·3	779·7	1867·0	81·3	33·5	114·8	459·5	846·6	1306·1	3287·9
2006	1139·8	815·1	1954·9	80·6	38·1	118·7	457·6	844·9	1302·5	3376·1
2007	1184·0	865·6	2049·6	84·3	39·2	123·5	472·3	852·7	1325·1	3498·2
2008	1170·9	889·5	2060·4	106·3	41·0	147·3	494·8	872·5	1367·3	3575·0
2009	1039·8	863·5	1903·3	234·0	82·4	316·4	505·6	874·9	1380·5	3600·2
2010	985·1	843·5	1828·6	257·6	98·2	355·8	529·2	884·6	1413·8	3598·2
2011	970·2	843·2	1813·4	260·7	103·4	364·1	540·1	881·5	1421·6	3599·1
2012	949·6	823·8	1773·4	265·2	108·0	373·2	546·5	896·9	1443·4	3590·0
2013	974·4	829·0	1803·4	227·7	102·3	330·0	557·8	895·0	1452·8	3586·2

(Source: Central Statistics Office http://www.cso.ie)

(a) Suggest two categories of people, aged 15 years and over, who might not be in the labour force.

(b) Find the median and the interquartile range of the total persons at work over the period.

10 marks awarded for the very easy part (a). 5 marks awarded for the more difficult part (b). Candidates performed very badly in part (b).

Solution

(a) Categories of people aged 15 years and over who might not be in the labour force includes:

Students, retired, stay at home persons, long term illness ...

Only two categories required.

(b) For the median, rearrange the 10 totals in ascending (or descending) order

1773·4, 1784·8, 1803·4, 1813·4, 1828·6, 1867, 1903·3, 1954·9, 2049·6, 2060·4

Median halfway

$$\text{Median} = \frac{1828·6 + 1867}{2} = 1847·8$$

For the interquartile range, rewrite the 10 totals

1773·4, 1784·8, 1803·4, 1813·4, 1828·6, 1867, 1903·3, 1954·9, 2049·6, 2060·4

Lower quartile   Upper quartile

Interquartile range = upper quartile − lower quartile

$$= 1954·9 − 1803·4 = 151·5$$

Example

45 students in a class each recorded the number of whole minutes, x,

spent doing experiments on Monday. The total of the results is $\sum_{i=1}^{45} x_i = 2{,}232$.

(i) Find the mean number of minutes the students spent doing experiments on Monday.

(ii) Two new students joined the class and reported that they spent 37 minutes and 34 minutes, respectively. Calculate the new mean including these two students.

Solution

(i) $$\text{Mean} = \frac{\text{Total}}{\text{Number of students}}$$

$$= \frac{\sum_{i=1}^{45} x_i}{45} = \frac{2{,}232}{45} = 49·6 \text{ mins}$$

(ii) Total for 47 students $= 2{,}232 + 37 + 34 = 2{,}303$

$$\text{New mean} = \frac{2{,}303}{47} = 49$$

Variability of data

Each of these sets of numbers has a mean of 4, but the spread of each set is different:

(a) 4, 4, 4, 4, 4   (b) 1, 3, $3\frac{1}{2}$, 4·2, 8·3   (c) −196, −49, 25, 66, 174

There is no variability in set **(a)**, while the numbers in set **(c)** are much more spread out than in set **(b)**.

key point

We have three ways of measuring the variability or spread of a distribution: the **range**, the **interquartile range** and the **standard deviation**. We already met the range and the interquartile range.

The standard deviation (σ)

The standard deviation (σ, pronounced 'sigma') is an important and useful measure of spread. It gives a measure of the deviations from the mean, μ. It is calculated using all the values in the distribution.

To calculate σ:

- For each reading x, calculate $x - \mu$, its deviation from the mean.
- Square this deviation to give $(x - \mu)^2$. Note that irrespective of whether the deviation was positive or negative, this is now positive.
- Find $\Sigma (x - \mu)^2$, the sum of all these values.
- Find the average by dividing the sum by n, the number of readings. This gives $$\frac{\Sigma (x - \mu)^2}{n}.$$
- Finally, take the positive square root of $\dfrac{\Sigma (x - \mu)^2}{n}$ to obtain the standard deviation, σ.

The standard deviation, σ, of a set of n numbers with mean μ is given by:

$$\sigma = \sqrt{\frac{\Sigma (x - \mu)^2}{n}}$$ (see *booklet of formulae and tables*, page 33)

Hence, the standard deviation for:

(a) 4, 4, 4, 4, 4 is calculated to find $\sigma = 0$
(b) 1, 3, $3\frac{1}{2}$, 4·2, 8·3 is calculated to find $\sigma = 2\cdot4$
(c) -196, -49, 25, 66, 174 is calculated to find $\sigma = 123\cdot3$

key point

Set **(a)**, with data not spread out about the mean, has $\sigma = 0$, while set **(c)** has a much higher standard deviation than set **(b)**, confirming that **(c)** is much more spread about the mean.

Properties of the standard deviation

- σ measures spread about the mean and should be used only when the mean is chosen as the measure of centre.
- $\sigma = 0$ only when there is *no spread*. This happens only when all observations have the same value. Otherwise, $\sigma > 0$. As the observations become more spread out about their mean, σ gets larger. We can say that the higher the standard deviation, the greater the variability in the data.
- σ, like the mean, μ, is affected by extreme values.
- The square root in the formula for $\sigma = \sqrt{\dfrac{\Sigma(x - \mu)^2}{n}}$ ensures that the x-values and the standard deviation are in the same units.

You can use your calculator to calculate the standard deviation, σ. Calculator instructions can be found at the end of this book.

The first five terms of an arithmetic sequence are e, f, 17, g, h. Calculate the mean of these five numbers. Justify your answer.

Solution

For an arithmetic sequence we can write:

$$a - 2d \qquad a - d \qquad a \qquad a + d \qquad a + 2d$$

To get the mean of five numbers we use $\frac{\Sigma x}{5}$:

$$= \frac{(a - 2d) + (a - d) + (a) + (a + d) + (a + 2d)}{5}$$

$$= \frac{5a}{5}$$

$$= a$$

$\therefore$ Mean = a = The middle term in the arithmetic sequence. e, f, 17, g, h is the given arithmetic sequence.

$\therefore$ Mean = middle term = 17.

The above work is my justification.

Sequences are covered by the chapters Pattern I and Pattern II in *LSMS Maths Higher Level Paper 1*.

The first four terms of a geometric sequence are:

$$\begin{array}{c|c|c|c}\hline x & 6 & 9 & y \\\end{array} \longrightarrow$$

   x 6   9 y

(i) Find the value of x.

(ii) Find the value of the common ratio of the sequence.

(iii) Hence, find:

  (a) the mean

  (b) the standard deviation of $\{x, 6, 9, y\}$ correct to one decimal place.

Solution

(i) In a geometric sequence:

$$\text{Common ratio} = \frac{\text{2nd term}}{\text{1st term}} = \frac{\text{3rd term}}{\text{2nd term}} = \frac{\text{4th term}}{\text{3rd term}} = \cdots$$

Gives $\dfrac{6}{x} = \dfrac{9}{6} = \dfrac{y}{9}$

Now $\dfrac{6}{x} = \dfrac{9}{6}$

   $(6)(6) = (9)(x)$ (multiply both sides by $6x$)

      $36 = 9x$

       $4 = x$

(ii) Common ratio $= \dfrac{6}{x} = \dfrac{6}{4} = \dfrac{3}{2}$

(iii) Now $y = \dfrac{3}{2}(9)$

   $\Rightarrow y = 13 \cdot 5$

  (a) Mean of $\{4, 6, 9, 13 \cdot 5\}$

    $= \dfrac{4 + 6 + 9 + 13 \cdot 5}{4}$

    $= 8 \cdot 125$

    $= 8 \cdot 1$ (correct to one decimal place)

(b) Standard deviation of {4, 6, 9, 13·5}

$$\sigma = \sqrt{\frac{\Sigma(x - \mu)^2}{n}}$$

$$\sigma = \sqrt{\frac{(4 - 8 \cdot 1)^2 + (6 - 8 \cdot 1)^2 + (9 - 8 \cdot 1)^2 + (13 \cdot 5 - 8 \cdot 1)^2}{4}}$$

$$= 3 \cdot 577$$

$\sigma = 3 \cdot 6$ (correct to one decimal place)

Alternatively, you may use your calculator to enter the data and find $\sigma = 3 \cdot 6$.

In the previous exam questions, basic knowledge of arithmetic and geometric sequence are required before you can successfully tackle the statistics question. This type of question, which involves cross-over of topics, features prominently in the exam.

Histogram

A histogram is often used to display information contained in a frequency distribution. It is similar to a bar chart with no gaps between the bars, and the two are often confused. The essential characteristic of a histogram is that the **area of each rectangle represents the frequency**, and the sum of the areas of the rectangles is equal to the sum of the frequencies.

Bar charts can only represent discrete data, while histograms can represent discrete or continuous data.

Distributions and shapes of histograms

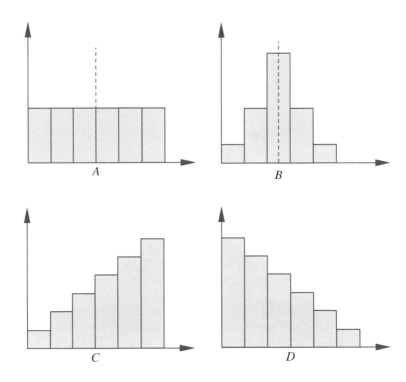

Histograms come in many different shapes. Above we have four histograms, all with different shapes:

A has uniform distribution and is symmetric (balanced).
B has a symmetric shape.
C has no axis of symmetry. It is negatively skewed, that is, there is a tail at the negative end of the distribution.
D has no axis of symmetry and is positively skewed.

The diagram below shows a skewed frequency distribution. Vertical lines have been drawn through the mean, mode and median. Identify which is which by inserting the relevant letter in the spaces below.

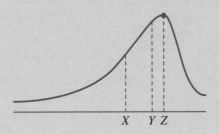

Mean =   Mode =   Median =

Solution

The mode (most common) is associated with the highest point on the curve $\Rightarrow$ mode = Z.

The median (middle) is between the mean and the mode $\Rightarrow$ median = Y.

Finally, the mean = X.

The shapes of the histograms of four different sets of data are shown below.

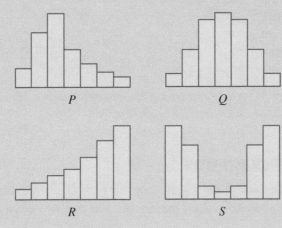

(i) Complete the table below, indicating whether the statement is correct (✓) or incorrect (×) with respect to each data set.

	P	Q	R	S
The data are skewed to the left				
The data are skewed to the right				
The mean is equal to the median				
The mean is greater than the median				
There is a single mode				

(ii) Assume that the four histograms are drawn on the same scale. State which of them has the largest standard deviation. Justify your answer.

Solution

(i)

	P	Q	R	S
The data are skewed to the left	×	×	✓	×
The data are skewed to the right	✓	×	×	×
The mean is equal to the median	×	✓	×	✓
The mean is greater than the median*	✓	×	×	×
There is a single mode	✓	✓	✓	×

*Note in Q and S the mean is equal to the median.

(ii) S has the largest deviation because a lot of the data are far from the mean.

Stem and leaf diagrams

Histograms provide an easy to understand summary of the distribution of data. However, they do not show the values themselves. For this we need a stem and leaf diagram.

Example

The ordered stem and leaf plot shows the times taken by 24 students to complete an exercise.

Stem	Leaf
0	6 8 8 9
1	1 4 5 7 7 8
2	0 1 1 3 4 5 5 6
3	2 2 6 6 7 8

Key: $0\,|\,9 = 9$ minutes

Use this stem and leaf plot to calculate the following.

(i) The range   (ii) The median   (iii) The lower quartile

(iv) The upper quartile   (v) The interquartile range

Solution

(i) Range = largest value − smallest value = $38 - 6 = 32$ minutes.

(ii) The median mark (Q_2) is the time value halfway through the distribution. The halfway value is between the 12th and 13th values.

$= \frac{1}{2}[21 + 21] = 21$

∴ The median = 21 minutes.

(iii) The lower quartile (Q_1) is the value one-quarter of the way through the distribution. This one-quarter value is between the 6th and 7th values.

$= \frac{1}{2}[14 + 15] = 14\frac{1}{2}$

∴ The lower quartile $(Q_1) = 14\frac{1}{2}$ minutes.

(iv) The upper quartile (Q_3) is the value three-quarters of the way through the distribution. This three-quarters value is between the 18th and 19th values.

$= \frac{1}{2}[26 + 32] = 29$

∴ The upper quartile $(Q_3) = 29$ minutes.

(v) The interquartile range

$= Q_3 - Q_1 = 29 - 14\frac{1}{2} = 14\frac{1}{2}$ minutes.

Always use an **ordered** stem and leaf diagram.

An educator believes that new Maths methods will help Leaving Certificate students improve their maths grades. She arranges for a Leaving Cert class of 21 students to take part in new Maths methods for a one-year period. A control class of 24 Leaving Cert students follow the traditional maths methods. At the end of the year a maths test is given to all students. The results in percentages are given on the ordered back-to-back stem and leaf plots.

4	3	1 9
5 4	4	2 2
8 7 6 2	5	1 3 7 9 9 9
8 6 6 3 3 1	6	0 6 2 8
7 6 3 2 2	7	1 1 3 5
8 5 4	8	1 2 8

Write down four errors in the above ordered back-to-back stem and leaf plots.

Although it is not used in this example, back-to-back stem and leaf plots allow us to compare two data sets.

Solution

Error 1: The plot does not indicate which group is traditional and which is new Maths.

Error 2: The right-hand line

6	0 6 2 8

is not ordered. It should read:

6	0 2 6 8

Error 3: There are 21 readings on both sides of the plot. One side should have 24 readings.

Error 4: No key on either side.

Right-hand side $7|3 = 73\%$

Left-hand side $6|5 = 56\%$

The population of Ireland is ageing, though less rapidly than in other developed countries. Here is an ordered stem and leaf plot of the percents of residents aged 65 and over in the 32 counties according to a recent census. The stems are whole percents and the leaves are tenths of a percent.

(i) There are two outliers: County Leitrim has the highest percent of older residents and County Dublin has the lowest. What are the percentages for these two counties?

(ii) Ignoring Leitrim and Dublin, describe the shape and spread of this distribution.

Stem	Leaf
5	9
6	
7	
8	
9	6 7
10	6
11	0 2 3 6 7
12	0 1 1 1 4 4 5 7 9
13	1 2 3 3 3 8 8
14	0 7 8 9
15	3 6
16	
17	6

Solution

(i) 17·6% for Leitrim
5·9% for Dublin

(ii) The mean is located at the *central stem* of the stem and leaf plot (or the central rectangle of the histogram), as in the diagram below. Since the mean is at the centre, the shape is symmetrical.

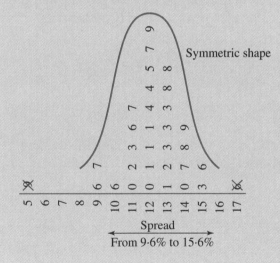

Symmetric shape

Spread
From 9·6% to 15·6%

key point

Outliers are values that are noticeably more extreme than the majority of scores.

13 Statistics III: Scatter Graphs and Correlation

aims
- ☐ Know where to find (and apply) the relevant statistical information in the *booklet of formulae and tables*
- ☐ Know how to describe correlation in words and numbers
- ☐ Know how to draw and interpret scatter plots
- ☐ Know how to find $(\bar{x}, \bar{y})$ and construct a line of best fit
- ☐ Know how and when to apply the numbers μ, σ, r found by using the calculator and work with $y = a + bx$ as the line of best fit

Correlation

Scatter plots (graphs)

Is the number of cigarettes smoked by an individual related to the age of their death?

Are your overall Leaving Certificate results related to the number of hours you spend at your part-time job?

To look at the relationship between two sets of quantitative data, we plot the points on a graph (similar to *x*-axis/*y*-axis). Data that come in pairs are called **bivariate data**.

Scatter plots are used whenever we are examining possible relationships between two variables (bivariate data).

When analysing scatter plots, we use the word 'correlation' to describe the strength of the linear relationship between two variables.

Scatter plot patterns

Here are three scatter diagrams that are typical of what we meet.

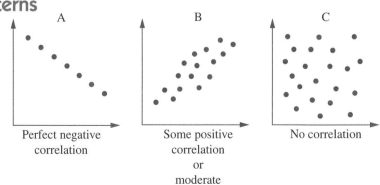

A	B	C
Perfect negative correlation	Some positive correlation or moderate positive correlation	No correlation

We get negative correlation where increasing values of one variable are associated with generally decreasing values of the other variable (case A above).

We get positive correlation where increasing values of one variable are associated with generally increasing values of the other variable (case B above).

We have no correlation when the points are randomly and widely spaced out (case C above).

key point

Correlation measures the strength of the linear association between two quantitative variables. Before using correlation, check the following.

1. Are both variables quantitative?
2. Check the scatter plot for evidence of 'straightness', i.e. can you visualise a straight line passing through the plot and representing the relationship? We call this the line of best fit by eye.
3. Check for outliers and extreme values (stragglers). Outliers are very important and always deserve special attention. Outliers can make a weak correlation look strong or can hide a strong correlation.

Example

The Type Fast secretarial training agency has a new computer software spreadsheet package. The agency investigates the number of hours it takes people of varying ages to reach a level of proficiency using this package. Fifteen individuals are tested and the results are summarised in the table below.

Age (x)	32	40	21	45	24	19	17	21	27	54	33	37	23	45	18
Time (in hours) (y)	10	12	8	15	7	8	6	9	11	16	t	13	9	17	5

(i) Given the mean time taken was 10·6 hours, calculate the value of t.
(ii) Plot the data on a scatter plot.
(iii) Comment on the strength and direction of the correlation of the scatter plot in (ii).

Solution

(i)
$$\frac{10 + 12 + 8 + 15 + 7 + 8 + 6 + 9 + 11 + 16 + t + 13 + 9 + 17 + 5}{15}$$

$$\Rightarrow \frac{146 + t}{15} = 10{\cdot}6$$

$$146 + t = 159$$

$$t = 13$$

(ii)

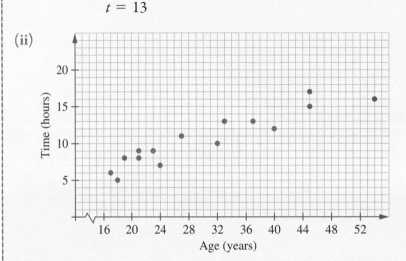

(iii) The correlation is moderate to strong and it is in the positive direction.

Interpreting scatter plots and calculating r, the correlation coefficient

We use scatter plots to help understand data, but now we have to understand scatter plots.

Interpreting a scatter diagram is often the easiest way for you to decide whether correlation exists. Correlation means that there is a linear relationship between the two variables. This could mean that the points lie on a straight line, but it is much more likely to mean that they are scattered about a straight line.

The correlation coefficient, *r*

Measuring correlation of scatter plots (scatter graphs)

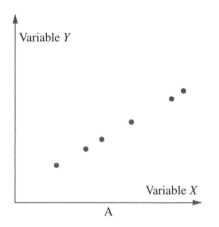

A

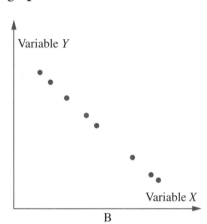

B

The points on scatter graph A are in a straight line. In this case we say there is **perfect positive correlation** between the two variables, X and Y.

We use the letter r to represent the correlation. We say that $r = 1$ when we have perfect positive correlation.

The points on scatter graph B are in a straight line. In this case we say there is **perfect negative correlation** between the two variables, X and Y.

We say that $r = -1$ when we have perfect negative correlation.

How the correlation, *r*, measures the direction and strength of a linear association:

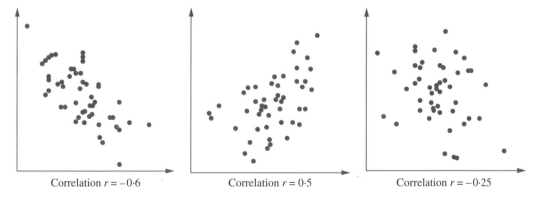

Correlation $r = -0.6$ Correlation $r = 0.5$ Correlation $r = -0.25$

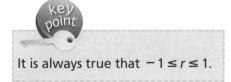

key point

It is always true that $-1 \leq r \leq 1$.

What *r* is not

- *r* is not the slope of the line of best fit.
- *r* is not resistant. This means *r* is strongly affected by outliers.
- *r* is never a value above 1.
- *r* is never a value below −1.
- *r* does not describe curved relationships.
- An *r* value of +0·58 is not better than an *r* value of −0·75. Do not assume a positive value of *r* is good or a negative value of *r* is not good.

How *r* is calculated is not examined on this course.

However, it is important that candidates can find *r* using a calculator. This is a skill you should learn. The instructions for using a calculator are at the back of this book.

If you cannot use your calculator on exam day, then you decide by observation from the given scatter plot whether *r* is negative or positive and write down your best guess for *r*, correct to one decimal place.

The line of best fit

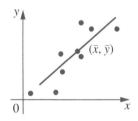

A line of best fit is drawn on a scatter diagram to find the direction of an association between two variables and to show the trend. The line of best fit can then be used to make predictions.

To draw a line of best fit by eye, draw a line that will balance the number of points above and below the line. For a more accurate line, plot the mean point $(\bar{x}, \bar{y})$ by calculating the mean of the *x*-values and the mean of the *y*-values. The line of best fit does not have to contain any of the individual data points or the origin.

The mean point is written as $(\bar{x}, \bar{y})$.

(2017 Q.2 (a)–(c))

An experiment measures the fuel consumption at various speeds for a particular model of car. The data collected are shown in Table 1 below.

Table 1							
Speed (km/hour)	40	48	56	64	88	96	112
Fuel consumption (km/litre)	21	16	18	16	13	11	9

(a) Find the correlation coefficient of the data in Table 1, correct to 3 decimal places.

Correlation coefficient =	

(b) Plot the points from the table on the grid below **and** draw the line of best fit (by eye).

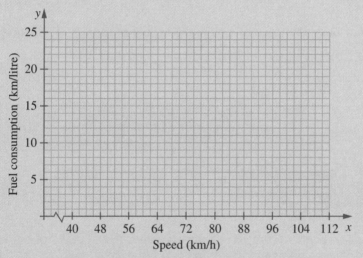

(c) The slope of the line of best fit is found to be −0·15. What does this value represent in the context of the data?

Solution

(a) Calculator → correlation coefficient = −0·957

(b)

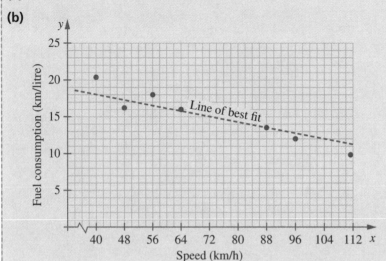

The line of best fit shown on the graph is one of many possible lines

(c)

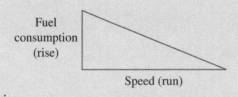

$$\text{Slope} = \frac{\text{rise}}{\text{run}} = -0{\cdot}15$$

$$\text{Slope} = \frac{\text{fuel consumption}}{\text{speed}}$$

In the context of the data this represents, the rate at which fuel consumption in km/h is decreasing as the speed in km/h increases.

Parts (a), (b) and (c) were awarded 5 marks each. 15 marks = 5%. Candidates performed well here.

Example

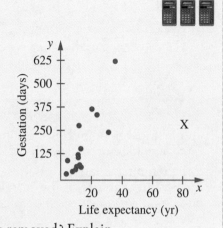

For women, pregnancy lasts about 9 months. In other species of animals, the length of time from conception to birth varies. Is there any evidence that gestation period is related to the animal's lifespan? The first scatterplot shows *gestation period* (in days) vs. *life expectancy* (in years) for 16 species of mammals. The point marked X at the far right represents humans.

(i) For these data $r = 0.49$ not a very strong relationship. Do you think the association would be stronger or weaker if humans were removed? Explain.

(ii) Is there reasonable justification for removing humans from the data set? Explain.

(iii) Here are the scatterplot and regression analysis for the 15 non-human species. Comment on the strength of the association, when $r = 0.8$.

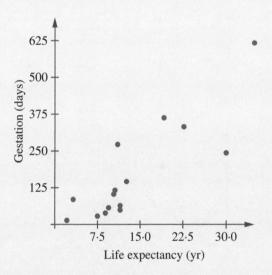

In the same way r was found, the calculator provides values $a = -53.2$ and $b = 14.1$.

Write the line of best fit, $y = a + bx$

(iv) Draw a line of best fit for the scatterplot that excludes the point (X) that represents humans.

(v) Interpret the slope of the line you drew.

(vi) Colobus monkeys have a life expectancy of about 22 years in the wild. Estimate the expected gestation period of a colobus monkey.

Solution

(i) Association would be stronger. The X point representing humans is an outlier. Hence, taking out the humans would increase the correlation (r) and the slope (m).

key point

In this case, the point representing humans is an outlier, that is, a value that is unusual (does not fit with) compared to the rest of the data.

If the sample is a large random sample, an extreme value (outlier) will not greatly alter the size of the correlation. However, if the sample is a small one, as above, an extreme data point can have a disproportionately large effect.

(ii) Restricting the study to non-human animals is justifiable. Removing an outlier may be useful (not always).

(iii) Correlation is moderately strong.

(iv) $y = a + bx$ becomes $y = -53\cdot2 + 14\cdot1x$

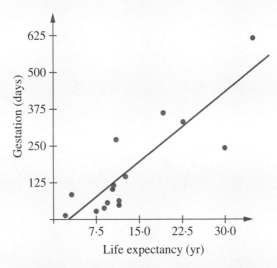

(v) Slope of line of best fit is approximately 14. This means for every year increase in life expectancy, the gestation period increases by about 14 days on average.

(vi) For $x = 22$ years, $y = -53\cdot2 + 14\cdot1(22) = 257$ days. In fact, gestation period for colobus monkeys is 170 days.

We need to be familiar with:

- Correlation + or −
- How to calculate r
- $(\bar{x}, \bar{y})$ point
- Line of best fit written as $y = a + bx$
- Correlation versus causality
- Outliers, see circled point in the diagram

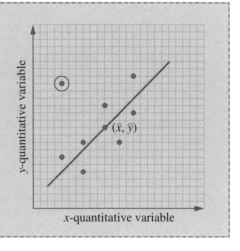

Causation

A correlation between two sets of data does not necessarily mean that one causes the other.

(2011 Q.2)

(a) Explain, with the aid of an example, what is meant by the statement 'correlation does not imply causality'.

(b) The data given in the table below and represented in the scatter diagram are pairs of observations of the variables x and y.

x	1	2	3	4	5	6
y	11	15	17	17	15	11

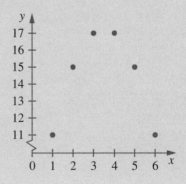

(i) Calculate the correlation coefficient.

(ii) What kind of relationship, if any, do the observed data suggest exists between x and y?

Solution

(a) Attracta said, 'We had a fire in our house recently. Five firemen and one fire engine were called to deal with it. The insurance company paid the claim of €17,000 for the damage.' Her friend Noreen replied, 'We had a fire in our house last year. Eighteen firemen and two fire engines were called to deal with it. The insurance company paid the claim of €235,000 for the damage. Those firemen caused a frightful mess.'

Correlation between two variables does not automatically mean that one causes the other, e.g. as the number of firemen fighting the fire rises, so does the insurance claim.

The size, strength, duration and ferocity of the fire increases the size of the claim, not the firemen. However, the number of firemen present is related to the dimensions of the fire.

A positive correlation between two variables does not mean that one is necessarily causing the other. For example, in a primary school there might be a correlation between reading ability and shoe size, but big feet don't make you read better and reading doesn't make your feet grow! In this case, both variables are connected to age – a 'confounding factor'.

(b) (i)   Calculator $\Rightarrow r = 0$

   (ii)   No (linear) relationship.

   The relationship may be quadratic. This type of relationship is not on the course.

14 Statistics IV: The Normal Curve, z-Scores, the Central Limit Theorem, Sampling and Standard Errors

aims

- ☐ To be familiar with the empirical rule and normal curves
- ☐ To be totally familiar with the material covered in the Probability chapter in the section headed: normal distribution and probability
- ☐ To read the z-tables (tables in the back of this book) for forward and backward cases
- ☐ How to apply the normal curve/z-scores to in-context questions
- ☐ To know about the Central Limit Theorem and its application to standard error of the mean and standard error of the proportion
- ☐ Gain the skills to apply standard error to in-context exam questions

The normal distribution and empirical rule

Many continuous variables, which occur naturally, have a shape like this.

This is called a normal distribution. It has a high probability density close to the mean and this decreases as you move away from the mean.

key point

The main features of normal distribution are that it is:

- bell shaped
- symmetrical (about the mean)
- mean = mode = median
- the total area under the curve is 1.

Examples of variables which are likely to follow a normal distribution are:

- the lengths of leaves from oak trees
- the times taken by 10-year-old girls to run 100 m
- the heights of adult males in Ireland
- the widths of car doors coming off a production line.

Empirical rule (68%, 95% or almost all) for the normal curve

For many large populations, the **empirical rule** provides an estimate of the approximate percentage of observations that are contained within one, two or three standard deviations of the mean.

- Approximately 68% of the observations are in the interval $\mu \pm 1\sigma$.
- Approximately 95% of the observations are in the interval $\mu \pm 2\sigma$.
- Almost all of the observations are in the interval $\mu \pm 3\sigma$.

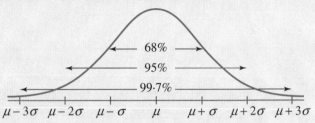

It is vital for candidates to know the empirical rule for the normal curve.

Example

Marks obtained on a national test (Test A1) are normally distributed with a mean of 100 and a standard deviation of 16.

(i) (a) Draw a large, neat diagram showing the distribution of marks. Label the points which show marks of 100, 116, 132 and 148.

(b) What percentage of the students who took Test A1 obtained marks greater than 116?

(c) What is the probability that a randomly selected student who took the test obtained a mark of less than 68?

(d) What are the end points of the interval which has its centre at the mean and within which 95% of the marks lie?

(ii) A new national test (Test B1) was constructed to have marks ranging from 100 to 250 and to be normally distributed for this range.

(a) What is the mean mark on Test B1?

(b) What is the median mark?

(c) If 84% of students obtained marks of less than 196 on Test B1, estimate the standard deviation of marks for this test.

Solution

(i) (a)

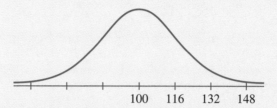

(b) We make use of this graph illustrating the empirical rule.

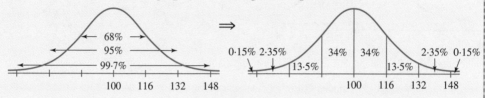

By observation from the above graph, the percentage of students scoring greater than 116 marks $= 13\cdot5\% + 2\cdot35\% + 0\cdot15\% = 16\%$.

$\therefore$ Approximately 16% of students scored greater than 116 marks.

The normal curve is symmetric about the mean.

(c)

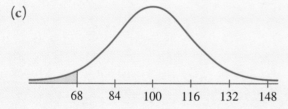

Approximately 2·5% of randomly selected students will obtain a mark of less than 68.

(d)

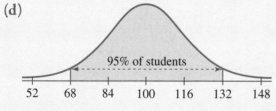

95% of students

End points of interval are [68, 132].

(ii) (a) and (b)

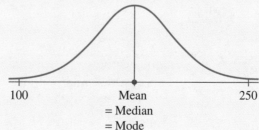

100   Mean   250
= Median
= Mode

$$\text{Mean mark on Test B1} = \frac{100 + 250}{2} = 175 = \mu.$$

Median mark = mean mark for normal distribution = 175.

(c)

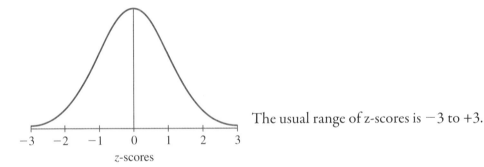

empirical rule

0·15% 2·35%   34%   34%   2·35% 0·15%

13·5%   13·5%

175   175 + σ   175 + 2σ   175   175 + σ

Notice: $0·15\% + 2·35 + 13·5 + 34 + 34 = 84\%$

From the empirical rule, 84% of students score $< \mu + \sigma$.

$$\therefore \mu + \sigma = 196 \Rightarrow 175 + \sigma = 196 \qquad \text{Answer: } \sigma = 21$$

Standard scores (z-scores)

The number of standard deviations that a value lies above or below the mean is called a **standard score** or **z-score**.

The usual range of z-scores is -3 to $+3$.

−3 −2 −1   0   1   2   3

z-scores

In general, if x is a measurement belonging to a set of data with mean μ and standard deviation σ, then its value in z-units is given below:

key point

$z = \dfrac{x - \mu}{\sigma}$, where x is the score or value

μ is the mean

σ is the standard deviation

Standard scores are very useful when comparing values from different normal distributions.

(2013 Q.2 (a))

A random variable x follows a normal distribution with mean 60 and standard deviation 5.

 (i) Find $P(x \leq 68)$

(ii) Find $P(52 \leq x \leq 68)$

Solution

(i)

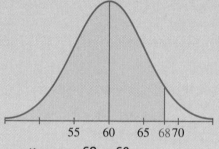 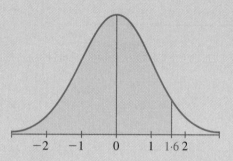

$$z = \frac{x - \mu}{\sigma} = \frac{68 - 60}{5} = 1 \cdot 6$$

$$P(x \leq 68) = P(z \leq 1 \cdot 6) = 0 \cdot 9452$$

(Read from *booklet of formulae and tables*, page 37)

Diagrams not required, included here for clarity.

(ii) $z = \dfrac{x - \mu}{\sigma} = \dfrac{52 - 60}{5} = -1 \cdot 6$

$P(52 \leq x \leq 68) = P(-1 \cdot 6 \leq z \leq 1 \cdot 6)$

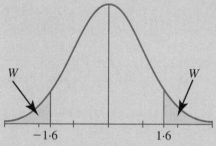

Shaded areas, W, are equal because the distribution is symmetric.

Area $W = 1 - 0 \cdot 9452 = 0 \cdot 0548$ (from part (i))

$P(-1 \cdot 6 \leq z \leq 1 \cdot 6) = 1 - W - W$

$\qquad\qquad\qquad\quad\;\; = 1 - 0 \cdot 0548 - 0 \cdot 0548$

$\qquad\qquad\qquad\quad\;\; = 0 \cdot 8904$

Part (i) was awarded 10 marks. Part (ii) was not well answered, it was awarded 5 marks.

The normal curve transformed

All normal distributions will have a mean (μ) and standard deviation (σ). Different values for μ and σ will give different normal distributions.

The first diagram shows two normal distributions with the same mean but different standard deviations.

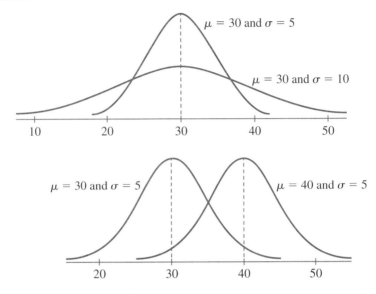

$\mu = 30$ and $\sigma = 5$

$\mu = 30$ and $\sigma = 10$

$\mu = 30$ and $\sigma = 5$

$\mu = 40$ and $\sigma = 5$

The second diagram shows two normal distributions with the same standard deviation but different means.

exam
Q

(2013 Q.2 (b))

(b) The heights of a certain type of plant, when ready to harvest, are known to be normally distributed, with a mean of μ. A company tests the effects of three different growth hormones on this type of plant. The three hormones were used on a different large sample of the crop. After applying each hormone, it was found that the heights of the plants in the samples were still normally distributed at harvest time.

The following diagrams A, B and C, show the expected distribution of the heights of the plants, at harvest time, without the use of the hormones.

The effect, on plant growth, of each of the hormones is described on the next page. Sketch, on each diagram, a new distribution to show the effect of the hormone.

Hormone A

The effect of hormone A was to increase the height of all plants.

Diagram A

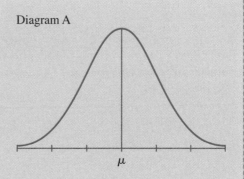

Hormones B

The effect of hormone B was to reduce the number of really small plants and the number of really tall plants. The mean was unchanged.

Diagram B

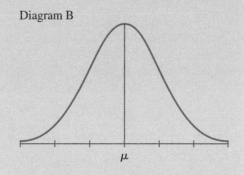

Hormone C

The effect of hormone C was to increase the number of small plants and the number of tall plants. The mean was unchanged.

Diagram C

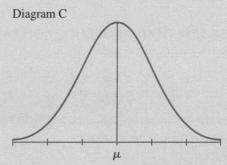

Solution

Hormone A

The effect of hormone A was to increase the height of all of the plants.

Diagram A

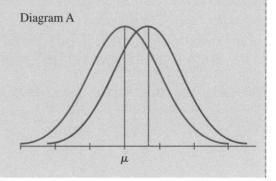

Hormones B

The effect of hormone B was to reduce the number of really small plants and the number of really tall plants. The mean was unchanged.

Diagram B

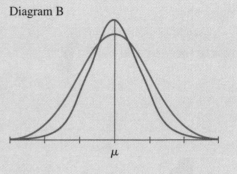

Hormone C

The effect of hormone C was to increase the number of small plants and the number of tall plants. The mean was unchanged.

Diagram C

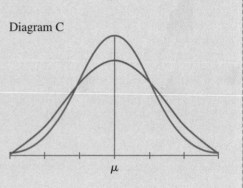

Reading normal distribution tables in reverse

Find the value of k, such that, $P(z \leq k) = 0.9750$ or find the value of z_1 given the shaded area of the standard normal curve.

The above question, asked in two different ways, has a solution which involves reading the tables in reverse.

In either case, the z-score associated with an area of 0.9750 can be found in the *booklet of formulae and tables*, page 37 or the extract here:

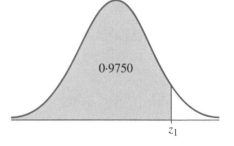

0.9750

z_1

z	0·00	0·01	0·02	0·03	0·04	0·05	0·06
1·9	0·9713	·9719	·9726	·9732	·9738	·9744	9750

The z-score associated with an area of 0.9750 is given in the tables as $z_1 = 1.96 = k$

Central limit theorem

This is a very powerful theorem used on our course to solve in-context questions where population samples of size n are used.

Instead of $z = \dfrac{x - \mu}{\sigma}$ for an individual case, in a sample mean (of size n) we use

$$z = \frac{x - \mu}{\sigma_{\bar{x}}}$$

where $\sigma_{\bar{x}} = \dfrac{\sigma}{\sqrt{n}}$ (see *booklet of formulae and tables*, page 34)

The **central limit theorem** says that regardless of the shape of the original distribution, the taking of averages of samples results in a normal curve. To find the distribution of $\bar{x}$, the sample means, we need to know only the original population mean and standard deviation.

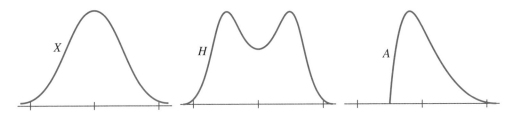

The three probability densities above all have the same mean and standard deviation. Despite their different shapes, when $n = 10$ (or more), the sampling distribution of the mean, $\bar{x}$, are nearly identical.

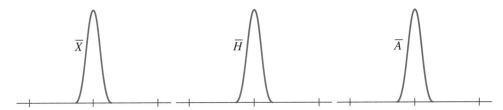

When taking samples, it is vital to remember:
- The mean of the samples = The mean of the original population.
- The standard deviation of the sample means = $\dfrac{\sigma}{\sqrt{n}}$ where σ is the standard deviation of the original population and n is the number of samples.

Why is this? Let's think about it for a minute. Means vary less than the individual observations. The mean age of groups of four randomly selected primary school students are shown.

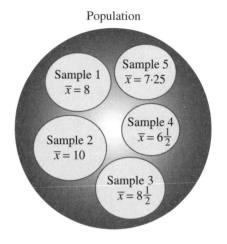

Population

	Age of students				$\bar{x}$
Sample 1	5	7	11	9	8
Sample 2	10	10	12	8	10
Sample 3	6	7	9	12	$8\frac{1}{2}$
Sample 4	7	7	5	7	$6\frac{1}{2}$
Sample 5	5	12	6	6	7·25

By observation, the results for $\bar{x}$, the mean of the samples, are less spread out than the individual observations.

Alternatively, think about this:

Which would be more surprising: having one student in your class of 30 who is over 2 m tall or having the mean of 30 students in your class to be over 2 m tall? The first event is fairly rare; there may be someone in your class over 2 m tall. But finding a class of 30 students whose mean height is over 2 m tall simply will not happen! The reason is that sample means have smaller standard deviations than individuals.

It goes down by the square root of the sample size. Finally, $\frac{\sigma}{\sqrt{n}}$ can be referred to as the standard error.

Spend some time working on the standard error, $\sigma_{\bar{x}}$. Many candidates find it challenging.

(2018 Q.8 (a) (i))

(a) (i) *Acme Confectionary* has launched a new bar called *Chocolate Crunch*. The weights of these new bars are normally distributed with a mean of 4·64 g and a standard deviation of 0·12 g. A sample of 10 bars is selected at random and the mean weight of the sample is found. Find the probability that the mean weight of the sample is between 4·6 g and 4·7 g.

Solution

(i)

Because the question has a sample $n = 10$, we use $\dfrac{\sigma}{\sqrt{n}}$ the standard error of the mean when calculating the z-score for the sample.

$$\sigma_{\bar{x}} = \frac{\sigma}{\sqrt{n}} = \frac{0·12}{\sqrt{10}} = 0·037947331$$

use $z = \dfrac{x - \mu}{\sigma_{\bar{x}}}$ twice

$$z_1 = \frac{4·6 - 4·64}{0·037947331} \qquad z_2 = \frac{4·7 - 4·64}{0·037947331}$$

$$z_1 = -1·05 \qquad z_2 = 1·58$$

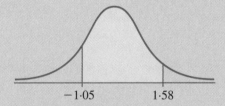

$$P(4·6 \leq x \leq 4·7) = P(-1·05 \leq z \leq 1·58)$$

Using the *booklet of formulae and tables*, page 36 and page 37, and the two diagrams:

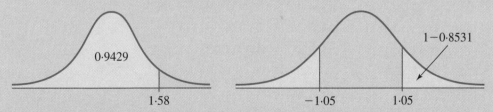

We write

$$P(-1·05 \leq z \leq 1·58) = 0·9429 - (1 - 0·8531)$$

$$= 0·796 \text{ or } 79·6\%$$

Population and sample proportions

Suppose there are two candidates in an election, A and B, and we want to estimate as a percentage e.g. 48% or as a decimal e.g. 0·48 the level of support for candidate A.

The population proportion is usually denoted by the letter p. Now suppose we then select a simple random proportion (sample) of 80 voters and ask them which candidate they support in the election.

The sample proportion is usually denoted by the letter $\hat{p}$, in this case $\hat{p} = 0·48$
The standard error of the proportion, $\sigma_{\hat{p}}$ is found using

$$\sigma_{\hat{p}} = \sqrt{\frac{\hat{p}(1 - \hat{p})}{n}} \text{ (see booklet of formulae and tables, page 34)}$$

Since we don't know p, we can't find the true standard deviation of the sampling distribution model. Instead we use $\hat{p}$ and calculate the standard error.

$$\sigma_{\hat{p}} = \sqrt{\frac{\hat{p}(1 - \hat{p})}{n}} = \sqrt{\frac{0·48(1 - 0·48)}{80}} = 0·0559 = 5·59\%$$

On our course, the central limit theorem tells us the sample distribution is normal, so its business as usual. Let's look at a sample exam question.

A survey is being conducted of voters' opinions on several different issues.

The Democrats, a political party, usually have support of 23% of voters.

(i) Calculate the standard error of the proportion in a random sample of 1111 voters.

(ii) Of the voters in the sample above, calculate the probability that 25% or more of them support the Democrats.

Solution

(i) Standard error of the proportion,

$\hat{p} = 23\% = 0·23$ $\sigma_{\hat{p}} = \sqrt{\frac{0·23(1 - ·023)}{1111}}$

$n = 1111$ $\sigma_{\hat{p}} = 0·0126$

(ii) use $z = \dfrac{x - \mu}{\sigma_{\hat{p}}} = \dfrac{0·25 - 0·23}{0·0126} = 1·59$

$P(x \geq 0·25) = P(z \geq 1·59)$

$= 1 - 0·9441$

$= 0·0559$

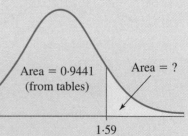

Area = 0·9441 (from tables)   Area = ?

1·59

Revision question

(i) Assume that the duration of human pregnancies can be described by a normal model with a mean of 271 days and a standard deviation of 12 days.

   (a) What percentage of pregnancies should last between 271 and 296 days?

   (b) Using the empirical rule, write down the 95% confidence interval for the mean pregnancy duration.

   (c) Suppose a certain doctor is currently providing prenatal care to 52 pregnant women. Let $\bar{h}$ represent the mean length of their pregnancies. According to the central limit theorem, what is the distribution of this sample mean? Specify the model, mean and standard deviation.

   (d) What is the probability that the mean duration of these patients' pregnancies will be more than 275 days?

(ii) The duration of human pregnancies may not actually follow a normal model as described in part **(i)**.

   (a) Explain why it may be somewhat skewed to the left.

   (b) If the correct model is in fact skewed, does that change your answers to parts **(a)**, **(b)** and **(d)** in **(i)**? Explain why or why not for each of the three parts.

Solution

(i) (a) $P(271 \leq x \leq 296) = P\left(\dfrac{271 - 271}{12} \leq z \leq \dfrac{296 - 271}{12}\right)$

$$= P(0 \leq z \leq 2\cdot08)$$
$$= 0\cdot9812 - 0\cdot5$$
$$= 48\%$$

(b) $\pm 2 = \dfrac{x - 271}{12}$ (empirical rule ± 2 standard deviations)

   $271 \pm 24 = x$

247⌈   ⌉295

(c) The distribution of these sample means is normal. Mean $\mu = 271$ and the standard deviation $\sigma_{\bar{x}} = \dfrac{\sigma}{\sqrt{n}} = \dfrac{12}{\sqrt{52}} = 1\cdot66$.

(d) $P(x > 275) = P\left(z > \dfrac{275 - 271}{1\cdot66}\right) = P(z > 2\cdot41)$

$$= 1 - 0\cdot9920 \quad \text{(from normal tables)}$$
$$= 0\cdot0080$$

(ii) (a) There are not as many very long pregnancies nowadays due to births being induced after a certain stage. Hence, the curve is skewed to the left.

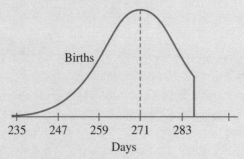

(b) For data that are significantly skewed, we cannot use the normal approximation on parts **(a)** and **(b)** in **(i)**.

However, since regardless of the initial shape of the original data the sample mean always follows a normal curve distribution, the answer for part **(i) (d)** is correct for this large sample size (52 women).

Statistics V: Margins of Error and Confidence Intervals

Margin of error

A margin of error tells you how many percentage points your results will differ from the real population value. For example, a 95% confidence interval with a 2% margin of error means that your statistic will be within 2% of the real population value, 95% of the time.

There are four ways to calculate the margin of error. The method used to calculate the margin of error is based on the information given in a question.

Method 1: If you *only* have the sample size, n: Margin of error, $E = \dfrac{1}{\sqrt{n}}$

Method 2: If you have the standard deviation and use the empirical rule:

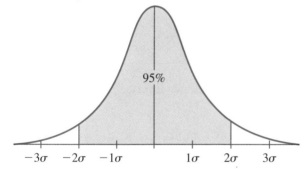

95% of the population are between -2σ and $+2\sigma$

Margin of error, $E = 2\sigma$

Method 3: If you have a sample, of size n, and the standard deviation of the population, we must use the standard error of the mean (as covered in the previous chapter).

> **Note:** The empirical rule is a rounded version of the correct values. More accurately, 95% of the population is within -1.96 and $+1.96$ deviations away from the mean.
>
> $$\text{Margin of error, } E = 1.96\sigma_{\bar{x}} \implies E = 1.96\dfrac{\sigma}{\sqrt{n}}$$

Method 4: If you have a sample, of size n, and the population proportion, we must use the standard error of the proportion (as covered in the previous chapter).

$$\text{Margin of error}, E = 1{\cdot}96 \; \sigma_{\hat{p}} \;\Rightarrow\; E = 1{\cdot}96\sqrt{\frac{\hat{p}(1 - \hat{p})}{n}}$$

The normal curve and 95% confidence intervals

In general, a confidence interval looks like this:

Estimate $\pm$ margin of error (E)

The more confident we want to be, the larger the margin of error must be.

The larger the sample size n, the smaller the margin of error. This means larger samples give more credible results.

The 95% confidence interval

We have four methods for calculating the 95% confidence interval. The four methods for calculating the margin of error, E, reappear!

Method 1: Using the simple margin of error for a sample

$$\bar{x} - \frac{1}{\sqrt{n}} \qquad\qquad \mu \qquad\qquad \bar{x} + \frac{1}{\sqrt{n}}$$

$$\bar{x} - \frac{1}{\sqrt{n}} \le \mu \le \bar{x} + \frac{1}{\sqrt{n}}$$

Method 2: Using the empirical rule

$$\bar{x} - 2\sigma \qquad\qquad \mu \qquad\qquad \bar{x} + 2\sigma$$

$$\bar{x} - 2\sigma \leq \mu \leq \bar{x} + 2\sigma$$

Method 3: Using the standard error of the mean for a sample   (see *booklet of formulae and tables*, page 34)

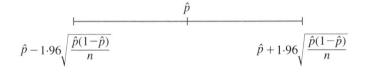

$$\bar{x} - 1\cdot96\,\frac{\sigma}{\sqrt{n}} \qquad\qquad\qquad \bar{x} + 1\cdot96\,\frac{\sigma}{\sqrt{n}}$$

$$\bar{x} - 1\cdot96\,\frac{\sigma}{\sqrt{n}} \leq \mu \leq \bar{x} + 1\cdot96\,\frac{\sigma}{\sqrt{n}}$$

key point

$\bar{x}$ and μ are often interchangeable

Method 4: Using the population proportion, $\hat{p}$, for a sample   (see *booklet of formulae and tables*, page 34)

$$\hat{p}$$

$$\hat{p} - 1\cdot96\sqrt{\frac{\hat{p}(1-\hat{p})}{n}} \qquad\qquad\qquad \hat{p} + 1\cdot96\sqrt{\frac{\hat{p}(1-\hat{p})}{n}}$$

key point

p and $\hat{p}$ are often interchangeable.

We now look at four examples to illustrate the above four methods.

Calculating margins of error and constructing 95% confidence intervals

Example

A survey of 1600 people chosen at random showed 47% support for the government.

Using the formula for margin of error, $E = \dfrac{1}{\sqrt{n}}$

(i) Calculate (at the 95% confidence level) the margin of error
(ii) Hence, create the 95% confidence interval for the survey in terms of x.

Solution

(i) $E = \dfrac{1}{\sqrt{n}} = \dfrac{1}{\sqrt{1600}} = \dfrac{1}{40} = 0\cdot025 = 25\%$

(ii) $\quad \bar{x} - \dfrac{1}{\sqrt{n}} \leq \mu \leq \bar{x} + \dfrac{1}{\sqrt{n}}$

$\qquad 47\% - 2\cdot5\% \leq \mu \leq 47\% + 2\cdot5\%$

$\qquad\qquad 44\cdot5\% \leq \mu \leq 49\cdot5\%$

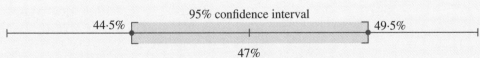

95% confidence interval

44·5%   47%   49·5%

What does '95% confidence' really mean?

What do we mean when we say we have 95% confidence that our interval contains the randomly selected value? Formally, what we mean is that '95% of randomly selected values will be captured/fall into the confidence interval'. This is correct, but somewhat long winded, so we usually say, we are 95% confident that the (randomly) selected value lies in our interval.'

Our uncertainty is about whether the particular (randomly) selected value is one of the successful ones or one of the 5% that falls outside the interval.

Example

In a survey, the IQ scores of people were recorded. The mean score was 100 points and the standard deviation was 15 points. Assuming that IQ scores are normally distributed

(i) Calculate (at the 95% confidence level) using the empirical rule, the margin of error of IQ scores.

(ii) Hence, create the 95% confidence interval for IQ scores.

Solution

(i) $E = 2\sigma = 2(15) = 30$ points

(ii) $\bar{x} - 2\sigma \leq x \leq \bar{x} + 2\sigma$

     $100 - 30 \leq x \leq 100 + 30$

       $70 \leq x \leq 130$

95% confidence interval

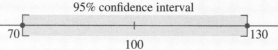

70   100   130

Example

A survey was carried out to find the weekly rental costs of holiday apartments in a certain country. A random sample of 400 apartments was taken. The mean of the sample was €320 and the standard deviation was €50.

(i) Calculate (at the 95% confidence level) the margin of error.

(ii) Hence, create the 95% confidence interval for the survey.

Solution

(i) $E = 1 \cdot 96 \dfrac{\sigma}{\sqrt{n}} = 1 \cdot 96 \left(\dfrac{50}{\sqrt{400}} \right) = 4 \cdot 9$

(ii) $\bar{x} - 1 \cdot 96 \dfrac{\sigma}{\sqrt{n}} \leq \mu \leq \bar{x} + 1 \cdot 96 \dfrac{\sigma}{\sqrt{n}}$

$320 - 4 \cdot 9 \leq \mu \leq 320 + 4 \cdot 9$

$315 \cdot 1 \leq \mu \leq 324 \cdot 9$

95% confidence interval

315·1   324·9

μ

Example

During the making of a movie, a survey found that out of 724 extras, only 181 were suitable for parts in a major movie.

(i) Calculate (at the 95% confidence level) the margin of error for the survey

(ii) Hence, create the 95% confidence interval for the survey.

Solution

(i) $E = 1 \cdot 96 \sqrt{\dfrac{\hat{p}(1 - \hat{p})}{n}}$ where $\hat{p}$ = sample proportion = $\dfrac{181}{724} = 0 \cdot 25$

$E = 1 \cdot 96 \sqrt{\dfrac{0 \cdot 25(1 - 0 \cdot 25)}{724}} = 1 \cdot 96(0 \cdot 016) = 0 \cdot 31 = 3 \cdot 1\%$

(ii) $\hat{p} - 1.96\sqrt{\dfrac{\hat{p}(1 - \hat{p})}{n}} \le x \le \hat{p} + 1.96\sqrt{\dfrac{\hat{p}(1 - \hat{p})}{n}}$

$$0.25 - 0.031 \le x \le 0.25 + 0.031$$
$$0.219 \le x \le 0.281$$

95% confidence interval

0·219 ┌───────────────┐ 0·281

0·25

Margin of error, working in reverse

In certain situations, a certain margin of error may be required. There is an inverse relationship between the sample size, n, and the margin of error. The smaller the sample size the larger the margin of error. If (say) a margin of error of 4% is acceptable, what sample size is required?

We then solve $\dfrac{1}{\sqrt{n}} = 0.04 \,(4\%)$

Then $\quad \dfrac{1}{n} = 0.0016 \quad$ (square both sides)

$$1 = 0.0016\,n$$
$$624 = n$$

Example

At the 95% confidence level, calculate the sample size, n, to have a margin of error of:

(i) 1·25%   (ii) 3%

Solution

$$\dfrac{1}{\sqrt{n}} = \text{margin of error}$$

(i) $1{\cdot}25\% = 0{\cdot}0125$

$$\frac{1}{\sqrt{n}} = 0{\cdot}0125$$

$$1 = 0{\cdot}0125\sqrt{n}$$

(multiply both sides by $\sqrt{n}$)

$$\frac{1}{0{\cdot}0125} = \sqrt{n}$$

(divide both sides by $0{\cdot}0125$)

$$\frac{1}{(0{\cdot}0125)^2} = n$$

(square both sides)

$$6{,}400 = n$$

(ii) $3\% = 0{\cdot}03$

$$\frac{1}{\sqrt{n}} = 0{\cdot}03$$

$$1 = 0{\cdot}03\,\sqrt{n}$$

(multiply both sides by $\sqrt{n}$)

$$\frac{1}{0{\cdot}03} = \sqrt{n}$$

(divide both sides by $0{\cdot}03$)

$$\frac{1}{(0{\cdot}03)^2} = n$$

(square both sides)

$$1111{\cdot}111111 = n$$
$$1{,}112 = n$$

Note: Always use the next whole number value of n, not to the nearest whole number.

Example

A poll shows that the government's approval rating is at 70%.

The poll is based on a random selection of 896 voters with a margin of error of 3%.

Show that the poll used a 95% level of confidence.

Solution

Confidence limits $= \pm\,(z)(\sigma_{\hat{p}})$ where z represents the % level of confidence

$$0{\cdot}03 = \pm\,(z)\sqrt{\frac{\hat{p}(1 - \hat{p})}{n}}$$

$$0{\cdot}03 = \pm\,(z)\sqrt{\frac{0{\cdot}7(1 - 0{\cdot}7)}{896}}$$

$$0{\cdot}03 = \pm\,(z)(0{\cdot}153)$$

$$\frac{0{\cdot}03}{0{\cdot}153} = \pm z$$

$$\pm 1{\cdot}96 = z$$

Hence, the poll is using the 95% level of confidence.

Two exam questions

We finish this chapter by working on two exam questions.

(2015 Q.2 (a))

A survey of 100 shoppers, randomly selected from a large number of Saturday supermarket shoppers, showed that the mean shopping spend was €90·45. The standard deviation of this sample was €20·73.

Find a 95% confidence interval for the mean amount spent in a supermarket on that Saturday.

Solution

$$E = \text{margin of error} = 1·96 \frac{\sigma}{\sqrt{n}}$$

$$= 1·96 \frac{20·73}{\sqrt{100}}$$

$$= 4·06$$

Confidence interval

$$\bar{x} - E \leq \mu \leq \bar{x} + E$$

$$90·45 - 4·06 \leq \mu \leq 90·45 + 4·06$$

$$86·39 \leq \mu \leq 94·51$$

95% confidence interval

86·39 ⌐   ⌐ 94·51
├────────────┴────────────┼────────────────┴────────────┤
                          μ

(2018 Q.8(a)(ii))

Acme Confectionary has launched a new bar called *Chocolate Crunch*. The weights of these new bars are normally distributed with a mean of 4·64 g and a standard deviation of 0·12 g.

(ii) A company surveyed 400 people, chosen from the population of people who had bought at least one *Chocolate Crunch* bar. Of those surveyed, 324 of them said they liked the new bar. Create the 95% confidence interval for the population proportion who liked the new bar. Give your answer to 2 decimal places.

Solution

(ii) Margin of error $= E = 1·96\sqrt{\dfrac{\hat{p}(1 - \hat{p})}{n}}$

$$\hat{p} = \frac{324}{400} = 0·81$$

$$n = 400$$

$$E = 1·96\sqrt{\frac{0·81(1 - 0·81)}{400}} = 0·0384$$

Confidence interval given by

$$\hat{p} - E \leq p \leq \hat{p} + E$$

$$0·81 - 0·0384 \leq p \leq 0·81 + 0·0384$$

$$0·7716 \leq p \leq 0·8484$$

$$0·77 \leq p \leq 0·85 \qquad \text{(correct to two decimal places)}$$

This very good, straightforward question was awarded 15 marks (5%). Be sure you know this technique.

Statistics VI: Hypothesis testing and *p*-Values

aims

☐ To understand the idea of null hypothesis
☐ To learn how to carry out a hypothesis test
☐ To apply hypothesis testing to in-context exam questions
☐ To calculate and apply the *p*-value for a test statistic as an alternative approach to hypothesis testing

Hypothesis testing

A hypothesis is a statement (or theory) whose truth has yet to be proven or disproven. Examples of hypotheses:

- More than half the population is satisfied with EU membership.
- Drinking fizzy drinks causes tooth decay.
- The age of marriage has increased over the past 20 years.

> **NULL HYPOTHESIS**
>
> The statement being tested in a test of significance is called the **null hypothesis.** The test of significance is designed to assess the strength of the evidence against the null hypothesis. Usually the null hypothesis is a statement of no effect or no difference. We abbreviate 'null hypothesis' as H_0.

Statistics help to make decisions

We can use statistics to accept or reject claims.

1. Is global temperature increasing?
   The null hypothesis, H_0, is that global temperature is not increasing, i.e. no difference in temperature. The alternative hypothesis, H_A, is that global temperature is increasing.

2. Is a new drug effective at treating Ebola?
   The null hypothesis, H_0, is that the new drug is not effective.
   The alternative hypothesis, H_A, is that the new drug is effective.

3. Is a survey on left-handed people biased if it indicates 24% of people are left handed?
   The null hypothesis, H_0, is that 24% of people are left handed, i.e. survey not biased.
   The alternative hypothesis, H_A, is that the survey is biased.

Often the people investigating the data hope to reject H_0. They hope:
  (i) their new drug is better than the old one

or

  (ii) the new ad campaign is better than the original

or

  (iii) the new machine is better than the existing one.

However, in statistics, it is essential that our attitude is one of skepticism. Until we are convinced otherwise, we accept H_0. In other words, we cling to the idea that there is no change, no improvement, no deterioration, no effect.

The reasoning behind hypothesis testing is that we usually prefer to think about getting things right rather than getting them wrong. A similar logic applies in trials by jury, where the defendant is considered innocent until it is shown otherwise.

Procedure for carrying out a hypothesis test

We can use the following 5 steps to carry out a hypothesis test.

Step 1. Write down H_0, the null hypothesis, and H_A, the alternate hypothesis.

Step 2. Calculate the margin of error, E.
Using either $1 \cdot 96 \frac{\sigma}{\sqrt{n}}$ or $1 \cdot 96 \sqrt{\frac{\hat{p}(1 - \hat{p})}{n}}$, whichever is appropriate.

Step 3. Write down the 95% confidence internal either
$\bar{x} - E \leq \mu \leq \bar{x} + E$ or
$\hat{p} - E \leq p \leq \hat{p} + E$, whichever is appropriate.

$$\begin{array}{c}\bar{x} - E \\ \hat{p} - E\end{array} \boxed{} \begin{array}{c}\bar{x} + E \\ \hat{p} + E\end{array}$$

Step 4. If the value of the given sample mean or the given population proportion is within the confidence internal, we **do not reject** the null hypothesis, i.e. we do not challenge the claim.
However, if the value of the given sample mean or the given population proportion is outside the confidence internal we **reject** the null hypothesis i.e. the null hypothesis is wrong.

Step 5. State the conclusion in words.

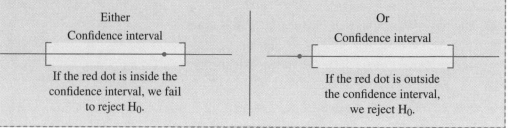

In the final analysis, testing the null hypothesis, H_0, simply involves a confidence interval and a red dot.

Either	Or
Confidence interval	Confidence interval
If the red dot is inside the confidence interval, we fail to reject H_0.	If the red dot is outside the confidence interval, we reject H_0.

(2017, Q.8 (a) (iii))

In 2015, in a particular country, the weights of 15-year-olds were normally distributed with a mean of 63·5 kg and a standard deviation of 10 kg.

(iii) In 2016, 150 of the 15-year-olds in that country were randomly selected and their weights recorded. It was found that their weights were normally distributed with a mean weight of 62 kg and a standard deviation of 10 kg. Test the hypothesis, at the 5% level of significance, that the mean weight of 15 year olds, in that country, had not changed from 2015 to 2016. State the null hypothesis and your alternative hypothesis. Give your conclusion in the context of the question.

When working with levels of confidence (or levels of significance), statisticians can use percentages ambiguously. In particular, the 5% level of confidence and the 95% level of confidence mean the same thing. That is to say, 5% of the time outside the confidence interval or 95% of the time inside the confidence interval.

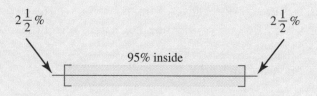

Solution

Step 1. H_0: Mean weight has not changed $\mu = 63.5$ kg.

   H_A: Mean weight has changed $\mu \neq 63.5$ kg.

Step 2. In this question $E = 1.96\dfrac{\sigma}{\sqrt{n}}$

   $n = 150$, $\bar{x} = 62$ and $\sigma = 10$

$$E = 1.96\dfrac{10}{\sqrt{150}} = 1.6003$$

Step 3. The 95% confidence interval given by

   $\bar{x} - E \leq \mu \leq \bar{x} + E$

   $62 - 1.6003 \leq \mu \leq 62 + 1.6003$

   $60.3997 \leq \mu \leq 63.6003$

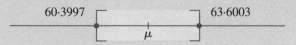

Step 4. 63.5 falls within this interval

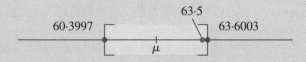

Hence, do not reject H_0 the null hypothesis.

Step 5. We conclude the mean weight has not changed.

This question was awarded 15 marks (5%). A great question for the well-prepared candidate.

Example

National data in 1970 showed that 58% of the adult population had never smoked cigarettes. In 2010, a national health survey interviewed a random sample of 880 adults and found that 52% had never smoked cigarettes.

(i) Construct a 95% confidence interval for the proportion of adults in 2010 who had never smoked cigarettes.

(ii) Does this provide evidence of a change in behaviour among the Irish?
   Write appropriate hypotheses.
   Using your confidence interval, test and appropriate hypothesis and state your conclusion.

Solution

(i) Use

$$\hat{p} - E \le p \le \hat{p} + E$$

where

$$\hat{p} = 52\% = 0{\cdot}52$$

$$1 - \hat{p} = 1 - 0{\cdot}52 = 0{\cdot}48$$

$$n = 880$$

Then

$$0{\cdot}52 - 1{\cdot}96\sqrt{\frac{(0{\cdot}52)(0{\cdot}48)}{880}} \le p \le 0{\cdot}52 + 1{\cdot}96\sqrt{\frac{(0{\cdot}52)(0{\cdot}48)}{880}}$$

$$0{\cdot}52 - 0{\cdot}033 \le p \le 0{\cdot}52 + 0{\cdot}033$$

$$48{\cdot}7\% \le p \le 55{\cdot}3\%$$

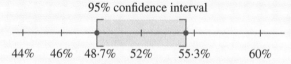

95% confidence interval

Based on these data, we are 95% confident that the proportion of adults in 2010 who had never smoked cigarettes is between 48·7% and 55·3%.

(ii) $H_0: p = 58\%$

$H_A: p \ne 58\%$

58% Falls outside this interval

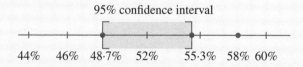

95% confidence interval

Hence we reject H_0

We conclude that the proportion of adults in 2010 who had never smoked was less than in 1970.

p-Values: an alternative approach to hypothesis testing

A p-value is:

- a probability
- used to make a decision on the null hypothesis, H_0
- a measure of the strength of evidence to reject or fail to reject the null hypothesis.

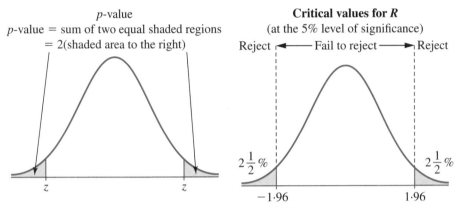

p-value

p-value = sum of two equal shaded regions
= 2(shaded area to the right)

Critical values for R

(at the 5% level of significance)

Reject ◄──── Fail to reject ────► Reject

$2\frac{1}{2}\%$ $2\frac{1}{2}\%$

-1.96 1.96

The decision to reject, or fail to reject, H_0 is based on the comparison of the p-value with the level of significance. On our course, we only use a two-tailed test at the 5% level of significance.

exam focus

It is vital to know that the critical p-value = 0·05 at the 5% significance level.
If $p \leq 0.05$, there is strong evidence to reject H_0
If $p > 0.05$, there is strong evidence to fail to reject H_0.
In summary: If p is low,
                    H_0 must go!

How to perform a hypothesis test using p-value

Step 1. State H_0 and H_A.
Step 2. Calculate the z score (this is often called the test statistic, T).
Step 3. Determine the p-value (a diagram is useful).
Step 4. If $p \leq 0.05$, reject H_0. If $p > 0.05$, fail to reject H_0.
Step 5. State the conclusion in words.

key point

Do not confuse p-value with the population proportion p. They have nothing whatsoever to do with each other!

Example

A company claims that the average weight of a packet of cereal it produces is 400 g with a standard deviation of 12 g. To test this claim, a random sample of 64 of these packets were weighed and found to have a mean value of 403 g.

 (i) Write down H_0 and H_A.

 (ii) Calculate the test statistic for this sample mean.

(iii) Calculate a p-value for this sample mean.

(iv) At the 5% level of significance, is there evidence to show that the mean weight of the packets of cereal is not 400 g? Justify your answer.

Solution

 (i) The null hypothesis, H_0: $\mu = 400$ g

The alternative hypothesis, H_A: $\mu \neq 400$ g

(ii) $\bar{x} = 403$, $\mu = 400$, $\sigma = 112$ and $n = 64$

The test statistic is given by:

$$z = T = \frac{\bar{x} - \mu}{\dfrac{\sigma}{\sqrt{n}}} = \frac{403 - 400}{\dfrac{12}{\sqrt{64}}} = 2$$

(iii) $P(T \geq 2) = P(z \geq 2)$

$= 1 - P(z \leq 2)$

$= 1 - 0 \cdot 9772$ (from *booklet of formulae and tables*)

$= 0 \cdot 0228$

The p-value $= 2\,(0 \cdot 0228) = 0 \cdot 0456$

key point

p-value = twice the shaded area.

(iv) Since $0 \cdot 0456 < 0 \cdot 05$ (*or* $4 \cdot 56\% < 5\%$), we conclude there is strong evidence to reject the null hypothesis, H_0.

We state that there is strong evidence to reject the claim by the company that the average weight of a packet of cereal is 400 g.

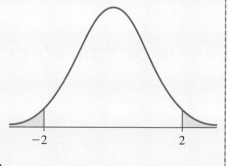

It is worth noting that the examiner often leads candidates step-by-step through a tough question, as seen in the above Example.

(2015 Q.2 (b) and (c))

A survey of 100 shoppers, randomly selected from a large number of Saturday supermarket shoppers, showed that the mean shopping spend was €90·45. The standard deviation of this sample was €20·73.

(b) A supermarket has claimed that the mean amount spent by shoppers on a Saturday is €94. Based on the survey, test the supermarket's claim using a 5% level of significance. Clearly state your null hypothesis, your alternative hypothesis, and your conclusion.

(c) Find the p-value of the test you performed in part (b) above and explain what this value represents in the context of the question.

Solution

(b) Step 1. H_0: Mean spend is €94

H_A: Mean spend is not €94

Step 2. Margin of error, $E = 1 \cdot 96 \dfrac{\sigma}{\sqrt{n}} = 1 \cdot 96 \dfrac{20 \cdot 73}{\sqrt{100}} = 4 \cdot 06$

Step 3.

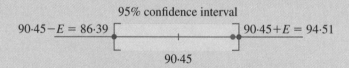

95% confidence interval

$90 \cdot 45 - E = 86 \cdot 39$ $90 \cdot 45 + E = 94 \cdot 51$

$90 \cdot 45$

Step 4. Mean spend = €94, is inside the 95% confidence interval, see red dot in diagram above.

We do not reject H_0, i.e we do not challenge the claim.

Step 5. In conclusion, the supermarkets claim may be correct. All we can say is there not enough evidence to reject their claim that the mean amount spent by shoppers is €94.

(c) Calculate the test statistic $T(= z) = \dfrac{\bar{x} - \mu}{\dfrac{\sigma}{\sqrt{n}}} = \dfrac{90{\cdot}45 - 94}{\dfrac{20{\cdot}73}{\sqrt{100}}}$

$$\text{Then } T = z = -1{\cdot}71$$

$$
\begin{aligned}
P(T \le -1{\cdot}71) &= P(z \le -1{\cdot}71) \\
&= P(z \ge 1{\cdot}71) \\
&= 1 - P(z \le 1{\cdot}71) \\
&= 1 - 0{\cdot}9564 \quad \text{(booklet of formulae} \\
&\qquad\qquad\qquad\;\; \text{and tables)} \\
&= 0{\cdot}0436
\end{aligned}
$$

$p - value = 2(0{\cdot}0436) = 0{\cdot}0872 > 0{\cdot}05$, hence fail to reject H_0

Meaning: If the mean amount spent really was €94, then the probability that the sample mean would be €90·45 by chance is 8·72%. It is because this is more than a 5% chance that we do not reject the null hypothesis.

Glossary of Statistical Terms

Arithmetic mean   A measure of central tendency that sums all the scores in the data sets and divides by the number of scores.

Asymptotic   The quality of the normal curve such that the tails never touch the horizontal axis.

Bell-shaped curve (normal curve)   A distribution of scores that is symmetrical about the mean, median and mode and has asymptotic tails.

Bias   Systematic errors in the way the sample represents the population. It can be caused by poorly worded surveys, non-response or undercoverage.

Bimodal   A bimodal data set (distribution) has two peaks of data, as in the diagram below.

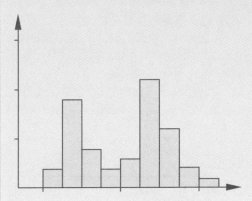

Bivariate data   A survey that examines the relationship between two variables (data sets). In our course, the two variables are usually quantitative variables.

Categorical data   Non-numerical data that can be counted but only described in words. Such data may be ordered or unordered.

Causality   The relationship between an event (the cause) and a second event (the effect).

Class interval   The upper and lower boundary of a set of scores used in the creation of a frequency distribution.

Confidence interval   A range around a measurement that conveys how precise the measurement is.

Confidence level   A measure of the reliability of a result. A confidence level of 95% (0·95) means we are 95% sure the result is reliable. Some confusion is caused by the use of the term 5% level to represent the 95% level.

Continuous numerical data   Data which can take any numerical value within a certain range.

Correlation coefficient (r)   A numerical index that reflects the relationship between two variables, constant between -1 and 1.

Critical value   The value necessary for rejection (or non-acceptance) of the null hypothesis.

Cumulative frequency distribution   A frequency distribution that shows frequencies for class intervals along with the cumulative frequency for each.

Data   An item, or items, of factual information derived from measurement or research.

Data point   An observation.

Data set   A set of data points.

Dependent variable   Often denoted by y, whose value depends on another variable. It is usually represented on the vertical axis.

Direct correlation   A positive correlation where the values of both variables change in the same direction.

Discrete numerical data   Data which can only have certain values.

Frequency distribution   A method for illustrating the distribution of scores within class intervals. Often given in tabular form (frequency distribution table).

Frequency polygon   A graphical representation of a frequency distribution.

Histogram   A graphical representation of a frequency distribution.

Hypothesis   An if–then statement of conjecture that relates variables to one another.

Independent variable   Often denoted by x, whose variation does not depend on another variable. It is usually represented on the horizontal axis.

Indirect correlation   A negative correlation where the values of variables move in opposite directions.

Inferential statistics   Tools that are used to infer the results based on a sample to a population.

Line of best fit (regression line)   The line that best fits the actual scores and minimises the error in prediction.

Margin of error   The extent of the interval on either side of the sample proportion.

Mean   The value where scores are summed and divided by the number of observations.

Measures of central tendency   The mean, median and mode.

Median The point at which 50% of the cases in a distribution fall below and 50% fall above.

Mid-interval value The central value in a class interval.

Mode The most frequently occurring score in a distribution.

Normal curve See *bell-shaped curve*. See also the diagram below.

Null hypothesis (H_0) The statement being tested in a test of significance is called the null hypothesis. The test of significance is designed to assess the strength of the evidence against the null hypothesis. Usually the null hypothesis is a statement of 'no effect' or 'no difference'.

Observed score The score that is recorded or observed.

Obtained value The value that results from the application of a statistical test.

One-tailed test Applies when interested only in extreme values on one side of the mean, i.e. one tail of the distribution.

Outliers Those scores in a distribution that are noticeably much more extreme than the majority of scores. Exactly what score is an outlier is usually an arbitrary decision made by the researcher.

Percentile point The point at or below where a score appears.

Population All the possible subjects or cases of interest.

Primary data First-hand data that you collect yourself or are collected by someone under your direct supervision.

Qualitative data A type of information that describes or characterises, but does not measure, data. Often referred to as non-numerical data.

Quantitative data A type of information that can be counted or expressed numerically.

Range The highest score minus the lowest score.

Sample A subset of a population.

Sampling error The difference between sample and population values.

Scatter plot A plot of paired data points.

Secondary data Second-hand data that have already been collected and made available from an external source such as newspapers, government departments or the internet.

Significance level The risk set by the researcher for rejecting a null hypothesis when it is true.

Skew or skewness The quality of a distribution that defines the disproportionate frequency of certain scores. A longer right tail than left corresponds to a smaller number of occurrences at the high end of the distribution; this is a *positively* skewed distribution. A shorter right tail than left corresponds to a larger number of occurrences at the high end of the distribution; this is a *negatively* skewed distribution.

Standard deviation (σ) A measure of dispersion (spread) of a set of values from their mean.

Standard error The standard deviation of the sample means $\left(\dfrac{\sigma}{\sqrt{n}}\right)$.

Standard score See *Z-score*.

Statistics A set of tools and techniques used to collect, organise, represent and interpret information.

Two-tailed test A test that applies when interested in the corresponding Z-score on both sides of the mean, i.e. both tails of the distribution. Sometimes called two-sided tests. See the diagram below.

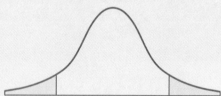

Type I error The probability of rejecting a null hypothesis when it is true.

Type II error The probability of accepting a null hypothesis when it is false.

Unimodal A unimodal data set (distribution) has one peak of data.

Univariate data A survey that looks at only one variable (data set). The variable may be either qualitative or quantitative.

Variability The amount of spread or dispersion in a set of scores.

Variance The square of the standard deviation, and another measure of a distribution's spread or dispersion.

Z-score Indicates the number of standard deviations that a value is above or below the mean:
$$z = \frac{x - \mu}{\sigma}$$

The Normal Curve Tables

Dóchúlachtaí don dáileadh normalach caighdeánach

I gcás z a thugtar, faightear ón tábla

$$P(Z \leq z) = \frac{1}{\sqrt{2\pi}} \int_{-\infty}^{z} e^{-\frac{1}{2}t^2} dt$$

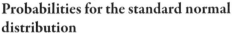

Probabilities for the standard normal distribution

For a given z, the table gives

$$P(Z \leq z) = \frac{1}{\sqrt{2\pi}} \int_{-\infty}^{z} e^{-\frac{1}{2}t^2} dt$$

z	0·00	0·01	0·02	0·03	0·04	0·05	0·06	0·07	0·08	0·09
0·0	0·5000	·5040	·5080	·5120	·5160	·5199	·5239	·5279	·5319	·5359
0·1	0·5398	·5438	·5478	·5517	·5557	·5596	·5636	·5675	·5714	·5753
0·2	0·5793	·5832	·5871	·5910	·5948	·5987	·6026	·6064	·6103	·6141
0·3	0·6179	·6217	·6255	·6293	·6331	·6368	·6406	·6443	·6480	·6517
0·4	0·6554	·6591	·6628	·6664	·6700	·6736	·6772	·6808	·6844	·6879
0·5	0·6915	·6950	·6985	·7019	·7054	·7088	·7123	·7157	·7190	·7224
0·6	0·7257	·7291	·7324	·7357	·7389	·7422	·7454	·7486	·7517	·7549
0·7	0·7580	·7611	·7642	·7673	·7704	·7734	·7764	·7794	·7823	·7852
0·8	0·7881	·7910	·7939	·7967	·7995	·8023	·8051	·8078	·8106	·8133
0·9	0·8159	·8186	·8212	·8238	·8264	·8289	·8315	·8340	·8365	·8389
1·0	0·8413	·8438	·8461	·8485	·8508	·8531	·8554	·8577	·8599	·8621
1·1	0·8643	·8665	·8686	·8708	·8729	·8749	·8770	·8790	·8810	·8830
1·2	0·8849	·8869	·8888	·8907	·8925	·8944	·8962	·8980	·8997	·9015
1·3	0·9032	·9049	·9066	·9082	·9099	·9115	·9131	·9147	·9162	·9177
1·4	0·9192	·9207	·9222	·9236	·9251	·9265	·9279	·9292	·9306	·9319
1·5	0·9332	·9345	·9357	·9370	·9382	·9394	·9406	·9418	·9429	·9441
1·6	0·9452	·9463	·9474	·9484	·9495	·9505	·9515	·9525	·9535	·9545
1·7	0·9554	·9564	·9573	·9582	·9591	·9599	·9608	·9616	·9625	·9633
1·8	0·9641	·9649	·9656	·9664	·9671	·9678	·9686	·9693	·9699	·9706
1·9	0·9713	·9719	·9726	·9732	·9738	·9744	·9750	·9756	·9761	·9767
2·0	0·9772	·9778	·9783	·9788	·9793	·9798	·9803	·9808	·9812	·9817
2·1	0·9821	·9826	·9830	·9834	·9838	·9842	·9846	·9850	·9854	·9857
2·2	0·9861	·9864	·9868	·9871	·9875	·9878	·9881	·9884	·9887	·9890
2·3	0·9893	·9896	·9898	·9901	·9904	·9906	·9909	·9911	·9913	·9916
2·4	0·9918	·9920	·9922	·9925	·9927	·9929	·9931	·9932	·9934	·9936
2·5	0·9938	·9940	·9941	·9943	·9945	·9946	·9948	·9949	·9951	·9952
2·6	0·9953	·9955	·9956	·9957	·9959	·9960	·9961	·9962	·9963	·9964
2·7	0·9965	·9966	·9967	·9968	·9969	·9970	·9971	·9972	·9973	·9974
2·8	0·9974	·9975	·9976	·9977	·9977	·9978	·9979	·9979	·9980	·9981
2·9	0·9981	·9982	·9982	·9983	·9984	·9984	·9985	·9985	·9986	·9986
3·0	0·9987	·9987	·9987	·9988	·9988	·9989	·9989	·9989	·9990	·9990

Calculator Instructions

Casio Natural Display Calculator

Before starting any procedures on the calculator, you should clear the memory:

To clear the memory:

Shift + 9 : CLR

3 : All

= : Yes

To find mean and standard deviation

To perform statistical calculations, we must create a frequency table.

To enter a frequency table, you must switch **Frequency on:**

Shift + Mode : Setup

Down Arrow

3 : STAT

1 : ON

To enter a table of data:

Mode

2 : STAT

1 : 1-VAR

Enter the data into the table, followed by the = sign each time. Once you have finished entering the data press:

AC button.

To analyse the data in the table:

Shift + 1 : STAT

4 : Var

Options are as follows:

2 : $\bar{x}$ (the mean of the terms, also known as μ)

3 : σx (the standard deviation)

For simplicity, to find the mean or standard deviation of a **single list of data**, create a frequency table and set all the frequencies to 1.

To find correlation coefficient, *r*

You must switch Frequency off:

Shift + Mode : Setup

Down Arrow

3 : STAT

2 : OFF

To enter a table of bivariate data:

Mode

2 : STAT

2 : A + BX

Enter the data into the table, followed by the = sign each time. Once you have finished entering the data press:

AC button.

To analyse the data in the table:

Shift + 1 : STAT

5 : Reg

Options are as follows:

3 : *r* (the correlation coefficient)

The line of best fit can be written as:
$y = A + Bx$
The values of *A* and *B* can be found on the calculator, in the same menu as correlation coefficient: 1 : *A*   2 : *B*

Sharp WriteView Calculator

Before starting any procedures on the calculator, you should clear the memory:
To clear the memory:

2nd F + ALPHA : M-CLR

1 : Memory

0 : Clear

To find mean and standard deviation

To put the calculator into Statistics mode:

Mode

1 : STAT

0 : SD

To enter the data:

Take each value and frequency as a pair of data.

Enter each pair, separated by a comma

Then press the DATA button

(e.g. enter: 2 , 13 DATA)

CHANGE

Once all the pairs of data have been entered, press:

ON / C

To find the mean or standard deviation of a **single list of data** press the DATA button after each value. Leave out the comma and frequency value.

To analyse the data entered:

ALPHA then 4 then $=$: $\bar{x}$ (the mean of the terms, also known as μ)

ALPHA then 6 then $=$: σx (the standard deviation)

To find correlation coefficient, r

To put the calculator into Statistics mode:

Mode
1 : STAT
1 : LINE

To enter the data:

Take each value and frequency as a pair of data.

    Enter each pair, separated by a comma

        Then press the DATA button

        (e.g. enter: 2 , 13 DATA)

CHANGE

Once all the pairs of data have been entered, press:

ON / C

To analyse the data entered:

ALPHA then $\div$ then $=$: r
(the correlation coefficient)

The line of best fit can be written as:
$y = a + bx$
The values of a and b can be found on the calculator by:

        Alpha then (then $=$: a
        Alpha then) then $=$: b

Practice exercise

Use your calculator to find the mean and standard deviation of the following table of data:

Value	2	4	6	8	10
Frequency	13	6	9	2	6

The answers are:

Mean $\mu = \bar{x} = 5$ Standard Deviation $\sigma x = 2 \cdot 88675$

Use your calculator to find the correlation coefficient of the following bivariate data:

Value X	1	2	4	6	9
Frequency Y	7	9	6	3	8

The answers is:

Correlation coefficient $r = -2 \cdot 09785$

Line of best fit: $y = 7 \cdot 26 - 0 \cdot 15\,x$